EUGENICS AND THE FIREWALL

Canada's Nasty Little Secret

EUGENICS AND THE FIREWALL

Canada's Nasty Little Secret

JANE HARRIS-ZSOVAN

Eugenics and the Firewall: Canada's Nasty Little Secret
First published 2010 by
J. Gordon Shillingford Publishing Inc.

Book design by Relish Design Inc.
Archival material used with permission of City of Lethbridge Archives (Galt Museum).
Printed and bound in Canada on 100% post-consumer recycled paper.

We acknowledge the financial support of the Manitoba Arts Council and The Canada Council for the Arts for our publishing program.

J. Gordon Shillingford Publishing Inc.
P.O. Box 86, RPO Corydon Avenue
Winnipeg, MB R3M 3S3
Canada

Library and Archives Canada Cataloguing in Publication

Harris, Jane, 1960-
      Eugenics and the firewall : Canada's nasty little secret / Jane Harris-Zsovan.

Includes bibliographical references and index.
ISBN 978-1-897289-51-8

      1. Eugenics—Canada—History. I. Title.

HQ755.5.C3H37 2010   363.9'20971   C2010-905339-7

TABLE OF CONTENTS

I: THE FOGGY PAST

I stood in the doorway, listening to adults with hushed voices whisper words pre-schoolers weren't supposed to understand. Their whispers were about the house across the alley where the old lady with the smeared red stuff on her cheeks lived. Her grown-up son was home and, as the adults assessed the situation in quiet voices, I made out some of my mother's words: Ponoka Operation.

I didn't know what an operation was, but from the worried tones I knew that even adults were afraid of people from Ponoka.

Today Ponoka[1] is pretty little town of 6500 people nestled in the rolling country of West Central Alberta. It's reputation for great rodeos, camping and fishing has been dwarfed by the image of the provincial mental hospital built a century ago, under the Liberal Premiership of Ernest Rutherford. Now called: The Centennial Centre for Mental Health and Brain Injury, the upbeat language on the hospital website gives little clue to its frightening past.[2] For most of the 20th century, "Send 'em to Ponoka", or "That guy belongs in Ponoka" were terrifying insults Albertans hurled at neighbours they didn't like.

Alberta Hospital in Ponoka was, for decades, an overcrowded, chronically cash-strapped provincial mental asylum just 54 kilometres northwest of the Provincial Training School for Mental Defectives at Red Deer. If the province locked you up inside either place, you might not be allowed to come home unless you had the operation.

The operation came in many forms: tubal ligation, hysterectomy, castration and vasectomy. Its goal: ensuring 'mental defectives' and 'insane' people did not reproduce and that their children would not overwhelm provincial social services, jails and hospitals.

Between 1928 and 1972, 2,822 Albertans, labelled insane or mentally defective, were sterilized by order of the four-person Provincial Eugenics Board. Many were wheeled into the operating room not knowing what was going to happen to them. Sometimes women expecting tubal ligations got complete hysterectomies. Other patients were told them they were getting appendectomies. Consent was often not necessary and, in many cases, parents and guardians did not know a family member had been sterilized.

Maybe we shouldn't be surprised at the stealth that was used to get people on the operating table. Patients, who knew what was happening to them might escape. While 2822 patients were sterilized between 1929 and 1972, another 1903 Albertans, declared unfit by the Eugenics Board, did manage to evade the surgeon's scalpel.[3]

The original act required a guardian to consent if the patient was unable to agree the operation. In 1942, the Social Credit Government expanded that *Sexual Sterilization Act* to make chronic illnesses like neurosyphilis,[4] epilepsy and Huntington's chorea grounds for sterilization. They removed the need for consent before operating on Huntington's chorea patients or people classified as mental defectives. By this time the Eugenics Board spent five minutes or less with each file before approving the operation.

Problems emerged. A board member was removed in the 1950s, when the first reports came out that several sane people of normal intelligence had been sterilized. Unknown to the public, mental patients became drug trial guinea pigs; testicles were removed from sterile Down's syndrome patients so the director of the Red Deer Training School could perform his laboratory experiments. Victims, who were well enough to be released, often tried for years to have families, until their doctors discovered the truth. When victims like Leilani Muir, a woman of normal intelligence, who was labelled a moron and sterilized at age 14, asked the government why they had been sterilized without their knowledge, government staff claimed to have no record of the operations.

The government of Alberta didn't acknowledge this horror story for decades. It remained hidden even after the *Sexual Sterilization Act* was rescinded in 1972. And it would have remained hidden if Leilani Muir had not taken the government to court and insisted on a public trial. Her lawsuit unleashed a flood of lawsuits as hundreds of former patients came out of the shadows to drag the reluctant government of Alberta to account.

A Lesson Unlearned

In 2007, former Member of the Alberta Legislature, David King, suggested that the 35th anniversary of the abolition of *Alberta's Sexual Sterilization Act*, might not be worth celebrating.

"We should be careful about celebrating the repeal of the Act. If we aren't careful, we may think we have nothing to learn, because we are celebrating having fixed the mistake. Maybe we should think of ourselves as marking the 80th anniversary (almost) of a grave public policy mistake which it took our community 44 years and much tragedy to fix," King told his audience.[5]

These were strange comments coming from the Member of the Alberta Legislature who introduced the 1972 *Sexual Sterilization Repeal Act* on the floor of the Alberta[6] Legislative Assembly in 1972.

In 1971, King was one of 45 Conservative MLAs who toppled Alberta's Social Credit dynasty. Their platform included protecting patients' rights by abolishing the *Sexual Sterilization Act* and re-writing the *Mental Health Act*.

Thirty-five years after his bill put an end to the Provincial Eugenics Board, King seemed worried that the political culture that allowed the *Sexual Sterilization Act* to remain law in Alberta for 40 years and that prompted many Alberta pundits and politicians to defend its injustices, was still be part of Alberta's political culture. King put it in that framework when he spoke to the "Eugenics and Sterilization in Alberta: 35 Years Later Conference" at the University of Alberta in April 2007.

"Our government tells us that our infrastructure crisis reflects the cost of mistakes made 15 years ago and since then. Now, we have to fix these mistakes, and we pay the price, both financially and in human terms—homeless people, insufficient extended care beds, etc. The mistakes, when they were made, reflected misplaced certainty; they also reflected an appalling lack of confidence in Alberta and in Albertans. The decision-makers of the day were wrong, and citizens were wrong to have been silent."[7]

To date, victims of the *Sexual Sterilization Act* have received little sympathy from the political heirs to the populist political movements that created and expanded the *Sexual Sterilization Act*.

When victims' fight for compensation from the province became media stories in the 1990s, print editorials throughout the province offered few apologies to the victims and many laments about the cost of reparations. The Conservative Government of Ralph Klein did not condemn wrongdoing by previous regimes or take credit for the Lougheed era emphasis on human rights that led Alberta to abolish its Eugenics Board. Instead, they tried to use the Notwithstanding Clause of Canada's Charter of Rights and Freedoms, to limit compensation to victims.[8]

The victims have been pretty much forgotten by Canada's political and media establishment. With an Ontario-born Albertan in the Prime Minister's Office, Canada's conservative bloggers and columnists[9] seem anxious to keep Alberta's political establishment untainted by its history of human rights violations. Instead, they blame the popularity of eugenics on Liberals or Co-operative Commonwealth Federation[10] politicians like the late Tommy Douglas. Michael Coren, in his column "Don't Blame Right-Wing Thugs for Eugenics, Socialists made it Fashionable," published in the *National Post*[11] in 2008, insisted that leftist politicians, like Tommy Douglas (who renounced forced sterilization after a trip to Europe in 1936) were solely responsible for the popularity of eugenics, not just in Canada, but in the United Kingdom, United States and Germany.[12] Many early eugenicists were leftists, but, most important, Social Darwinist ideas behind right-wing eugenics absolved the wealthy of responsibility to help the poor.

Coren's piece is only one example of Canadian articles and blogs that leave the messy histories of Alberta and British Columbia untouched. Conservative moral values played a leading role in legalizing forced sterilization of mental and moral defectives in Canada's two most western provinces.

In Alberta, the non-partisan United Farmers of Alberta passed the first sexual sterilization act in the British Empire in 1928. The UFA's successor, Social Credit governments, led by a radio-evangelist, William Aberhart, and then his protégé, Ernest Manning, removed the need to obtain patient or family consent when the Eugenics Board ordered mental defectives or Huntington's chorea patients with dementia sterilized. (Wards of the court were also sterilized without family or patient consent.) British Columbia, the only other province to enact a *Sexual Sterilization Act,* passed its eugenics law in 1933. Like Alberta, B.C. dealt with a rash of wrongful sterilization lawsuits by former patients in the mid-1990s.

Still, the British Columbia Eugenics Board, which authorized sterilization of a few hundred patients, was a pale shadow of its counterpart on the eastern slopes of the Rockies.

In Alberta, where nearly three thousand citizens were sterilized, lied to, experimented on, and, subjected to daily abuse at hands of provincial staff, generations of politicians showed little empathy for the victims. After a few magazine articles and documentaries in the 1990s, the media lost interest too. Many Albertans have forgotten Leilani Muir and the other victims who made headlines during the court cases of the 1990s. Tar sands, oil royalties, environmental policies, and making sure provincial interests remain at high on the federal agenda top headlines. Perhaps the pundits and politicians fear igniting regional antagonisms. Surely, Canada's Confederation is not too fragile to deal with our history honestly.

The important questions remain unanswered.

How could a province that claims that 'strong and free' as its motto, deny basic freedoms to so many of its own citizens? Why does the extent of Alberta's eugenics past and its link to the Manning/Aberhart legacy remain the unacknowledged moral blind spots in Canadian politics?

Do dwindling voter turnouts, low citizen involvement, and the pack mentality of Alberta politics make put vulnerable Albertans at risk? As Alberta becomes one of the political and economic powerhouses of our Confederation, what does that mean for Canada? Does Canadian unity really depend on us not asking hard questions of provincial governments that put provincial autonomy above the rights of vulnerable Canadians?

II: BEGINNINGS

I propose to show in this book that a man's natural abilities are derived by inheritance, under exactly the same limitations as are the form and physical features of the whole organic world. Consequently, as it is easy, notwithstanding those limitations, to obtain by careful selection a permanent breed of dogs or horses gifted with peculiar powers of running, or of doing anything else, so it would be quite practicable to produce a highly-gifted race of men by judicious marriages during several consecutive generations.

—Sir Francis Galton, 1822-1911[13]

What Is Eugenics?

Eugenics is a quaint, genteel sounding word derived from the Greek word 'eugene'. It is usually translated as 'well-born' in English. The *Canadian Oxford Dictionary* says eugenics is the science of improving the (esp. human) population by controlled breeding for desirable inherited characteristics.[14]

Eugenics is often divided into sub-categories. Positive eugenics encourages couples to select healthy, intelligent mates and provides incentives to encourage eugenically 'fit' couples to have babies. Incentives may include tax incentives, childcare, or baby bonuses. Education programmes may encourage the fit to live healthy lifestyles that protect their future children from damage. They may also counsel people with mental or physical defects to be sterilized.

Negative eugenics is often coercive. It includes forced segregation of the 'unfit' into institutions or camps, forced sterilization, genocide and, at its extreme, killing the severely handicapped. There's nothing quaint or genteel about that.

Did Albertans invent eugenics?

No. Albertans didn't invent eugenics.

The man usually called the 'father of eugenics' is a half-cousin of Charles Darwin named Francis Galton. He believed the idea, which caught fire after the American and French Revolution, that we are all born equal, is a dangerous lie.

Galton developed 'probabilistic statistics' to help himself analyse heredity. He and his followers believed they could improve humanity the same way they improved their race horses and hunting dogs: through selective breeding. Galton's books make interesting reading, not just because of the lucidity of his writing, but because they illustrate the frank and unabashed bigotry of the 19th century.

In this 1873 letter to the editor, Galton asked readers to support his proposal to convince 'industrious, order-loving Chinese' to immigrate to East Africa to supplant the native blacks that he describes as 'lazy, palavering savages'.

AFRICA FOR THE CHINESE:

"Sir, in a few days Sir Bartle Frere will return to England, and public attention will be directed to the East Coast of Africa. I am desirous of availing myself of the opportunity to ventilate some speculations of my own, which you may perhaps consider of sufficient interest to deserve publication in *The Times*. My proposal is to make the encouragement of the Chinese settlements at one or more suitable places on the East Coast of Africa a part of our national policy, in the belief that the Chinese immigrants would not only maintain their position, but that they would multiply and their descendants supplant the inferior Negro race. I should expect the large part of the African seaboard, now sparsely occupied by lazy, palavering savages living under the nominal sovereignty of the Zanzibar, or Portugal, might in a few years, be tenanted by industrious, order loving Chinese, living either as a semi-detached dependency of China, or else in perfect freedom under their own law. In the latter case they would be similar to that of the inhabitants of Liberia, in West Africa, the territory which was purchased 50 years ago and set apart as an independent state for the reception of freed Negroes from America."

—Francis Galton, letter to the Editor of *The Times*, June 5, 1873.

In *Hereditary Genius* (first published in 1869), Galton used the 'pedigrees' of prominent British families to back up his claim that genius runs in families and that heredity determines destiny in both animals and human beings. (Galton did not consider environment to be a significant factor in human ability.)

Galton proposed to increase the fitness of humanity by arranging marriages between men and women who proved to be fittest. Using a system of positive and negative eugenics, society would benefit by increased fertility among the fit and low fertility among groups he believed are unfit.

His eurocentric hierarchy of race put white Northern Europeans at the top of the heap. Whites from Southeast Europe come next, then Asians, Native Americans, and Africans. He ranked Australian Aborigines as the most inferior of peoples. These theories helped justify class systems, imperialism, and racism. Not surprisingly, eugenics became most popular in Britain, Northern Europe and among prosperous whites in the United States where the upper and middle classes felt threatened by foreigners and the poor.

Galton's followers refined his ideas about incentives and deterrents: positive eugenicists (influenced by ideas of social and moral reformers outside the eugenics movement), proposed incentives to build a healthy population. Family allowances, health clinics, and education to encourage healthy families to grow, and to deter the unfit from reproducing. Negative eugenics advocates wanted to prevent the unfit from reproducing: segregating them by putting them in institutions, sexual sterilization of the unfit, and allowing only the fit to marry. They looked down on positive eugenicists, with its utopian values that provided charity to the poor, equalized education to opportunities between classes, and urged government to re-distribute wealth between classes. According to the Social Darwinists, progressive social reformers ignorantly violated natural laws by interfering with 'survival of the fittest'. Social Darwinists pointed to the work of economist Thomas Malthus and Galton's cousin, Charles Darwin, as the scientific basis for their ideas.

Malthus was revered among Victorians, England's intellectual class. Charles Darwin even claimed that reading the work of Malthus, a classical liberal free market economist, had helped him understand how plants and animals adapted to their environment.

"In October 1838, that is, fifteen months after I had begun my systematic enquiry, I happened to read for amusement *Malthus On Population*, and being well prepared to appreciate the struggle for existence which everywhere goes on from long-continued observation of the habits of animals and plants, it at once struck me that under these circumstances favourable variations would tend to be preserved, and unfavourable ones to be destroyed. The result of this would be the formation of new species. Here, then, I had at last got a theory by which to work..."[15]

Economist Thomas Malthus (1766-1834) believed that letting inferior humans, particularly the poor, procreate without restrictions, would serve to destroy civilization. He thought that the poor reproduced more rapidly and, if not restricted, their fertility would cause the human population to explode beyond the food supply. He also believed that unrestricted breeding would cause humanity to become degenerate because the poor (whom many in the middle and upper classes believed were criminals, moral defectives, chronically ill, unemployed, lazy, and feeble-minded) reproduced their inferior traits.

These ideas which made sense to more than just the academics, fuelled the fears of members of the middle and upper classes in the British Empire, Northern Europe and the United States. These 'respectable' classes were terrified that the bad-mannered, irresponsible, immoral lower masses were about to outnumber them and push civilization into chaos, poverty, and insanity.

The term 'race suicide' describe their deepest fear: that they would be outnumbered and replaced by those they now ruled.

American Eugenics

The ruling question for eugenicists: why do the feeble-minded tend so strongly to become delinquent? The answer may be stated in simple terms. Morality depends upon two things: (a) the ability to foresee and to weigh the possible consequences for self and others of different kinds of behaviour; and (b) upon the willingness and capacity to exercise self-restraint. That there are many intelligent criminals is due to the fact that (a) may exist without (b) On the other hand, (b) presupposes (a) In other words, not all criminals are feeble-minded, but all feeble-minded are at least potential criminals. That every feeble-minded woman is a potential prostitute would hardly be disputed by anyone. Moral judgment, like business judgment, social judgment, or any other kind of higher thought process, is a function of intelligence. Morality cannot flower and fruit if intelligence remains infantile.

—Lewis M. Terman, *The Uses of Intelligence Tests* (1916)[16]

American eugenicists shared their British cousins' fondness for 'pedigree analysis'. In 1912, an American psychologist, Henry Herbert Goddard, published pedigree analysis of a family he named the Kallikaks (Greek for beautiful (Kalos) and bad (Kakos). He claimed the Kallikaks descended from one man who had children with two women. The descendents from the respectable wife, he declared, were healthy and productive, while those from the feebleminded barmaid were alcoholics, criminals, prostitutes, or 'feebleminded' half-wits.

Goddard's study stoked the fears of prosperous white Americans, who were already suspicious that imbeciles, moral degenerates, black Americans and poor, often illiterate, immigrants from Eastern and Southern Europe would soon outnumber them. Even though, the Hardy-Weinberg theorem, developed in 1908, predicted that it would take 40 generations of negative eugenics to rid society of degenerates, they were eager to at least stem the tide.

Gregor Mendel's[17] studies of recessive traits in plants helped convince many eugenicists on both sides of the Atlantic that heredity determines human genius. Mendel's work on recessive genes shows that heredity is more complicated than Galton suggested; eugenicists considered it a valuable addition to their understanding.

The Austrian monk's work was most influential in the United States. American eugenicists also liked negative eugenics strategies. Thanks to their fervent pitches to politicians, women's groups, churches, doctors, and middle class Americans demanded laws to stop the epidemic of feeble-mindedness and moral depravity they were convinced was overwhelming the United States. The first eugenic sterilization bill to become law passed in Indiana in 1907 (two earlier sterilization laws, in Michigan (1897) and Pennsylvania (1905), were never enacted). Thirty-one American States eventually passed sexual sterilization laws.[18]

Even before the American Eugenics Society was officially founded in 1926, American eugenicists convinced many of their countrymen to support eugenics policies including segregating and sterilizing the chronically and mentally ill, mentally handicapped, criminals, alcoholics, epileptics, and Huntington's chorea patients. They also pressured politicians to restrict immigration by Southern and Eastern Europeans, enact racial segregation laws, and make intermarriage between blacks and whites illegal. American eugenicists also brought intelligence testing to the forefront where it could be used to help diagnose those unfit to reproduce.

In 1933, an American Eugenics Society 'model sterilization law' was adopted in Nazi Germany. The *Law For the Protection of Hereditary Health* came into effect in Germany on July 14, 1933. It was the first plank in the

Nuremberg Laws that formed the legal basis for the killing of the disabled, political dissenters, Gypsies, Jews, homosexuals, and religious minorities under the Nazi regime between 1933 and 1945.

While the U.S. had its share of Social Darwinists, most American eugenicists believed reforming society was the only way to ensure future generations would be mentally and physically fit. They promoted birth control and child spacing to ensure children were healthy and could be well cared for. Others promoted early marriage to raise birth rates among the white middle class. Still others joined the prohibition movement to stamp out the moral degeneration they believed was caused by drunkenness.

Their love for negative eugenics didn't stop Americans from creating effective positive eugenics programs. It was quite the contrary. American eugenicists excelled in launching energetic education campaigns, writing marriage guides, medical articles and school textbooks, offering 'free lectures', and showing the dangers of 'degenerate breeding' in silent movies like *The Black Stork* (1917). It was based on a case in which a Chicago doctor, Dr Harry Haiselden, convinced a couple to let their baby, born with congenital syphilis, die. The movie portrayed the tortured life the child would have had if it had been allowed to live. Eugenicists didn't want all babies to die. They also excelled at organizing community events including Better Baby and Fitter Families contests where 'respectable' people could show off their broods, win prices and be photographed for the local paper.

British Influence

Darwin's son and other speakers at 1921 New York Eugenics Conference.

True Lovers Need Not Fear 'Eugenics', declares Darwin. New York, Sept 23. True lovers need not shy off at mention of the word 'eugenics'.

Eugenicists do not desire to abolish love as a guide to the selection of mates in marriage, but only wish to purify it of ill harmful effects. This is the message brought by Major J. Conrad Darwin, one of England's leading eugenicists and son of Charles Darwin, originator of the Darwinian theory of evolution, speaking before the Second International Congress of Eugenics which opened last night.

Major Darwin deplored the popular misconception which credits to eugenicists with the desire to substitute cattle breeding principles for romance.

If young people were always allowed to follow their natural inclination, he declared, the mating usually would be wise from the standpoint of eugenics.

But many marriages which are made for wealth or social position do not lead to better the human race. Segregation of the feeble-minded and other sub-normal types is a most important end for which eugenicists are striving, Major Darwin added.

It's hardly surprising that an eminent Brit, like Major Darwin, would be invited to speak to the American crowd.

Prior to World War I, British activists shared their American cousins' commitment to segregating the mentally ill, alcoholics, and mentally handicapped. A few considered euthanasia as a possibility for the severely handicapped. After the First World War, British eugenicists became less interested in preventing 'degenerate' births than in recovering the shattering loss of 994,138 soldiers and civilians.

Between the World Wars, British eugenicists focused on eugenics education: promoting eugenic marriage and social reforms would lead to a utopian society and replace brutish individualism with communitarian enlightenment. They put their energies into fighting for family allowances and tax relief to allow working and middle class families to grow and prosper.

While some British eugenicists liked Germany's 1933 *Law for the Protection of Hereditary Health*, the paths between the British and German eugenicists diverged over the issue of consent. The British Eugenics Society rejected compulsory sterilization and Hitler's Nuremberg Laws.

Unlike their American counterparts, British eugenicists failed to convince politicians to pass laws forcing sterilization of the unfit. The British Parliament rejected a 1931 Private Member's Bill by Labour MP Major A. G. Church that would allow forced sterilization.[19]

Eugenics Comes to Canada

Canadian eugenicists adopted their fellow British subjects' utopian dreams and their American cousins 'fear of being overwhelmed by foreigners and degenerates'.

British-style social reforms, like baby bonuses and family allowances, did improve the lives of Canadian families. But many Canadians were more concerned with what they perceived as an onslaught of immigrants, moral laxness, and insanity; this favoured restricted immigration, sterilization of defectives, and segregating the unfit from mainstream society.

Canadians picked up on the latest news about the new 'eugenics' science from newspapers and travelling speakers from Britain and the United States.

Men and women eager to improve the lot of the mentally ill and mentally handicapped were influenced by these ideas too. A Toronto psychiatrist, Dr Charles Kirk Clarke, who along with physician and medical inspector Dr Clare Hincks founded the Canadian National Committee for Mental Hygiene (the precursor to the Canadian Mental Health Association) in 1918, borrowed the ideas of American eugenicists as he linked rising numbers of the 'feeble-minded' with immigration.

His colleague and Hincks' boss, Dr Helen McMurchy,[20] took the eugenics messages to thousands of women involved in Canadian charity, suffragette and social reform organizations. Groups like the National Council of Women, The Women's Christian Temperance Union and some locals of the United Farm Women of Alberta liked her message that healthy families, low crime rates, eradicating poverty, and ridding society of alcoholism, child abuse and insanity depended on ensuring that the unfit did not fill 'the cradles with degenerate babies'.[21]

In order to prevent a racial poisoning disaster, experts also advised Canadian women to wear corsets to develop their unborn offspring and to attend education sessions on eugenics. Like their sisters elsewhere, Alberta women gladly complied, believing that it was their duty to help stem the tide of lunatics and mental defectives.

Local community groups followed the American example, organizing baby contests. These contests were particularly successful in western Canada. Even tiny communities, like Fort Macleod, Alberta, could muster up a couple of dozen prize babies for the judges' consideration.[22]

Larger Alberta communities also drafted their most notable citizens, like Mayor Hardie of Lethbridge, Alberta, to make the tricky choice of their city's annual crop of infants who entered the Lethbridge Baby Contest in 1914.[23]

Baby Contest at Lethbridge

Who says Lethbridge is depopulated?

One wouldn't have dared make such a wild assertion when the baby contest was in progress. There were sixteen babies entered: small ones, fat ones, thin ones, big ones. Mayor Hardie was given credit for knowing something about babies, and acted as judge. He looked over the lot, and at once picked out the sturdiest, the four-months-old child of Mrs Hislop, a boy of course. The best looking girl this time, strange to say, won second.

She was a mighty winsome young lady to the daughter of Mrs Whitfield. The Mayor explained after his strenuous 'task' was over, that he judged the little ones as beef type first. The strongest first, the best looking second. (Eugenics)[24]

In Western Canada, where Ottawa's policy of rapid development and mass immigration caused social unrest, and overloaded schools, jails, and mental hospitals, eugenics was an easy sell. Not surprisingly, the most fervent lobbying for eugenics legislation to place on the eastern slopes of the Rockies, in Alberta.

III: FEDERAL IMMIGRATION POLICES IN THE NORTH WEST

Sir John A. Macdonald's government started it. Ottawa's policy of rapid settlement of Western Canada began in the 1870s under the Liberal Conservative administration of Canada's first Prime Minister, but it didn't stop when he died suddenly in June 1891.[25] Conservative and Liberal successors made rapid settlement of the Northwest Territories, Canadian government policy, until World War I made the focus of Prime Minister Robert Borden's (1917-1920) wartime coalition winning the war without allowing conscription to further alienate Quebec.

In 1901, under Borden's predecessor, Sir Wilfrid Laurier, immigration reached 55,747 immigrants. Most of them settled in Western Canada.

On a visit to Western Canada in September 1910, Sir Wilfrid Laurier, a Liberal, praised Canada's first finance minister, the Conservative Sir Alexander's Tilloch Galt, for his dedication to settling Western Canada. As High Commissioner to London in the 1880s, Galt had gone beyond the British Isles in search of immigrants: facilitating the settlement of Russian Jews in portions of the Northwest Territories that included modern Alberta and Saskatchewan. He was over 60 when he retired as Canada's High Commissioner to London to launch a major mining settlement project in the District of Alberta. The Galt Mines in Lethbridge were among the first in Canada to recruit miners from Hungary when the supply of Canadian and British workers ran short.[26]

Laurier's Minister of the Interior, Clifford Sifton, also went beyond the British countryside to find farmers. His search extended to the United States, where he targeted recent European immigrants and expatriate Canadians; to Northern Europe, where Scandinavians and Germans answered his call; and to Central and Eastern Europe, where Doukhobors, Mennonites, and Ukrainians eagerly answered Canada's invitation to settle the prairies.[27]

Simmering Discontent

Heavy immigration furthered the federal government's goal of populating the west. It also brought profits for railways, land speculators and industrialists. But Anglo-Saxon shopkeepers, middle class professionals, farmers and tradesmen often felt overwhelmed and threatened by the newcomers.

More Figures from the Census of Canada

While British immigration was still dominant in Canada, Dominion census results also showed rising numbers of Germans (many of these new immigrants were ethnic Germans fleeing Russia or Eastern Europe) and Austro-Hungarians.

> "The increase in population in ten years, 1901 to 1911, amounted to 1,835,328, being an increase of 34.1 percent. Of this increase the English contributed 562,251 or 34.17 percent, the Irish, 61,663 or 3.35 percent, the Scotch, 137,726 or 10.77 percent, the Welsh, 11,713 or .64 percent, the French, 405,519 or 2.09 percent, the Germans, 82,819 or 4.51 percent, the Austro-Hungarians 110,925 or 6.03 percent.
>
> The British races (English, Irish, Scotch, Welsh, etc.) make up 833,790 or 45.2 percent, of the total increase, and with the French and German account for 1,322,128 or 72 percent of the total increase in the decade. The Scandinavians, Jews, Italians, Poles, Dutch and Finnish stand in the order named."
>
> —*Lethbridge Daily Herald*, 12 September 1913, page 3.

It didn't help that the local newspapers told Albertans lurid stories of murder, madness, drunkenness, and debauchery in their back yards.[28] People who once boosted immigration now rang warning bells.

You couldn't find a bigger booster for Western Canada than Charles Alexander Magrath. After a stint as a clerk in the House of Commons in Ottawa, the transplanted Ontarian took up surveying. Upon his arrival in the District of Alberta in 1885, he took a job at the Northwest Coal and Navigation Company in Lethbridge and soon became Elliott Galt's assistant. Charles Magrath and Elliott Galt spent decades building towns and selling lands to settlers. Charles eventually got into politics. As Lethbridge's first Mayor and MLA, Magrath dedicated himself to growth.

Lethbridge is the youngest town in the Canadian Northwest and possesses advantages unequalled by any of her sister towns. We are all of one opinion as to her future and I am sure that there will not be the slightest doubt existing in the minds of any one present that will be called upon to witness, if we live to the allotted three score and ten, a large and flourishing city in our present town site.[29]

It was he who convinced Canada's Minister of the Interior, Clifford Sifton, to refund the Galts' survey dues in order to fund irrigation projects that created towns.

In 1910, Charles Alexander Magrath was married to Elliott's sister, Mabel, and writing a book. As he assessed Canada's potential in Canada's growth and some problems affecting it,[30] Magrath's attitude toward non-British immigration remained generally positive. In fact, he insisted that the British Empire's definition of citizenship was not ethnic but represented adherence to a civic culture and British Parliamentary institutions. But with labour unrest threatening mining in southwest Alberta, potential social unrest on the prairies clouded his optimism about any economic benefits of rapid settlement. He urged Canada to take a more stringent attitude to screening immigrants.

Magrath worried that 'negative' immigration, was being fostered by Laurier's Liberals. He suggested that physical and mental exams in Canadian ports were sloppy. The result: moral, mental physical defectives were threatening to drag down Canadian productivity. In his opinion, these poor-quality immigrants also created the backlash against immigration in Western Canada.

Rapid expansion of the Canadian Northwest allowed two new provinces, Saskatchewan and Alberta, to be carved out of the Northwest Territories in 1905. The federal policy of mass immigration to Western Canada had created ethnic tensions, crime, and even industrial slums in the mining towns of the Northwest. The new Province of Alberta, in particular, was also home to a strong women's movement, a proudly progressive electorate, and a large immigrant population. This was fertile ground for the eugenics lecturers to travel through.

IV: SLUMS AND STRANGE WAYS IN ALBERTA

WORLD GETTING CRAZIER, HE SAYS. IN A FEW HUNDRED
YEARS THE WHOLE EARTH WILL BE OUT OF ITS MIND

London, Aug.1. The vision of a mad world and an era of lunacy was
prophesied by Dr Forbes Winslow yesterday while expressing his dissent
from the statement made at the Eugenics Congress by Dr Mott that increase in lunacy is more apparent than real. Dr Winslow said: "There will
be more lunatics in the world than sane people three hundred years hence.
This prophecy is based on the present rate of the growth of lunacy revealed
by recent returns. We are rapidly approaching a mad world. In every part
of the world civilization is advancing and so insanity is bound to advance.
There were 36,763 lunatics in 1850. There are now 136,000."

—*Lethbridge Daily Herald*, 02 August 1912, page 7.

When No News is Good News

Albertans didn't know what their world was coming to. Every train that
stopped in town dropped off dowdy-looking people wearing strange clothing,
speaking unintelligible words, and doing bewildering things. After supper,
they stretched out their local newspapers at the kitchen table, hoping to
read some local gossip or the MPs report from Parliament. Instead, alarming
stories about racial suicide and an epidemic of lunacy leapt up at them from
the newsprint.

The early 20th century was a golden age for Canada's newspapers. In
1913, Canada boasted 138 daily newspapers for its 7,632,000 people.[31, 32]
Alberta, a province of less than 470,000 people,[33] had more than two dozen
newspapers.[34]

Turn-of-the-century Alberta newspapers were filled with stories about
scientific advances, better babies, the scourge of alcoholism and, of course,
the coming onslaught of lunatics. Headlines like "Cities Very Bad, The
Insanity Is Astounding," linked rising population, crowding and alcoholism,
especially in crowded cities, to rising lunacy rates.[35]

Albertans reading about the 1912 World Eugenics Conference in London discovered that learned men and women thought an explosion of emotionality was ruining the initiative of Anglo-Saxon society on both sides of the Atlantic: the British race was 'becoming small, dark, and emotional'.

WHAT EUGENICS CONGRESS LEARNED: VERY FEW MEN OF FIRST RANK ABILITY IN THE WORLD SAY SAVANTS

London, July 30. Tile, phlegmatic Briton, has been accused of being in danger of losing his poise and attitude of unconcern and of becoming emotional. It happened yesterday at the Eugenics Congress, the accuser being: Mrs Dr Whetliari, who declared that the small, dark race, which is now an ingredient in the British population, is harmful when dominant. An auditor interrupted with the suggestion that Lloyd-George, who is small and dark, be dismissed from the government on eugenic principles. Dr Whetliari went on to say: "It is possible that the British nation and all western nations generally are becoming shorter and darker, less able to take and keep the initiative, less persistent and more emotional, whether in government, science or art."

Canadians, who always suspected they were on the right side of the American Revolution, had their loyalty validated as American delegates revealed their great admiration of the British aristocracy.

Dr Woods, of the Harvard Medical School, said he had analyzed the forty-seven Americans in the Hall of Fame in New York and then prepared a list of 3,500 people distinguished enough to appear in standard works of biography and found that half of those in the Hall of Fame were closely related to someone in the second group. This, he mentioned to illustrate the idea that eminent men have an average of one able relative each, when from the aristocracy, and less than that when from the middle classes, presumably for the reason that there is more selective mating in aristocracy than in the middle classes. Dr Woods handed royalty a bouquet by declaring that men of genius among royalties were about a hundred times as many as among other people, that of 12 monarchs he had analyzed, forty could rank with any man of genius such as Gustavus Adolphus, William the Silent and Prince Eugene.[36]

Further, local newspapers revealed, in shocking detail, the 'eugenic' secrets of darkest Africa to farmers, housewives and shopkeepers.

IT'S NICE OF THEM TO HAVE THE FUNERAL

Chicago, Sept. 16. A club is the solution of the eugenics problem among the Zulus of Africa, said JH Halmer for 32 years a resident of that country, before the International Lyceum Convention here last night. When a baby is born to Zulu parents and he appears to be below the Zulu standard, it is given a gentle wallop over the head, he explained. After that there is a funeral.[37]

When the British Empire went to war against Germany, Alberta mothers, fathers, and wives kissed their young men good-bye. Then they came home to headlines proclaiming The Great War as the latest battle in an epic evolutional structure that began before history that only the fittest could survive.

CAUSE OF THE WAR

London, May 10. Dr William Ridgway a professor of archaeology at Cambridge University, in an address last night before the Eugenics Society, declared the present war resulted from cautionary racial struggles. Hard facts seen from a scientific viewpoint said Dr Ridgeway, "indicate the present war is the first of a long series and that the new struggle will be more serious. The earth's waste places are getting filled up and these wars are part of evolutionary racial struggles for existence, and not the result of mere kingly ambitions."[38]

But sacrificing 60,661[39] citizen soldiers for king and country didn't stop vice, poverty, or insanity in Canada. The racial poisoning experts at the 1912 World Eugenics Conference feared what was taking root seemed to be tightening its grip on the upright, moral, and Anglo-Saxon parts of Canadian society.

Albertans sought to understand its causes: population growth, stress, and poorly thought out marriages. Claims that 20% of madmen were drunks reinforced the moral conservatism of the middle class.[40]

"If only clergymen would have more children, society would become more eugenically fit," said William T. Ellis as he mused about the implications of the American Eugenics Society's cold statistics.

"On the other hand, what are the fruits of even our most imperfect Christianity? I leave the reader to make his own answer: reminding him merely that on January 9, 1930, in the annual meeting of the American Eugenics

Society, which is by no means a particularly pious organization, where it was seriously proposed, 'as measure of racial benefit', that there be provided 'a special stipend' for the rearing of every child born to a clergyman."

This measure was advocated because cold statistics have proved that the best quality of leaders arose from the progeny of the clergy. Verily, "By their fruit shall ye know them."[41]

Clearly, there wouldn't be enough preachers' kids to clean up Canada's moral climate. Another plan was needed. Positive eugenicists pitched the importance of teaching young Canadians how to develop their own eugenic fitness and how to choose mates that would ensure the fitness of future generations.

DISCUSS SOCIAL HYGIENE

TORONTO, ON. (CP)—Social hygiene. In relation to boys' and girls' work and the education of children was the subject discussed at a special meeting under the auspices of the Canadian Social Hygiene Council at the University of Toronto during the recent meeting of the British Association for the Advancement of Science, and the speakers were distinguished members of the British Association.

Dr Lydia Henry, warden of the Social Science department of King's College for Women, London, was the first speaker, and opened her address with a brief explanation of the meaning of the term, social hygiene. She pointed out that its aim was to procure normal environment and upbringing for every individual in the community. It implies sound recreation and the development of the talents of the child, also good home conditions and the organization of all methods which will provide the fullest opportunity for each person. This can only be achieved, Dr Henry remarked, by the co-operation of the state, the community and the individual.

SPECIAL CLINICS

With reference to her own work in England, the speaker described the special clinics for girls and women, with her instruction of hundreds of interested boys and girls in the fundamentals of the origin of life. She showed the importance of a psychological understanding of each age, on the part of teachers and mothers, and a knowledge of the differences of mental condition between boys and girls. "The control of venereal, which is not a disease, but a symptom of the wrong way of looking at life, is only one part of the social hygiene movement."

Dr McCurdy, of Cambridge University, speaking as a psycho-pathologist, outlined his work of dealing with problems of mental peculiarity and instability, and also his conclusions with regard to various social customs.

"The great achievement of material science," he said, "have cost more than they are worth." He balanced in particular the advance in the industrial world, which has a great bearing on the problem of the mentally subnormal. Modern industry puts a premium on stupidity, for the amount of thinking is now greatly reduced among the workers, "busy fingers and idle heads make for unrest," he said.

"We must change the compulsory system of education of today," said Dr McCurdy, "so that only the child of marked intelligence will be given an education, and those who are feeble mentally will have ordinary tasks."

The speaker feared that social legislation and organized charily have tended to increase and maintain the relative number of unfit citizens.

APPEAL TO WORK TOGETHER

Prof William D. MacDougall, professor of psychology at Harvard University, in acknowledging the broad scope of the social hygiene movement, made a strong appeal to all organizations having the general welfare at heart, to work together to this end, and to avoid the succumbing to destructive rivalry which too frequently develops. He emphasized the necessity for thinking of both heredity and environment in our endeavour to improve the race. R.A. Fisher, Honorary Secretary of the British Eugenics Education Society, gave an interesting address on the aims of his society.[42]

V: CHANGING IDEAS ABOUT CHRISTIAN DUTY

Protestant clergymen in Britain and the United States agreed with the eugenicists' view that society was heading for disaster. For 1900 years, the church had been trying to convince a sceptical public that their taste for vice was sliding society straight to hell.

Turn-of-the-century preachers could not help but notice that 'scientific' lectures by travelling eugenicists held their congregation's attention while sermons on the seven deadly sins put them to sleep. Not surprising they started tacking on lessons in eugenics 'science' to their sermons denouncing drunkenness, extra-marital sex, lack of discipline, and laziness.

In Alberta, local churches drew the public in by hosting lectures by travelling eugenicists. To the delight of the church boards, these meetings were usually packed. Some pastors, like the minister of Westminster Church in Lethbridge, put together their own eugenics lecture series. Men's groups learned how bird breeding could help them understand how to improve their own chances of developing better progeny. Borrowing the eugenicists' message that clergy produce better offspring, the minister at Westminster compared the offspring of evangelist Jonathan Edwards to the degraded, moronic, immoral descendents of 'a well known assassin'.

Christians now believed that not only would they inherit the Kingdom of God in Heaven, their children would be smarter, richer, and more respected than the ungodly. Eugenics must be right because it supported church doctrine. Christian duty wasn't just following the Ten Commandments anymore, it was cutting off the supply of 'demon alcohol', preventing society from being overrun by defectives, and ensuring Christian morality was enforced.

When a Miss Miller of Lethbridge disagreed with Christian morality in a letter to the editor, an upright citizen wrote in to say that it was a woman's duty to ensure her offspring were healthy, and that Christian chastity was the key to the health of the species. The writer pointed to the successes of the eugenics movement as evidence of the need to enforce Christian morality.

> Such unchastity, Miss Miller, is wrong and contemptible to humanity…
> no human being has the moral, social or legal right to such indulgence…
> anyone who does so is a violator of every known law of biology, eugenics,
> human anatomy, hygiene, morality, society and the law of the land. In the
> face of this, would you contend that there remains one excuse for illicit
> intercourse? No, your heart tells you a thousand times no…[43]

As Alberta's churches took an active interest in eugenics, church-based social
reformers came to accept Galton's belief that 'degenerate breeding' was both
a result and a reason for what they saw as a rising tide of vices. Unchecked
'degenerate breeding' would produce slums full of lunatics and morons.

Many middle and upper classes no longer wanted to protect the vulnerable, they wanted protection from them. This siege mentality among the
prosperous in society represented a dramatic theological turnaround.

Just a generation before, anti-slavery reformers, like William Wilberforce,
anti-poverty workers, like Wilson Carlile and William Booth, and advocates
of 'moral treatment' of the mentally ill, like the Quaker, William Tuke, were
motivated by the Christian tradition of mercy.

The idea that those now called 'defectives' were a threat to society, rather
than its victims, was a radical departure from the tradition of mercy found in
this early 19th-century prayer for the mentally ill and mentally handicapped.

> …we that have reason can deserve heaven no more than these can; but
> these do not deserve hell so much as we have done. Impute not to them
> their follies that are unavoidable, nor the sins which they discern not, nor
> the evils which they cannot understand; keep them from all the evil and
> sad mischances and make supply of their want of the defences of reason by
> the special guard of angel…[44]

And this Prayer for Madmen:

> Pity the evil they suffer, and pardon the evils they have done, and impute
> not unto them the evils which they rather bear than act; and let not their
> entry into this calamity be an exclusion from their future pardon. Lord,
> restore them to their health and understanding; take from them all violent
> passions, and remove all evil objects far from their eyes and ears. (p. 356)[45]

Previously unthinkable ideas now crept into Protestant thinking: sexual sterilization of the unfit might stop society from becoming a moral

cesspool. Christian-based activist groups, like the Women's Christian Temperance Union, who were also targets of lobbying by eugenicist, Dr Helen McMurchy, soon adopted the idea. So did the Young Men's Christian Association. In Alberta, YMCAs organized classes for physical development of girls according to eugenic principles.[46]

This shift in thinking toward eugenics in Alberta was dramatic. Before 1914, most of Alberta's women reformers emphasized Christian charity and work with immigrants by organizations such as the Traveller's Aids or nursing missions.[47]

The success of these outreaches was acknowledged even before Alberta became a province. In March 1904, the Superintendent of Neglected and Delinquent Children wrote an article about the benefits of the child saving movement as a way to prevent delinquency and rising crime rates. In it, he decries the institutionalization of children because a child needs love as a flower needs sunshine. Environment was more important than heredity, according to Chadwick.

"If every child born into the world were given proper care, education, and wholesome home environment the great stream of pauper and criminals now passing into our prisons and refuges, to be maintained at tremendous expense, would almost be entirely cut off," he wrote.

SUPT. CHADWICK GIVES INTERESTING INFORMATION ON THE SUBJECT.

At the request of the Herald, R. B. Chadwick of Edmonton, superintendent of neglected and delinquent children has contributed another article on the matter of providing for such children. Mr Chadwick says during the past thirty years the care and training of the child has engaged the thoughtful attention of thinking men, the world over. It is now generally recognized that if every child born into the world were given proper care education, and wholesome home environment the great stream of pauper and criminals now passing into our prisons and refuges to be maintained at tremendous expense would almost be entirely cut off. This work is not provided for as a government work, but is brought about by a combination of municipal and personal philanthropy, each society taking care of its own finances, and providing the funds to meet the expenditure necessary to success of the work, but operating under the supervision of the Department of the Attorney General of the Province the belief has been spreading steadily for the past thirty years that such children can be better provided for by being placed in good homes, under the normal conditions of life. A child needs love as a flower needs sunshine. The monotony of institutional life, with its rules for all actions, and its system of directing every thought and moment of time by a discipline of the most rigid character, has proven the bane of many a child's life.

This monotony is unavoidable when children are massed together. The result of this monotony of existence has produced a type which is known as the 'institutionalized' type, a dull, spiritless individual who as a rule, lacking force of individuality...[48]

VI: DO SOMETHING, PLEASE!
(TO STEM THE TIDE OF LUNATICS
AND MORONS)

E dmonton, Alberta, 1907—Premier Alexander Cameron Rutherford
has a problem. Since becoming Premier of the new Province of Alberta
in 1905, his government has continued the Northwest Territories Legislature's policy of sending the mentally ill to 'the mental' at Brandon, Manitoba.
Voters want a cheaper, more modern asylum in Alberta. They also want a
provincial home for mental defectives.[49] The numbers of insane and feeble-
minded Albertans are growing, but it's not feeble-minded folk that worry
Rutherford. It's the bill for housing the insane at the Brandon 'Mental'. In
1907, Rutherford introduces the *Insanity Act*. To his relief, the bill is passed.

The Insanity Act (1907)

The Insanity Act became law in Alberta when it received Royal Assent March
15, 1907. It looked a lot like the 1888 *Ordinance Respecting Insane Persons of
the Northwest Territories*.[50]

The mentally ill were still rounded up and brought before a justice of the
peace. They were still put on trial and, if they were judged insane and dangerous, they were thrown in jail or sent home (as long as their relatives would
take them), until the Attorney General of Alberta decided whether or not to
send them to an asylum. The new act did allow families four days to appeal
the court's decision, something not allowed under the NWT legislation, and
relatives could accompany their family member to the asylum, if he did not
want a NWMP constable to do the job. Rutherford's government also added
a provision to release the prisoner (patient) on the grounds that the person
'is not insane or thought insane and is not dangerous'. The new Act put the
insane in care of the Attorney General rather than the Lieutenant Governor.
Both the NWT and Alberta Acts reflected realities. Treatment options were
scarce in Western Canada, and often the local jail was the only secure place
to put a mentally ill person until someone could be found to take them to the
nearest asylum, in Brandon, Manitoba.

Clashing Philosophies and Resources

Moderately mentally handicapped people usually found a place in rural society—milking the cows, helping out in the garden, setting the table for dinner. Unless they were severely disabled, there was generally no need to make special arrangements for them. Severely mentally disabled and mentally ill people were harder to integrate in daily life.

For centuries, society had a dual personality when it came to the mentally ill. The church may have thought that the insane needed prayers for protection and forgiveness, but governments, with widespread public support, often took a more pragmatic approach. Both Henry VIII, who founded London's notorious Bedlam in the 16th century, and Dr Thomas Bond, who established an asylum in Pennsylvania in 1755, thought the insane should be locked away in madhouses, not just for their own protection, but for society's. These early madhouses were more like jails than hospitals. In the 19th century, religious men like Phillipe Pinel in France, William Tuke in Britain and Dr George Peters in the colony of New Brunswick, introduced moral treatments into asylums. Rather than feared, the mentally ill were treated with kindness in these new asylums. Not everyone was convinced moral treatment was a good idea, though, and both types of asylums competed with each other throughout the 19th century.

But as proudly progressive Albertans considered what kind of asylum they wanted to build, the consensus was clear. They wanted a modern asylum built according to the best science. They also wanted mental defectives removed from their communities. Above all, they preferred the moral treatment model which treated patients with kindness. The Liberals delivered.

When Alberta Hospital in Ponoka opened in 1911, it was a humane refuge for both the severely 'feeble-minded' and 'insane'. It also fulfilled the government's need to protect the inmates from harm and to protect the public from inmates who could not be held accountable for their actions.

Within months, the place was filled to capacity. Another men's ward was added, then another women's ward. It wasn't enough. By the time World War I broke out in 1914, patients were sleeping on mats on the floor of the once stately day room. And there was no end to the influx.

As the Great War raged in Europe, the province knew they would be in even worse shape as wounded soldiers returned home and needed both physical and mental care. With the constantly burgeoning population of mentally ill, the cost of providing moral treatment Albertans once envisioned was now beyond reach.

By the end of World War I, many of Canada's top public health officials, including Dr Charles Kirk Clarke and Dr Clare Hincks, co-founders of the Canadian National Committee for Mental Hygiene, along with Dr Helen McMurchy, Ontario's Director of the Feeble-Minded, were even more concerned about the spread of low intelligence from one generation to another than they were about the epidemic of insanity. McMurchy, in particular, was successful in convincing Canadian women's groups that sterilizing the mentally defective was key to their goals of improving the lot of women and children.

The eugenicists' insistence that alcoholism and venereal disease were 'racial poisons' passed on by heredity dove-tailed nicely with the prohibitionist, morality-minded agenda of church-going ladies who joined Canada's women's organizations.

Thousands of women in the Women's Institute, Women's Christian Temperance Union, and some locals of the United Farm Women of Alberta put aside their reservations about birth control in the face of the 'evidence' presented by the medical establishment. As they began lobbying for sexual sterilization of the insane and feeble-minded, their cry was loudest in Alberta.

Women Enter Alberta Politics

FEARS RACIAL POISONS GAINING STRONG GRIP

TORONTO, May 18—Dr C. W. Salesby, of London, England, noted authority on eugenics, addressed a general meeting of the National Public Health Convention here last night and declared that racial poisons had gained a grip on the English races and he feared were eating away the virility of the English people. One of the cankers eating at the heart of the empire, Dr Salesby said, was venereal disease. He asserted that prohibition was of assistance in fighting venereal disease.[51]

Alberta's women, who received the provincial vote on 19 April 1916, took their fight for better education, health care, prohibition, and women's rights into city councils and the legislature well before the armistice was declared 11 November 1918.

In 1917, Hannah Rollinson Gale, who helped establish municipal hospitals and reform prisons in Calgary, was elected to Calgary's city council, becoming the first female alderman in Canada.[52] Earlier in the year, Women's Christian Temperance Union member, Louise McKinney was elected to the provincial legislature in 1917 as a Non-Partisan League MLA (precursor of the United Farmers of Alberta, who formed the government in 1921). Lt Roberta Catherine Price, née MacAdams, was elected at the same time as McKinney to represent soldiers away from their homes fighting in WWI. She was the first woman in the British Empire to introduce legislation.

Another WCTU member author and activist, Nelly McClung, was elected as a Liberal Member of the Legislature in 1921-1926. Alberta was also home to Canada's first woman magistrate, Emily Murphy. Among this group of powerful women was Hon Irene Parlby of Alix, who served as president of the United Farm Women of Alberta from 1916-1919, and minister without portfolio under the UFA government during its first term (1921-1926). In 1922, Parlby's local UFWA chapter introduced a contentious motion supporting birth control and eugenics. The Alix Chapter's motion tabled for further study after a raucous debate threatened to split the UFWA.[53]

VII: GETTING MENTAL DEFECTIVES OFF THE STREETS

C ries from mental health activists and women's groups that the insane asylum in Ponoka wasn't getting mental defectives off the street put Premier Charles Stewart and his Liberals in a budgetary pickle.

So when the Alberta Legislature passed a motion on February 20, 1917 to purchase land in Red Deer 'for the purpose of the work on behalf of the feeble-minded',[54] the government ignored the motion. Instead, they used the land for a soldiers' hospital. In March 1918, MLA Dr Stanley, asked the Hon Mr. Boyle, Minister of Health, what steps had been taken toward creating a home for the feeble-minded, Boyle gave him the bad news.

"The government does not intend to take any steps toward establishing a school or home for the feeble-minded until the end of the war, but intend taking what steps are necessary to get the fullest information regarding the number and classification of feeble-minded persons in the province," said Boyle.[55]

The debate was off to a bad start.

As discussion continued about the lack of care for foster children, the mentally ill, the deaf, mute and blind, it was obvious that the opposition UFA were fed-up with the Liberals' handling of the files.

Non-Partisan League MLA Louise McKinney made another motion, seconded by Dr Stanley, that "in the opinion of this house, the government should at once take definite steps to provide for the care and training of the feeble-minded in our public schools and also in our adult population." She got nowhere. In frustration, she withdrew her motion.[56]

Act Respecting Mentally Defective Persons

Facing allegations that they refused to solve the problem, the Liberals came up with their own plan to segregate the province's mental defectives. The Government's *Act Respecting Mentally Defective Persons* received Royal Assent 17 April 1919.

According the Act, a mentally defective person was "any person afflicted with mental deficiency from birth, or from an early age, so pronounced that he is incapable of managing himself or his affairs, and who is not classified as an insane person within the meaning of *The Insanity Act*."[57]

The Act made the already overcrowded Edmonton Home for Mentally Defective Children a public institution which would accept children from anywhere in the province and gave anyone in Alberta the right to ask the Minister of Education to declare a person 'mentally defective'.

> Whenever it is reported to the Minister that any person in the province is a mentally defective person the Minister may cause inquiry to be made and, if as the result of such inquiry it appears that any person should be provided for in an institution for mentally defective persons, and that the parents, guardians or others, having control of such persons refuse to consent to his being so taken care of, the Minister may cause proceedings to be instituted before a justice of the peace in the manner herein provided for.[58]

Municipalities would pay the costs of caring for the mentally defectives from their communities at the Edmonton Home, but they could retrieve those costs from the individual's estate or family. The Act created a provincial guardian of the estates of mental defectives, the Administrator of Lunatics' Estates, and made the Minister of Education the guardian of 'any infant received under this Act'.[59]

In 1920, plans were completed to expand the Edmonton Home For Defective Children onto a 1000-acre site at Oliver, on Edmonton's northern outskirts. With its own farm and garden, the site was large enough to produce food and housing for 500 children. But more space was needed.

As Lieutenant Governor Robert G. Brett read the Throne Speech, February 15, 1921, he finally revealed the Liberals' agreement to turn the soldiers' hospital in Red Deer into a home for the feeble-minded:

"It has been decided by my government to establish a permanent home for the feeble minded during the coming season, thus providing a necessary and welcome addition to the humane public institutions of the province."[60]

Some doctors and women's activists had hoped Stewart's government should go a step further and introduce a bill to force mental defectives to be sexually sterilized as many American states had done.

Premier Stewart had no plans to bring in a eugenics bill. His Liberal MLAs knew most Albertans weren't demanding sexual sterilization of mental defectives. The locals of the populist United Farmers of Alberta and United Farm Women of Alberta were still scrapping over the issue. And the most prominent Liberal MLA supporting sexual sterilization, Nelly McClung, might not even get re-elected because voters were fed up with her support for prohibition.

VIII: POLITICS WITHOUT POLICIES: ALBERTA'S GRAND EXPERIMENT

Want to understand Alberta politics? Forget the left-right political spectrum they talk about at the University of Calgary, Manning Centre for Democracy, or the Canada West Foundation. It just doesn't explain the pragmatic way most Albertans think. Nor does it explain the outcry in 2009 that forced the province to reverse its plans to cut health-care and Assured Income for the Severely Handicapped. Alberta's non-partisan streak began in the days when the province was part of the Northwest Territories. Even today, you won't find municipal candidates, mayors, reeves, or councils showing their party stripes on the job.[61]

Alberta's never-ending, ever-changing political movements usually have progressive underpinnings along with conservative roots. That's because they owe their existence to a pragmatic populist heritage that helped a non-partisan farmers' rights group, the United Farmers of Alberta, replace the Liberal party as Alberta's second political dynasty.

They said it in the Papers

A few weeks after the summer election of 1921, readers of the *Lethbridge Daily Herald* are treated to a learned analysis of the surprising consequences of the provincial election. Many eyes wander from the journalists' rundown of what policies and cabinet picks they might expect from the non-partisan farmers' organization that now controls of the legislature.

The attraction for their wandering eyes is a small box at the bottom of the page. Inside it, a tiny news story conveys the fears of an American university professor. He's afraid the current craze for passing laws making it illegal for the unfit to marry might spark a revolution.

TOO MUCH EUGENICS WOULD CAUSE REVOLT

NEW YORK, Sept. 27—A eugenic law forbidding the unfit to marry would breed revolution, Prof Rudolph M. Binder of New York University, told the eugenics congress, in session here yesterday. A better course to pursue, he said, would be to make the unfit fit.

—*Lethbridge Daily Herald*, 27 October 1921, Page 8.

Leave it Up to the Voters

The 21st-century incarnation of the United Farmers of Alberta is one of the most successful farmers' cooperatives on the prairies—selling everything from rubber boots to fishing supplies to gasoline. It bears little resemblance to the farmers' rights organization founded in 1909.[62] Back then the goal was ensuring Alberta's often city-bound politicians didn't forget to look out for the farm families in their constituencies.

When the UFA decided to run candidates in provincial elections, members insisted they were not forming an old style political party. They didn't need have a platform because UFA MLAs would vote according to the wishes of their constituents. And they would not act as partisans in the legislature.

Just to prove the sceptics wrong, UFA premier Herbert Greenfield included an opposition Liberal MLA in his first cabinet.

The UFA Members of the Legislature expected Albertans to tell them what they thought should be done with the province's overloaded mental health system. They did. Even within the UFA, the debate was loud and angry.

When the Attorney General and MLA for Ponoka, John Brownlee, walked into the 1922 United Farm Women of Alberta Convention, he may have expected to be served tea and cookies. Instead, he found himself in the middle of a nasty fight over birth control and eugenics.

The UFA MLA from Alix, Irene Parlby, tried to urge the women's wing of the UFWA to support eugenics science. To back her up the Alix UFWA chapter presented a motion on birth control and eugenics. The ruckus that ensued nearly broke up the convention, and the motion was tabled.

The ladies then put on a united front, urging Brownlee to diligently enforce prohibition. Happy to be taking on a less contentious topic, Brownlee assured the women he'd found just the man to enforce those prohibition laws. Brownlee told the UFWA that he wasn't so sure their tough line on prohibition was what the voters wanted because the issue of prohibition was one of levity among the general population.

RESUME OF PROCEEDINGS OF THE CONVENTION
OF UNITED FARM WOMEN

(by Elizabeth Bailey Price)

All news wires led to Alberta, turbulent, progressive Alberta, last week, when the city of Calgary was the scene of the UFA and the UFWA conventions.

Throughout the province itself and throughout the other provinces, the women, especially the rural women, were watching, waiting and wondering just what demands the farm women would demand of the Farmer Government of Alberta as their spoils of victory.

Hon Irene Parlby, Minister without portfolio, was one of the speakers and she heralded a note of caution. She said that she found that the women were especially pressing for many reforms such as homes for delinquent boys and girls, homes for the aged and infirm, institutions for the mental defectives, but no government, no matter how sympathetic it was to these reforms, could travel as fast as was expected and to bear in mind that the provincial purse was limited and the people had reached their limit of taxation.

After this, the first and only resolution asking for a money grant from the government was tabled. This was to the effect that the Women's Institutes be made self-supporting or the UFWA placed on the same basis. It was decided that no protest would be lodged against the grant to the Women's Institutes and that the UFWA would continue to remain an independent group of voters and ask no favours in the way of money grants.

DISCUSS BIRTH CONTROL

The most heated discussion of the whole convention centred around a resolution dealing with birth control which originated in the Alix local and which read as follows: "Whereas one of the primary necessities for family and therefore for public health is an intelligently determined interval between pregnancies to be secured by regulating the inception of life and not by interfering with life after it starts and whereas the lack of knowledge as to how to secure such an interval frequently results in serious disaster for mother and babies and indirectly or directly for the entire community. Be it resolved that this convention urge the speedy removal of all barriers due to legal restrictions, tradition, prejudice or ignorance, which now prevents parents from access to such scientific knowledge on this subject as is possessed by the medical profession."

For two hours this occupied time of the convention. Mrs M.S. Roper, of Alix, spoke to the resolution and in support of it read a carefully prepared report containing statistics and arguments in favour of it. Men bear arms, but women bear children, said the speaker. That is the birth politics of men. In England 25 percent of the soldiers were rejected as physically unfit. In America 20 percent, which means that one out of four of the male population is not fit even for war. Fewer and better babies is what we want, a control of birth so that pregnancy will not be perpetual, unregulated, haphazard and miserable.

She referred to the economic side of the question. Statistics showing that 50 percent of the families in the United States were living on $800.00 per year and 70 percent, on $1000.00. No one can educate his children, can feed them, clothe them, fit them for citizenship or even for soldiers on such a wage. It is quality not quantity that should be considered.

In the United States there are three million children who grow up annually to compete with their parents in the field of labour, forcing wages down and making conditions harder for all. The injustice to the child who is brought into the world, where there is insufficient food for him, overwork and ill health and, lack of opportunity for education was also pointed out. The recent war was brought on by the over-populated nations and has proven the fact that men were slaughtered to keep down the population.

The speaker then gave a brief history of the birth control movement in Holland, and what a boon it had been to that country. Every baby born is wanted and Holland has the sturdiest happiest babies in the world. Birth control clinics are established throughout the country and parents are taught the fundamental facts. In fact, women considered it obligatory to pass this information on and, although the birthrate is not so high as in other countries, the death rate is so very much lower that there is a greater proportion in the increase in population in these countries than in others where birth control is prohibited.

In conclusion: Mrs Roper moved the resolution.

DIVINE WILL OF GOD

Immediately on this, one of the delegates arose and moved that the motion be tabled, without discussion as they thought no one should take steps to interfere with or prevent the divine will of God in the creation of life. This was voted down and the pros and cons were then discussed heatedly. Many of the members felt that this involved a sacred matter, that in voting for it was contrary to the dictum of the Bible which said: "Be yea fruitful and multiply." Others felt that the organization should not be heralded through the newspapers as having, voted on this and indicated that if such a resolution went through it would be their duty to retire from the organization.

Thank God my mother didn't believe in birth control, exclaimed another delegate, emphasizing this statement with a thunderous knock on the table. Other delegates believed that this information should be secured for diseased parents, or to prevent the multiplying of the feeble-minded, but in the case of healthy parents already there were too many women now who wanted to shirk the arduous duty of raising a family. Another raised the point of having 'such books' around where the young people were that 'our girls' and 'our boys' already knew too much and such knowledge would increase the problem of illegitimacy.

It was pointed out that in Holland because of birth control illegitimacy and prostitution had decreased.

Case after case was cited of tired, hopeless mothers with large families which they could neither clothe nor feed, that these conditions had resulted in mothers losing their minds or being completely broken down by health.

Legislative remedies for these conditions were suggested by those opposing the resolution such as giving every child a bonus, and making it compulsory to have health certificates at the time of marriage.

Another delegate pointed out that knowledge alone would not accomplish for the country all that was needed but that moral education must accompany knowledge and that boys and girls should be taught the sacredness of parenthood. As many of the delegates did not want to take on the responsibility of voting on this and certain locals had not received it in time for discussion, it was decided to refer it back to the locals, the subject to be brought up again next year.

WANT ENFORCEMENT OF PROHIBITION

The most discussed subject in the whole convention was the enforcement of the prohibition laws. Concerning this Hon J.B. Brownlee made his first announcement regarding his policy of the administration of the liquor act: he said he had determined upon the appointment of a man to take general charge of the administration of the act, a man who would have the confidence of the people. Also another man at the head of the police squad was to be appointed. The man who could not be bought and one with a keen sense of his responsibility in the enforcement of this act. These names would be announced shortly.

He stated that the enforcement of this act would be determined by the backing of the people behind it. He asked the members to report any information, in any of the districts in which they knew that this law was being broken. He said it was not necessary to prove their case, that their communications would be treated absolutely confidential but that it would be passed on to the police squad who would immediately investigate the conditions. The greatest difficulties that confronted the enforcement of this act were still involving the difference between the provincial and Dominion authority in the laws concerning this and the levity with which the whole prohibition matter was considered by the public in general.[63]

While sterilization remained a contentious issue, the UFA was serious about getting the defectives off the streets. They amended the *Mental Defectives Act* to create a new Provincial Training School for Mental Deficiency at Oliver to serve the whole province. They also gave the superintendents of provincial institutions the power to admit patients and to deny parents the right to remove their children from the institution. Inmates committed by the Minister of Health could only be released by order of the Minister.

In 1925, they amended the Act again: parents who received permission to remove their children must provide reports to the superintendent in January and July. Adults released must report every three months. School inspectors were required to report mentally defective children to the Minister of Health.

IX: THE BRITISH EMPIRE'S FIRST SEXUAL STERILIZATION ACT

W hy give the unfit free room and board for life when more fit Albertans needed schools, roads and hospitals?

Housing one mentally handicapped child in the provincial training school cost the government $10 every month up to the child's sixteenth birthday. By that time, most of the feeble-minded teenagers were fit enough to milk cows or wash floors. Why not put them to work?

No way, said the eugenicists! Once out of the segregated wards, unfit youths and recovered lunatics were liable to pass on their mental defects by having children of their own. Even worse, those babies were liable to be illegitimate.

The government needed to come up with a way to discharge able-bodied morons and recovered lunatics without fuelling cries that they were adding to the epidemic of lunacy. Otherwise, Alberta's feeble-minded just might drain the provincial treasury.

By 1928, Premier John Brownlee, gauged the electorate's frustration and brought in eugenics legislation. The eugenicists themselves offered a solution: sterilize the unfit before releasing them into the community.

The Province of Alberta *Sexual Sterilization Act*, which received Royal Assent March 21, 1928, created a four person Eugenics Board composed of Dr E. Pope of Edmonton, Dr E.G., Mason of Calgary; Dr J.M. McEacheran, of the University of Alberta in Edmonton, and Mrs Jean H. Field of Kinuso, Alberta. The new act stipulated that replacements to the board would be appointed by the Lieutenant Governor. The board would always be made up of two physicians, one nominated by the Senate of the University of Alberta and the other nominated by the Alberta College of Physicians and Surgeons. Replacements for the two non-physicians on the board would be appointed by the Lieutenant Governor in council.

The Act stated that sterilizations could only be done upon release of a patient back into the community, with the consent of the patient, his next of kin or guardian. A loophole in the consent clause allowed for ministerial approval for sterilization when patients could not give informed consent and had no next of kin in the province. Even then, the operation could only be approved if the only obstacle to letting the patient resume life in the community was his or her ability to pass on a mental defect to potential offspring.

> When it is proposed to discharge any inmate of a mental hospital, the Medical Superintendent or other officer in charge thereof may cause such inmate to be examined by or in the presence of the board of examiners.
>
> If upon such examination, the board is unanimously of opinion that the patient might safely be discharged if the danger of procreation with its attendant risk of multiplication of the evil by transmission of the disability to progeny were eliminated, the board may direct in writing such surgical operation for sexual sterilization of the inmate as may be specified in the written direction and shall appoint some competent surgeon to perform the operation.
>
> Such operation shall not be performed unless the inmate, if in the opinion of the board, he is capable of giving consent, has consented thereto, or where the board is of the opinion that the inmate is not capable of giving such consent, the husband or wife of the inmate or the parent or the guardian of the inmate if he is unmarried has consented thereto, or where the inmate has no husband, wife, parent, or guardian resident in the province, the Minister has consented thereto.
>
> No surgeon duly directed to perform any such operation shall be liable to any civil action whatsoever by the performance thereof.[64]

This didn't solve problems in the Mental Health system. The Liberal Opposition let the government know they were not pleased with their successor's handling of the Mental Health system they had begun to build before they lost the 1928 general election. In March 1929, the Honourable N.G. Reid, provincial treasurer, defended the UFA's Minister of Health against charges from Liberal Leader, J. Shaw, K.C.

Shaw alleged that Ponoka hospital was overcrowded, dark, and had little fresh air. They claimed the place didn't offer patients enough occupational therapy and employed inefficient staff. Insisting that the Provincial Mental Hospital at Ponoka matched the best standards in Canada, Reid declared:

> We have heard much from the other side of the house about public opinion and how the people felt toward the minister and the administration of his department. Personally I am content to leave the whole question to

public opinion and will do so in the firm belief that the valuable work done by the minister on behalf of the health of the people of this province will be recognized and appreciated. The public will weigh the capabilities and the personalities of the leaders opposite who have attacked the minister and then will weigh him and his work with the result that in my opinion the minister will survive when they go under.[65]

The Conservatives didn't like the new direction either. In particular, they thought the government had picked the wrong man to study Alberta's mental health system. They said that the pro-eugenic stance of Dr Clare Hincks, co-founder of the National Committee for Mental Hygiene, would lead to Alberta choosing the wrong policies in their attempt to make the province's mental health system more effective.

"From the point of view of public confidence for reasons which give to my mind, Dr Hincks was not a happy choice as commissioner. Dr Hincks is the greatest protagonist in this country of the idea unaccepted as yet in most civilized countries, indeed accepted in but very few states of sexual sterilization," charged Col C.Y. Weaver, a Conservative MLA from Edmonton.[66]

Weaver conceded that he and his Conservative colleagues in the legislature would support most of the Hincks-Farrer report, but they would not endorse any recommendations supporting sexual sterilization and he alleged that the government was listening too closely to its consultants and not closely enough to the people of Alberta. "Opinion is very much divided here. Dr Hincks and the ministry worked in very close sympathy with one another as those who have waged a fight together inevitably become, and I think it unfortunate that the minister should have turned to dally in his time of difficulty," said Weaver.[67]

Weaver supported Liberal claims that the Minister of Health was negligent in his supervision of the Ponoka hospital.

"In reply to my questions on the order paper, the Minister replied that there was no record of the number of his visits to the hospital during the past eighteen months. That, I think. Mr Speaker, was a direct and intentional evasion of the question. It implies in the light of the fact that the deputy minister made fourteen visits and the assistant deputy eight visits during that time, many of which being before the last sitting of the House, and made verbal reports that there could be no possible excuse for the minister not taking the members of the legislature into his confidence," said Weaver.

The UFA government was undeterred by the accusations. In 1933,[68] they toughened up government control over the lives of mental defectives by amending the *Mental Defectives Act*.[69]

The 'power of procreation' was reinforced as a valid reason to deny mental patients freedom. The Act read: "The superintendent may discharge any mentally defective person from any institution in any case in which the superintendent considers such that such person is capable of earning the legitimate livelihood and conforming to the law, and that the power of procreation no longer exists."[70]

Once released the patient could be forced back into the institution if he could not work, lost a job, got into trouble with the law, or 'pursues any mode or manner of living', unsatisfactory to the institution's superintendent. Released patients could be apprehended and conveyed to any institution "established under this Act for the reception of mental defectives." The superintendent could now order patients moved to other institutions without patient or guardian consent.

X: HOLD YOUR HORSES!
(MAYBE THIS ISN'T SUCH A GOOD IDEA)

Peoples Forum
STERILIZATION
Editor *Herald*

Sir, with considerable interest we read, early in the winter, that several ladies representing various organizations whose chief object is to promote the welfare of their fellow citizens, had presented several resolutions to the government; one of which suggested that the scope of *The Sterilization Act* be extended to apply to men who commit sexual crimes.

The proper treatment of men who commit sexual crimes is eunuchation, it terminates sexual desire and lust, and prevents the perpetration of such crimes. Unfortunately, the Criminal Code of Canada does not make provision for such salutary, restraining measures. The Criminal Code of Canada is entirely within the Jurisdiction of the Federal Government, so the Provincial Government had no jurisdiction in that matter, nor in the matter of sterilization.

The Premier's reply, to the effect that sterilization is in experimental stage, and that the government thought it well to go slowly, although very meagre, is somewhat frank and gratifying, as it indicates that some of the members of the government and legislature have given the subject some thought and study. It is gratifying to learn, during the session, that the Act has not been put into operation, as such acts have been found very unsatisfactory in nearly all of the American States, in which they have been tried, and even declared unconstitutional by the courts, in most of them, although each state has its own criminal code with powers over life and death of the citizens, which powers the Canadian provinces have not. We commend the Government for using caution in the matter, as sterilization results in an increase in vice, crime and disease; the far-reaching consequences of which are physical and mental deficiency and moral delinquency, consequently increasing the evil that it is intended to remedy.

—John Halloway 11049 127 St. Edmonton[71]

Activists barraged the UFA government to expand the scope of the *Sexual Sterilization Act*, even beyond the legal limits of the British North America Act. But many Albertans had their doubts that the sometimes extreme views of the eugenicists had any basis in logic. When a Mrs Harrison showed up at the offices of the *Lethbridge Daily Herald* to spout eugenics and communist doctrine, the weary editor was brought out his afternoon doldrums by her alarming theories about childcare.

> She told me that she considered 'family life' absolutely subversive to the interests of the Communists, that children should from birth be regarded as the property of the State, that they would develop a much more genuine sense of responsibility in the atmosphere of the institution reproducing communists than in the home, which is under the influence of the patriarchal system. As regards the relationship of the sexes, she felt that it should exist merely for the purpose of reproducing the race without restraint except those imposed on by observance of the laws of eugenics in pursuance of her theories. She has planned a new system of motherhood endowment with pre-natal and post-natal care for mothers and babies. It was all very interesting, though I mentally took issue with her on every point.[72]

All this eugenics talk of sex seem a bit dodgy to moral conservatives. Their suspicions were confirmed when W.M. Davidson, a homeopath and eugenics lecturer, was convicted in Calgary on two charges of selling printed matter tending to corrupt morals and publishing an advertisement regarding the restoring of virility. Davidson was given the choice of paying a fine of $500 plus costs of his trial or spending three months in jail.[73]

As the debate over sexual hygiene continued internationally, the Pope and his cardinals condemned eugenics. In Britain, Cardinal Bourne fought a proposal contemplated by the British Ministry of Health to teach sexual hygiene.

"They should not admit interference with the liberty of marriage in adult men and women, nor any element of the horror known as eugenics. They could not admit what was called sex teaching, or any one of the whole series of propositions regarding sexual hygiene. Neither could they admit the claim of the state over the children as against that of the parents," wrote the cardinal.

The cardinal asked his hearers to keep in mind the proposed attack on moral law and the consequent infringement of individual liberty. They were dealing with people, said the cardinal, referring to outside supporters of such projects, who no longer accepted Christian law, men who he had been termed after-Christian.[74]

Even people who thought humans needed improving weren't sure humans were smart enough to know what a better human being was. Perhaps the most eloquent of this position was George Bernard Shaw.

WORLD NEEDS BETTER BRED PEOPLE, SAYS G.B.S.

NEW HAVEN, Conn., Feb. 11—A detailed selection of human beings is impossible because the sort of human beings that ought to be produced is not known, Bernard Shaw, British dramatist, had told the American Eugenics Society, which queried him as to his attitude toward eugenics. Mr Shaw wrote, I am fully sensible to the world's need for better bred people. But the effect of the qualities of income and consequent restrictions and perversion natural selection produced by capitalism, are so omnipresent that the first step in practical eugenics must be to make the whole community inter-marriageable and leave the result to nature. Only within very narrow limits dare we say with any confidence what sort of human beings ought not to be produced.[75]

But the naysayers faced a losing battle against experts, like the President of the American Medical Association, and the plethora of newswire stories touting eugenic successes. The AMA President, a Social Darwinist named Dr Pusey, was a fan of Calvin Coolidge's wise statesmanship in taking a definite stand against the federal support of a wide range of socialized activities.[76] Pusey lamented social reforms, including subsidized maternity care, for coddling individuals and fostering incompetence. Instead, he proposed birth control for the poor and eugenics.

Limitation of population rather than increase is the logical social ideal of the time, Dr William A. Pusey, president of the American Medical Association told the AMA annual convention in 1924.

If no effort is made at birth control, nature will take charge of the situation by eliminating those least able to resist. When this condition of saturation arrives, the humane plans of socialistic situation of today will be wrecked in the struggle by society for mere existence. Today there is no longer a frontier.

The United States has in 120 years passed 100,000,000 population. Within the span of children now living, our population will reach 175,000,000. The haphazardness of marriage and the possibility of public education on proper public education on proper marital choice in the absence of hope for a more scientific method of Eugenics.[77]

Across the Atlantic, the Rev Dr Ernest William Barnes, a mathematician who became the Anglican Bishop of Birmingham, U.K., was a eugenics activist. In 1924, he told the Eugenics Education Society that repressive measures against breeding of the unfit would be in accordance with the plan by which 'God brought humanity this far on its road'. The good Bishop described the 'unfit' as an impediment to the creation of what Christians termed the Kingdom of God on earth. Rev Barnes looked forward to the day when Christians would abandon their moral wariness and give full support to laws supporting forced sterilization of the unfit.[78]

Closer to home, Rev George Kerby, a Methodist Minister and President of Mount Royal College, said the 'greatest crime on the calendar was to bring into the world a misfit child, a mental cripple'. July 1, 1936, Kerby told the Canadian National Federation of Home and School Associations in Toronto, that Alberta's law requiring health certificates before marriage was the first step to eugenic marriage and said it should be followed elsewhere. He also compared the disabled to 'helpless animals' who ought not to reproduce. "Such crimes are being committed at such a rate that there are more persons in mental institutions than in all of the colleges and universities of Canada," said Kerby.[79]

Kerby endorsed Germany's alertness to the dangers of 'misfits' being allowed to marry and have children, he added that "the German example was" the first step toward universal eugenic marriage. In Canada, he advocated educating children about the functions of every part of their bodies, through physiology courses in every school.[80]

Dr Kerby said he wished he had never seen the inside of an asylum. "It would make you sick to see men so helpless that they had to have serviettes tucked under their chins—like babies—just helpless animals. The time is rotten ripe for something to be done about the situation," he explained.[81]

Three months after Kerby's speech, the United Church of Canada (which now included Methodists like Kerby) came out in favour of birth control and sterilizing the 'unfit'.[82, 83]

The Eugenics Society of Canada, which wanted other Canadian provinces to follow Alberta by passing their own sexual sterilization acts,[84] was now so powerful that when CBC Manager Gladstone Murray refused to broadcast a lecture by Dr Luke Teske of Toronto that linked venereal disease to eugenics in February 1937, Dr W.L. Sutton protested to the national media on behalf of society. A few months later, Murray was up before the House of Commons radio committee defending himself. He dared not question the mission of the Eugenics Society as he defended the CBC. Instead, he said that he doubted the accuracy of some statements in Teske's address and assured the Commons committee that the CBC was already in discussions with the Eugenics Society of Canada 'for an authoritative series of broadcasts'.

According to the Eugenics movement, even Canadian Aboriginals benefitted when they adopted 'eugenics science'. International newswires hummed as the incredible story of a First Nations clan in northern British Columbia led by a Métis patriarch named David. Like the wise Old Testament patriarchs, David reportedly ensured his clan remained pure by separating them from the moral pollution of neighbouring clans. But there was a modern twist to David's story: he apparently used eugenic principles to keep his new tribe healthier and brighter than the neighbours.

> The story of the unusual experiment in tribe-building one of the most interesting and practical examples of eugenics known to mankind has been brought here by Provincial Constable Thomas Van Dyke, who has just returned from the far-off tramp and trading post at Fort Graham. David was a man of remarkable ideals and self-restraint. He scorned the habits that had humbled other Indians and breeds. He was industrious and became one of the most successful hunters and trappers in the vast region over which he wandered. He avoided village life for he dreaded the sight and companionship of the majority of Indians who had fallen into a life of idleness and intemperance. Yet he cherished a pride in his native ancestry and he began to dream of a tribe of super Indians that one might be developed worthy of the country they were to inhabit. With this ideal in mind, he chose his mate carefully. He wed a Steance woman, the handsomest and strongest woman of her tribe. There were four daughters and when the time came for them to be married he sought afar for suitable bridegrooms, tall in stature, free from disease and bad habits and powerful in physique. The four daughters of David and their four husbands form the nucleus of the tribe that now numbers fifty-four and soon the search will start for suitable grooms for the many granddaughters who are coming of age.[85]

XI: TAKING THE ELECT TO THE PROMISED LAND

T he schoolteacher turned preacher William Aberhart burst upon Alberta's political scene like an early morning locomotive—waking up sleepy prairie towns and farms, pulling shopkeepers, farmers, teachers, and housewives aboard for what he promised was an exciting journey. Aberhart, a Calvinist preacher and schoolteacher who claimed to interpret "end-time prophecy," promised to transform Alberta first, then recreate all of Canada into a Social Credit[86] Promised Land—where worthy citizens (the elect) would joyously await the Second Coming of Christ and enjoy their due reward even before the Second Coming.[87] To build their Promised Land, Albertans would tear apart the existing economic system, fire the banks, print their own money, control pricing, give every adult a dividend they could live on, and ban greed and profiteering.

Who was this guy?

When adversaries angered him, William Aberhart's fiery face often boiled over with 'righteous anger'. At 250 pounds, balding with dark-rimmed glasses, he looked every inch the school principal he was. His preference for grey suits apparently made him look so much like a British battleship sailing toward the enemy that it prompted one of his admirers to call him 'the dreadnought'. That same follower described his hero as 'a trout among minnows'.[88,89]

Aberhart, a graduate of the Ontario Normal School and Queen's University, was an Ontario school principal and part-time preacher who came west in 1910 at age 32. In Calgary, he picked up where he left off in Brantford, teaching and preaching. As a principal, he marshalled students and teachers in four Calgary schools over the next 25 years. But teaching school was never enough for Aberhart. He also preached and taught Bible Classes, establishing the Calgary Prophetic Bible Conference in 1918 and turning his Sunday afternoon lectures into a radio show called the *Back to the Bible Hour* in 1925. It was these programs that made him a member of the family to thousands in Canada's four Western Provinces as well as the northwest United States. (Many rural folk could not get to church every Sunday, especially during harsh winters, but young and old family members could gather around the radio and listen breathlessly to radio preachers, like Aberhart, interpret scripture). When Aberhart discovered Major Douglas' Social Credit economic theories, he spread the message to his radio listeners, preaching Social Credit along with the scripture.

Science and Social Credit

When William Aberhart and his disciple Ernest Manning started making the rounds of Alberta churches and halls—speaking about their newfound way to political salvation—Social Credit still went by the name 'Douglasism' in honour of its Scottish founder. Major Clifford Hugh Douglas' 1924 book *Social Credit* inspired enough interest in the Dominions of the British Empire to get him invited to speak to the Canadian Select Committee of the House of Commons on Banking and Industry in Ottawa in 1923.[90]

As newspaper editors, politicians and old-timers in small town coffee shops argued about what caused the Depression—perhaps it was loss of buying power? Or was it just the Stock Exchange crash—William Aberhart told his congregations that he had found a scientific way to save Alberta from the scourge and conspiracy of bankers and financiers.

"Social Credit is in reality a scientific method of distributing the goods and services which we have in abundance in our province to the greatest advantage of everyone of our citizens," Aberhart told his radio audiences and those who gathered to hear him speak in towns and cities across the province.[91]

Aberhart believed there would be plenty for all once Canadians got international financiers and Canada's 'fifty big shots' off their backs. Poverty in Alberta was caused, he claimed, by financial interests that kept profits out of the hands of the masses, preventing consumers from acquiring the goods and services they needed.

"Furthermore, as far as the individual province is concerned, I am of the opinion the solution is not to be found in the realm of monetary reform, that is a federal matter. The question, as I see it, finds its greatest focus in connection with the lack of purchasing power found in the hands of consumers. Social Credit attacks the problem, at that point,"[92] said Aberhart.

According to Aberhart, Albertans didn't need to work longer hours or increase their productivity to escape poverty. Social Credit would spark prosperity by getting money into the hands of consumers.

"I am satisfied the problem is not to be found in the question of the number of hours per week the labourer must work. I am also convinced the problem is not bound up wholly in the matter exports and I believe that sabotage for the purpose of increasing prices is really criminal," said Aberhart.[93]

Aberhart was an educated man, a true believer in science. And like most educated people of his generation, he was inclined to believe eugenicists' assertions that 'science' had proven them right. Under Social Credit, Alberta's health care system would be modern, scientific, and designed to ensure that Albertans were healthy contributors to the nation's prosperity. That meant Alberta's health care system would provide free maternity and infant care as well as free care for polio, cancer and tuberculosis patients. But it must go further, to ensure more of the 'unfit' were identified and rendered incapable of reproducing.

Preaching Economic Salvation

It was a meeting like Aberhart's followers had set up in Blairmore, Vulcan, Granham, and dozens more small towns and cities. But tonight, the Social Credit evangelistic crusade was at the Lethbridge arena. The energetic Salvation Army band had put the congregation in a mood to hear the 'Social Credit Gospel' and fill the collection plates with their nickels and dimes. As the preacher from the Prophetic Bible Institute steps forward, ready to make the same pitch he's made on the radio and in other towns and cities across the province, the crowd goes quiet. "The inevitable crisis is upon us. The rapture and appearance of Christ is at hand. We will start a new social order," Aberhart shouted. As he pounded on the lectern, he proclaimed a new age of economic salvation for the people of Alberta.

Damnation for the Bankers

Aberhart delighted in proclaiming damnation on ungodly bankers, financiers and politicians and debunking their ideas about how to end the Depression. His elect, the people of Alberta, would bring Salvation to all of Canada, by defeating these Goliath 'Sons of Satan'. First Canada, then the entire British Empire, would take up his offer of salvation.

"The people have been getting to realize that there is a solution to preventing problems of poverty and death and misery in this vast dominion so bountifully blessed with all of the needs of mankind. That solution lies fundamentally in the distribution of more purchasing power," shouted Aberhart.[94]

Like an Old Testament prophet, Aberhart warned the faithful that if they did not heed this economic 'altar call' they and their children might die with their dreams unrealized:

"May I say this, men and women, unless you seize this election opportunity to demand monetary reform in Canada at once your chance may be gone forever because in the next five years, the impending financial crash may come to engulf us to the chaos of ruined homes farms and business that it will leave in its wake. This is your task. This, your challenge. Fight through, I charge you for the sake of your sons and daughters. If not for yourself, so that they at least may live secure, happy and unfettered in a new democracy that shall cover this great Dominion from sea to sea."[95]

Science and Faith

To sway the more scientific minds, he used another analogy. He put up a chart that compared debt and credit cycles to the human bloodstream. One of the congregation described the lecture.

"I remember going to another meeting. This one was in the Bible Institute and Mr Aberhart, when he stood up to speak. He had an old coat and it was covered with multi-coloured patches, a red one, a plaid one, and so on. And as he spoke about other people's ideas of help for the economic system, you see, he would say, 'Well, that won't work,' and he'd tear off a patch and finally he tore off the whole old coat and stood there in what I must say was a handsomely tailored model and said this is what represents Social Credit and it really brought down the house."[96]

But there was no need to understand this miracle to be saved, only to grasp the free gift of social credit salvation offered to all who would hear the message. Fred Kennedy was a reporter at the *Calgary Herald* when Aberhart led provincial voters to the Promised Land.

"Mr Aberhart came along with his philosophy: his social credit type of philosophy. It would take too long to try and describe what social credit was or is or what it means, but to use Mr Aberhart's own words, it was a dividend of $25 a month and a lower cost to live. Those were the words he used on the platform on many occasions...I don't think they understood anything about it. And he told them on occasion not to worry about that. You don't have to understand the philosophy of social credit to enjoy the benefits of it. That was the message that he gave the people," said Kennedy.[97]

One Man's Faith is Another's Scam

His political opponents didn't find Aberhart's theories reasonable or his tactics democratic. J.F. Lymburn, Q.C., who served as Attorney General in the UFA government, put it this way:

"He said, time and again, to his Prophetic Bible Society or whatever he was preaching from, that there was no doubt about his ability to ensure $25 a month for every adult and, of course, that is just nonsense. Either he was grossly ignorant of economics and finance or else he was deliberately putting up a (bait?) to get the people of the province to vote for him."[98]

But Social Credit faithful, like A.V. Bourcier, a candidate who joined Aberhart in the Legislature after the party's 1935 election victory, and Clifford Wilmot, who worked with Aberhart as an aide, considered Aberhart's character beyond question. It was Wilmot who dubbed Aberhart 'the dreadnought'.

"Occasionally, I called him chief, yes. He weighed 250 pounds, which of course, is an eighth of a ton and quite frequently dressed in grey which suited him very well and I used to refer to him as the dreadnought, which of course, is a style of British battleship and I got into trouble one day calling him the dreadnought. It was somebody who didn't understand what I was getting at, and I had to apologize and backwater. But, yes, he was always a dreadnought to me. He was like a trout among minnows. Other men around him seemed to pale into insignificance. You know he had quite a temper, but it wasn't mean or nasty temper. It was a righteous wrath and there were times when I did things that I shouldn't have done. I remember once that he accused me of soft-soaping the CCF, but he was a great man. I loved him. There's no doubt about that. I loved him," said Wilmot.[99]

Men and Women with a Mission

Potential MLAs, like Bourcier, would travel across railway tracks, through rain, in and out of ditches and over barbed wire fences to get to the meeting with voters.

"I remember on one occasion when I travelled to a meeting, I think there were three different modes of transportation. I remember travelling in an old jalopy, in a wagon, and in a truck and then, finally, all of these means came to an end. I mean they went into a ditch. It was impossible to go on. I climbed on to a high wire fence on to the railroad track and I walked four miles in the rain, arriving at about 10 o'clock at night for a meeting that was scheduled for eight, but everyone was there, that's the spirit that existed at a time. Everyone was there waiting. They knew that a social credit speaker would come," said Bourcier.

Aberhart and the Unions

Like the other Prairie Provinces, in the 1930s, Alberta was a hotbed of Canada's Depression-angered labour, socialist and communist movements. Aberhart's anti-capitalist, anti-bank policies, and wealth redistribution platform appealed to members of Alberta's CCF, Labour and Communist parties.[100] Aberhart was not shy about recruiting members of Alberta's organized labour unions. Talks like the one he gave the pro-union, often socialist, miners gathered in the Columbus Hall in Blairmore in December 1934 threatened to upset the CCF, Labour, Communist power base. His message to the miners promoted easier credit and increased purchasing power. Aberhart told them that, under a social credit plan, miners could provide their families with a better standard of living, by working only four to six days a week.

> ABERHART DECLARES SOCIAL CREDIT WOULD BE REAL BOON TO COAL MINES ADDRESSES LARGE AUDIENCE AT BLAIRMORE. WOULD INSURE FLOW OF CREDIT FROM OUR OWN CORRESPONDENT.
>
> BLAIRMORE, Dec. 23—Under the Social Credit system the mines in Alberta would work from four to six days a week due to the increased purchasing power of the people of Alberta under the system of Social Credit.
>
> This was the pronouncement of William Aberhart of Calgary, leader of Social Credit for Alberta, when he addressed a large audience in the Columbus hall Thursday evening. The meeting sponsored by the Social Credit Study clubs of the Crow's Nest Pass, was presided over by Rev A.E. Larke of Blairmore. Mr Manning to Mr Aberhart was the first speaker of the evening. He stated that they had spoken the previous evening to 200 people in Edmonton, where movement was slow in being started and appreciated. They did come to Blairmore to discuss politics, he stated, but only desired social get-together to discuss the economic situation of the province and what Social Credit would do to eliminate much misery and suffering.
>
> THREE BARRIERS
>
> He stated that the three barriers to the successful operation of the system were selfishness, being the indifference of the people to any new system;

blind prejudice, afraid to try any new system because it was never tried out before, and finally, misrepresentation.

He touched on the Australia election where advocates of the Douglas system in that country had failed to elect one candidate in the last general election...he attributed to the lack of purchasing power in the hands of the consumers. He said there is only one way of solving this problem, the government must put purchasing power directly and periodically into hands of the consumers.

How can this be done? The speaker demonstrated the method which purchasing power of 95 percent of present business is distributed by the banks and other financial agencies in the way of cheques, drafts etc. If Social Credit is introduced in tills, province, he explained, would pattern its procedure after the present method with the one exception that the credit would be issued by the provincial credit house instead offered by the banks. The proposal is, he declared, that the state credit house shall issue to each bona fide citizen of Alberta a monthly basic dividend of, say $25, sufficient to purchase the bare necessities of life, food, clothing and shelter, whether he works or does not work, and he never be asked to pay it back. Answering the question, where is the money coming from, he replied that it will come from a levy included in the 'just price' of goods, much the same as the gasoline tax is secured today.[101]

As Social Credit Study groups popped up all over the province and petitions circulated asking the UFA government to adopt Social Credit; both the government, the left-wing opposition worry that their votes will split even more and the result will be a Conservative government in Alberta.

LETHBRIDGE. "The result of the Australian elections, where despite all the propaganda and effort spent, the Social Credit group failed to elect a single representative, while the Labour Group made a gain of seven seats, should be an object lesson to Lethbridge people who are wasting their time trying to figure out such impossibilities as 'theorems', 'basic dividends', and other such myths. The time is not far distant when we will be in the thick of a general election fight, to say nothing of the provincial election, and it would seem that the part of wisdom would be for everybody whose interests lie in that direction to get solidly behind the Co-operative Commonwealth Federation; the one and only thing "which is a cure for our present difficulties; get the best men available lined up so that when the time comes we will be to a strong enough position to put them over. This can be done if everybody who should be doing some serious thinking began to do so and got lined up behind the movement. The time for chasing will-of-the-wisps is past. Grab yourself a copy of the C.C.F. manifesto, study it, preach it to everybody with whom you come in contact, so that when election time comes around you will be ready to take your place and do your part in the campaign work."[102]

XII: THE AGRICULTURAL HEARINGS

O verwhelmed by the growing numbers of true believers in the Social Credit gospel, UFA Premier Brownlee was mulling over the idea of giving Social Credit economics a trial run in Alberta.[103] In March 1934, a provincial sub-committee recommended that Major C. Douglas, founder of Social Credit, to be invited to speak to the Agricultural Committee of Alberta Legislature. The UFA MLAs may have hoped Social Credit would solve Alberta's problems. Their goal may also have been to get the UFA off the hook Aberhart's followers had them on by getting Social Credit's founder to admit that his plan would not work in the province because banking was under federal jurisdiction.

MAY BE INVITED TO VISIT ALBERTA—SUB-COMMITTEE RECOMMENDS CALLING OF ORIGINATOR OF SOCIAL CREDIT PLAN

Whether or not the social credit scheme can advantageously be applied as a provincial measure in Alberta, apart from other parts of the Dominion, is the question that will be put in particular to Major Douglas, if he comes. He is now returning via Canada from New Zealand. Some difference of opinion has developed among advocates of the plan as to the feasibility of provincial operation. Larkham Collins, Calgary chartered accountant, who gave evidence to the committee Tuesday, said that the Social Credit League of Canada does not believe it can be adopted successfully in the province, thus opposing the views of William Aberhart as expressed in his evidence the day before.

Prof G.A. Elliott of the department of economics of the University of Alberta, was another witness dealing with a number of general economic questions involved in the social credit proposals.[104]

But why not start closer to home? As the agricultural committee toyed with debt adjustment ideas and ways to increase protection for debtors, they called Larkham Collins, of Alberta's Douglas Social Credit League, and radio preacher William Aberhart as witnesses.

The Baptist schoolteacher/preacher stole the stage by announcing that a Social Credit government could pay each adult (over 21) in the province $25 per month from the surplus purchasing power. He also offered $1250 of his own savings to offset the cost of bringing Major Douglas to Alberta to testify before the committee.

ABERHART'S STARTLING PROPOSAL $25 PER MONTH TO ALL OVER 21 YEARS TO BE PAID BY PROVINCE UNDER DOUGLAS CREDIT SCHEME.

(by *Herald's* Special Legislative Correspondent.)

EDMONTON, March 19—Twenty-five dollars a month for every person in Alberta of 21 years and over, to be paid by the province out of social credit or unearned increment, was the startling proposal made to the agricultural committee of the legislature Monday in an exposition of the Douglas credit scheme by William Aberhart, Calgary. Such a payment of 'social dividends' was shown to be an essential and basic feature of the plan, the credit to be non-negotiable and to be used for the purchase of goods only, to the end that purchasing power and production might be more nearly balanced. The Douglas proposals are being investigated by the legislature through its agricultural committee in view of considerable interest displayed in the subject, and will be taken by us again Tuesday, when Larkin Collins, another advocate of the plan, and Prof G.A. Elliott of the university will be heard. Investigation of the question should go still farther, Mr Aberhart suggested, to the extent of inviting Major Douglas himself to come to Alberta. If necessary, he said, he would assume responsibility for the $1,250 such a visit would involve, believing that if Major Douglas, who is now in New Zealand, could be secured for addresses in Edmonton and Calgary they would finance themselves. Such an opportunity should not be allowed to pass, he submitted. Mr Aberhart based his exposition of the theory on an official statement in the Canada Year Book to the effect that the Dominion's 'national income is necessarily less than its national production', and therefore the necessity of increasing purchasing power to absorb the surplus production.[105]

When the Major's finally arrived in Alberta, his frosty, high-falutin' tone didn't go over very well with either Aberhart or members of the Agricultural Committee. The UFA government quickly decided Social Credit wasn't something they wanted in Alberta's future.

Voters were grateful that the UFA had, at least, considered Social Credit as a way out of Alberta's problems and it looked like Brownlee would be re-elected. That is, until Premier Brownlee got himself embroiled in a lurid sexual scandal. The revulsion to Brownlee's purported dalliances with a young legislative clerk caused a visceral negative reaction among Alberta's still largely British/Protestant voting population. Mr. Brownlee's resignation, his subsequent vindication, and the appointment of a new UFA premier, Richard Reid, didn't undo the damage. Social Credit activists, who once hoped that the UFA would adopt Social Credit, now cut their ties with the farmers' party and prepared to run their own candidates in the general election.[106]

Even though the fiery preacher was not running for election, it looked like he'd created enough of a fuss to, at least, split the vote. Aberhart's alliance of fundamentalists, shopkeepers, farmers and miners were expected to do exactly what the opposition feared, take away enough votes from the UFA, Labour, Liberal, and CCF parties, to allow the Conservatives to form a government.

XII: PREMIER ABERHART

A ugust 22, 1935, Albertans went to the polls. 300,000 Albertans voted; a huge turnout for a province with a total population of 676,781 (many of whom were under the voting age of 21).[107] The Social Credit party took 53 of the 63 seats in Alberta's legislature. Bible Bill Aberhart hadn't run in the election, but that didn't matter on election night. He even allowed his followers to indulge in a little idolatry before they got down to the business of finding him a riding to represent.[108] The night of Social Credit's victory, Aberhart went back to the Prophetic Bible Institute to celebrate. When someone in the crowd shouted: "Arise and worship Aberhart, the son of God," he shouted back: "Fear not, for I am with thee."[109]

Aberhart's most devoted pupil was Ernest Manning, a Saskatchewan farm boy who left home and family after listening to Aberhart's *Back to the Bible Hour* altar call. "It got me," he said of Aberhart's message. After graduating from the institute, Manning moved in with the Aberhart family and became the Prophetic Bible Institute founder's right hand man, first, in the ministry, and later, when they crusaded to bring Social Credit to Alberta. When Manning married Muriel Preston, the bride was escorted down the aisle and given away by William Aberhart.

Modern pundits often claim that Manning took Alberta in a more conservative direction than Aberhart envisioned. Manning probably never saw it that way. He remained a follower of Aberhart and Social Credit into old age. Decades after Aberhart's death, Premier Manning proclaimed William Aberhart one of the greatest men ever born in the Dominion of Canada. "In my honest opinion, Mr. Aberhart was one of the most outstanding men that the nation has produced," he said in his retirement speech during the Provincial Social Credit's December 1968 Leadership Convention.

Manning was far from the only follower of Aberhart to remain devoted to the man decades after his death: "I certainly think he was the man of the hour. Yes, I do think that he was raised up to give that message and wherever he is now you may be positively assured that he's doing a tremendous work and it'll be a work for good," said Clifford Wilmot when he was interviewed by the CBC in the 1960s.[110]

Aberhart Meets His Match: Another Baptist Preacher Ain't So Sure "Bible Bill" has Heard from God

Turning Alberta into 'The Promised Land' was harder than he thought it would be. Premier Aberhart and his cabinet tried to introduce Social Credit 'scrip'[111] as a substitute for Canadian currency in Alberta. It failed after a few months. The government passed its 1936 *Act Providing for the Recall of Members of the Legislative Assembly*, then rescinded it within a year. He also fought off a revolt by Social Credit hardliners within his own party. Things only got worse.

Social Credit plans to reform the banking system and to limit freedom of the press, ran aground when another Baptist Preacher, the new Lieutenant Governor, John Bowen, didn't quite see the prophetic nature of some of the Aberhart's proposed legislation.[112]

In October 1937, Bowen refused to grant Royal Assent to two laws passed by the Alberta Legislature. The legislation would have intruded on federal jurisdiction by giving the province power to tax and license banks: *The Bank Taxation Act*[113] and *Credit of Alberta Regulations Act*.[114] The Lieutenant Governor believed the Acts were unconstitutional and advised the Premier that he was referring them to the Governor General. The Governor General and, later, the courts, agreed with Bowen.

Bowen, the King's representative in the province, also refused to sign a law that would have had even more serious consequences to Albertans: *The Publication of Accurate News and Information Act*.[115] Its intention was to force newspapers to publish government propaganda and reveal their news sources to the government at the order of a powerful Chairman of the Social Credit Board.

Section Six of the *Accurate News And Information Act* made the Lieutenant Governor responsible for its most draconian enforcement measures, including banning reporters who did not toe the Social Credit line and banning anti-government sources from being used in provincial newspapers. The Act would have forced the Crown to close newspapers at the whim of the Chairman of the Social Credit Board:

In the case of the proprietor, editor, publisher, or manager of any newspaper has been guilty of any contravention of any of the provisions of this Act, the Lieutenant Governor in Council, upon the recommendation of the chairman, may by order prohibit, the publication of such newspaper either for a definite time or until further order the publication in any newspaper of anything written by any person specified by order the publication of any information emanating from any person or source specified in the order.

Section Four exempted the government from libel action by those who felt they had been misrepresented by the government's pronouncements.

"No action for libel shall be maintainable on account of the publication of any statement pursuant to this Act against any person who is the proprietor, editor, publisher, manager, or printer of the newspaper publishing the same or against any employee or any such person or against any person on account of any such statement."

Many Albertans were surprised that Bowen had deemed the situation serious enough to use the Reserve Power of the Crown. As the *Edmonton Bulletin* put it: "The duty of a Lieutenant-Governor, as of a Governor General, to accept the advice of his Premier so long as the Premier can command a majority in the legislature has been well established."[116] But others chastised Aberhart for using 'Alice in Wonderland' economics to gain re-election and making impossible promises to overthrow the big shots and strike it rich.

A government that clearly intends to profit by delay in retaining the emoluments of office bringing in legislation of a contentious nature which allow for this delay, with the people offered a 'meal of pottage'. In the shape of dividend which premier Aberhart and his government must know is no nearer fulfilment than it was two years ago when the Social Credit Government came into being. There are people suffering while the Aberhart Government is placing them under a delusion.

Mr Aberhart proposes to go to the country and make the banks 'the goat'. He'll attack the financial interest, put the blame on them for the failure of Social Credit and raise a great 'ballyhoo' to stir op the fast dwindling forces of Social Credit against the 'big shots', the 'capitalistic press' and call the balderdash that has characterized his utterances since he came to power. "The People's Weekly", which is not friendly to the existing financial system, any more than William Aberhart, is not hoodwinked by the

Banking Legislation. It is most outspoken in treating the legislation as pure buncombe… Tar sands, oil and gasoline have now become the playthings of our premier. The fountain pen has been thrown aside. It won the last election and will not win the next. He turns to natural resources, especially to those Alberta does not own and which he declares shall not own since he refuses to take away our public property from the private corporations which now own it.[117]

Aberhart was angered by his critics and by Bowen's[118] decision to refer the Bills to the Governor General. In the next budget, he made sure Bowen lost his driver and his official residence. But when Prime Minister Mackenzie King, Governor General Lord Tweedsmuir, the Supreme Court of Canada[119] and the Judicial Committee of the Privy Council at Westminster, England, all agreed with Bowen, Aberhart took to the radio waves, where 350,000 Albertans listened to him each week, whipping up his rhetoric with biblical allusions, accusing his opponents of being agents of Satan. These attacks were repeats of an earlier tirade, one year after his elections, when Aberhart blamed disunity in his own party on bankers and financiers. "These plotters, those money barons, those Sons of Satan, they shall not oppose the will of the people of Alberta," was his cry.[120]

Aberhart perfected the tradition of Alberta politicians using the Government of Canada as a foil to distract voters from their failure to enact policies they promised at election time. The strategy is nearly always effective in Alberta. This time was no exception. Instead of throwing out the guy who never fulfilled his election promises, voters re-elected enough Social Credit MLAs to keep Aberhart in power in 1940. His party, which never did reform the economic system or pay out its promised dividend to Alberta voters, remained in power until 1971.

To the end of his life, Aberhart took particular delight in revving up crowds with accusations that Alberta was being treated badly by Ottawa and that his government was standing up for them. He delighted in captivating crowds with tales of his latest trip to Ottawa to take on the infidels to Social Credit. Voters gazed in wonder as he recounted how, unafraid of their power, he'd 'looked them straight in the eye'.[121]

Aberhart's rhetoric was a little less intense after Canadians went to war against Hitler, in 1939, but as the Premier and Lieutenant Governor joined forces to urge Albertans to buy war bonds and stand strong against the Nazis, Aberhart still indulged in a little Ottawa bashing now and then.

ABERHART CHARGES SOCIAL SECURITY SCHEMES
MERELY NATIONAL SOCIALISM

EDMONTON, March 16 (CP)—"Every measure for the post-war period, compulsory contributory unemployment insurance, compulsory contributory health insurance, compulsory contributory old age pensions, all involve the perpetuation of state bureaucracy and all carry us another step towards the supreme state of national socialism." he said. "This is causing us to wonder what is the purpose of it all, and who is behind it."

"Tell me, is it not true that in some quarters within the British Empire, there are those who are striving most vigorously and diligently to set up a system of state socialism that is patterned after the nazi type?" He said that under the stress of war conditions, increasing power. "The disturbing feature about it all is that a barrage of propaganda is being let loose, intended to prepare us for the continuation of these controls and more and more controls after the war. We have foolishly allowed a private monopoly to get control of the money system and to dictate to the people how much money shall be issued and the conditions under which it shall be issue, virtually a hidden super-government which can bring to pass every desire of the people."[122]

In its first term, the Social Credit Party had eleven of its bills rejected, but the old teacher was able to reorganize the education system, give financial aid to farmers and beef up the *Sexual Sterilization Act* by widening the definition of "mental defective".

XIV: GETTING RID OF THE DEFECTIVES

"For the middle class, it was very comforting to be told that crime, poverty and prostitution were not social problems but medical problems for which there was a convenient medical solution,"

—University of Alberta Law Professor Gerald Robertson, June 1995, Testimony, Leilani Muir trial.

William Aberhart's economic policies may have been controversial, but the province's education, religious, and medical establishment loved his tough line with the feeble-minded and mental defectives as much as the shopkeepers, housewives and the farmers loved his dividend promises.[123]

The Queen's Representative in Alberta, John Bowen, did not refuse or even dally in signing amendments to the *Sexual Sterilization Act*. Even if he had objections, he would have been on shakier ground than he was when he refused to sign the banking legislation and the *Accurate News and Information Act*.

Unless a law passed by a parliament or a legislative assembly is unconstitutional, the Canadian Crown must give it Royal Assent. The amendments did not tread on federal authority. Health care was clearly a matter of provincial jurisdiction. Secondly, Canada had no federal or provincial human rights legislation during Aberhart's Premiership.[124] Neither the Province of Alberta nor the Government of Canada had passed their Bill of Rights. The *Canadian Charter of Rights and Freedoms* did not come into effect until 1982.

Broadening the Definition of Mental Defective

In 1937, the Social Credit Government broadened the definition of 'mental defective' and removed the possibility of civil suits being brought against it from sterilized patients or their family members who objected to the decisions of the Eugenics Board.

As of 1 April 1937, the definition of 'mental defectives' included: "Any person in whom there is a condition of arrested or incomplete development of mind existing before the age of eighteen years, whether arising from inherent causes or induced by disease or injury."[125]

Another amendment made it possible to bring outpatients of mental hygiene clinics before the Eugenics Board. By replacing Section 4 of Alberta's *Sexual Sterilization Act*, which required the Medical Superintendent or person in charge of a mental hospital bring a patient to the attention of the Eugenics Boards, the government made it possible for anyone in charge of a mental hygiene clinic to bring patients before the Board. The Eugenics Board now toured the province looking for unsterilized defectives living in local communities.

The legislature struck out Section 5 of the *Sexual Sterilization Act* and replaced it with separate provisions for the sterilization of psychotic and mentally defective persons.

Section 7 beefed up protection for those ordering and performing the surgery. Instead of only protecting the surgeon from lawsuits, the Act now protected the guardian, family member or the Minister who gave consent, the medical superintendent of the institution or the medical practitioner in charge of a mental hygiene clinic, members of the Eugenics Board, the anaesthetist, and the surgeon.[126] Was the inclusion of Section 7 an admission that the government foresaw legal problems with the Act or that they suspected former patients or their families, who might launch legal action, must have their legal right to sue abolished by the legislature?

The *Mental Diseases Act* was also amended to include drug and alcohol addicts.[127]

With fewer restrictions, the empowered Alberta Eugenics Board moved out into the province, weeding out defectives in clinics held in Alberta communities. Mental hygiene clinics, like the one held at the Lethbridge Nursing Mission, where Albertans who burdened by stress, money problems and the blues went to find help, now became tools in the Eugenics Board's mission to find people, especially unmarried mothers or simple-minded girls, who could be sterilized.

The Nursing Mission's 1937 Annual Report describes one of these new-fangled community clinics. According to the article, this mental health clinic was held ten times each year, and appointments had to be made in advance to avoid disappointment:

A wide range of patients avail themselves of the opportunity of free examination and advice by trained mental specialists. The probation officer brings us delinquent or problem boys and girls. The jail warden sends inmates from his institution of whose sanity he is doubtful. The mental defective, others with shattered nerves, the positively insane are all numbered in our clinic. The understanding and sympathy shown to them gives new courage and hope to many who come hopeless and depressed. Sixty percent of them sent to mental institutions are discharged normal.

In connection with delinquents sent us, usually by the probation officer or police, most of these were young and inexperienced. Three girls were sent to the Beulan Mission where they received medical and nursing care. Their babies were adopted through the department at Edmonton. They are now re-established in their homes and community, sadder and wiser from their experience and without the public knowing of their errors. Two have married; one whose mental capacity is below normal was examined by the Eugenics board and recommended for sterilization, which has been done. She has secured employment in another city. We have kept in touch with all except one who stayed four days then disappeared, only coming to light a few weeks ago when she came in looking very nice indeed, and is now married and living in the city.[128]

In the years just after the UFA-dominated legislature passed the *Sexual Sterilization Act*, the Alberta Eugenics Board spent an hour reviewing each patient's file. By 1935, the year the Social Credit Party took control of the legislature, the Eugenics Board had whittled down the time they spent reviewing each file to five minutes. Instead of doing their own research, Board members relied on the recommendations of the physicians and medical superintendents who brought patients before the Board.[129]

In 1942, the province gave itself the power to pay for the patient's upkeep with proceeds from his or her estate and added epileptics, as well as Huntington chorea and neurosyphillis patients to the list of who could be sterilized. While syphilis patients or their guardians still had to consent to sterilization, Huntington chorea patients and the 'mentally defective' could be sterilized without consent.[130]

By now Aberhart, who had never fulfilled his promise to give every adult Albertan a $25 a month provincial dividend, was well into his second mandate. It was smaller than the first one. Voters were beginning to wonder if Social Credit economics was more superstition than the science Aberhart insisted it was, and the press hadn't gotten any kinder to Aberhart.

"…for another, in an attempt to set up a system of government which, to paraphrase a saying of the late W.E. Gladstone in regard to the tyranny of the King of Naples, is the 'negation of justice erected into a system of government'. Instead of dealing with the pressing problem of unemployed relief by giving immediate consideration to one of the principal recommendations in the report of the special relief committee appointed by the government, namely, the centralization of relief, it has been shelved until the next session. Dr Cross, the Minister in charge of relief, stated in the House that the Government was fully cognisant of relief conditions in the province."[131]

The opposition parties were beginning to think they might defeat Social Credit next time a general election was called. But Aberhart stunned them again.

On 23 May 1943, William Aberhart, 64, died at his daughter's home in Victoria of liver cancer. Few in Alberta could even imagine their raging prophet being sick. Aberhart, on the other hand, probably never imagined Lieutenant Governor John Bowen and Mackenzie King eulogizing him.

BOWEN'S TRIBUTE

EDMONTON, May 24 1943—J.C. Bowen, lieutenant governor of Alberta, today added his tribute to Premier William Aberhart who died in Vancouver yesterday morning and said "he was not lacking in the courage of his convictions." (text of Mr. Bowen's tribute) The passing of Premier Aberhart has come to most Albertans as a very great surprise. He has been active in his duties and frequently broadcasted to the people until he left for a brief visit to the coast. Few even of his close friends knew he was conscious of any disability. His unremitting faith was doubtless taking a heavy toll of his energy and vitality. Mr. Aberhart was a man of very definite ideas and fixed judgments. He gave constantly of himself promoting the cause he espoused. He was not lacking in the courage of his convictions. In his religious principles and in his political philosophy, he was fearlessly outspoken. Those who followed him will miss his voice and leadership. Those who disagreed with him will now let the mantle of charity cover their opinions.[132]

XV: THE PERSONAL IS POLITICAL: ERNEST MANNING

MANNING'S STATEMENT

VANCOUVER, May 24 (CP)—Death of Premier William Aberhart of Alberta here Sunday "has caused a sense of irreparable loss in the hearts and minds of his thousands of friends throughout the entire Dominion," Hon E.C. Manning, provincial secretary and acting premier, said in a statement to The Canadian Press.

Mr. Manning's statement: In the death of Premier William Aberhart, the people of Alberta and of Canada have lost one of their greatest statesmen. His untimely passing has come as a terrible shock and has caused a sense of irreparable loss in the hearts and minds of his thousands of friends throughout the entire Dominion. In a very real sense Mr Aberhart gave his life in the service of his fellowmen. The boundless energy with which he applied himself to his work and the unselfish zeal with which he laboured tirelessly on behalf of others took their inevitable toll of his vitality and contributed to the illness that has resulted in his death at the very height of his outstanding career. Of him it may be truly said: "He fought a good fight." His name will go down in history as one of Canada's greatest economic reformers. His memory will live on in the hearts of thousands who knew him as the great Christian gentleman that he was. The influence of his life and service long will continue to inspire those who were privileged to be associated with him to carry on, with unrelenting determination, the work from which he has been called. The heartfelt sympathy and the prayers of his thousands of friends will be with Mrs Aberhart and the family in their bereavement.[133]

Irreparable Loss

When he spoke of the death of William Aberhart as Alberta's 'irreparable loss', acting Premier Ernest Manning was not paying empty homage. William Aberhart's death was a deeply personal loss for Manning.

Ernest Manning was Aberhart's most loyal disciple. Back in 1927, at age 18, he accepted Aberhart's *Back to the Bible* radio altar call—leaving his parents' farm in Saskatchewan to become Aberhart's student at the Prophetic Bible Institute. Aberhart took Manning into his home, taught him the Bible, made him Secretary of the Prophetic Bible Institute, and even walked the bride down the aisle the day Ernest Manning and Muriel Aileen Preston married. When Aberhart discovered Social Credit, he schooled Manning in his interpretation of the economic theory, just as he had schooled his favourite student in interpreting Bible prophecy.

Alberta Unhinged

May 1943 was a month of uncertainty in Alberta. For weeks, stories circulated that the premier wasn't simply visiting his daughters in British Columbia. Some sources suggested he was near death. Aberhart's protégé, Ernest Manning, shot down each rumour as soon as it surfaced.

When the news broke that William Aberhart was dead, the populace were dumfounded. Hadn't the Provincial Secretary assured them only a few days ago that the premier was fine? More questions flooded their minds. Was this the end of Social Credit? Who would lead the province now?

The Social Credit caucus met May 23 to calm the crisis. They chose the man who worked most closely with Aberhart to lead them: Ernest Manning.

The Star of Alberta's Progressive Politics

At 26, Aberhart's protégé, Ernest Manning, had been the youngest cabinet minister in the British Empire. Now, at 34, Ernest C. Manning, the Provincial Secretary and Ministry of Industry and Trade, was Premier of Alberta. He was now the youngest First Minister[134] in the British Empire.

The Opposition, already buoyed by the grumbling over Aberhart's failure to bring in the reforms he promised, predicted Manning's downfall and the end of Social Credit rule in Alberta. But young Manning, less given to angry outbursts and more conciliatory to opponents, soon won the voters over. Manning brought in an even bigger majority and attracted admiration across the British Empire. The multi-member electoral district of Edmonton was a dynamic entry into the usually dour world, of imperial politics. British subjects in far-flung dominions were intrigued with the young husband and father of two little boys credited with helping turning the economic tide for Depression-burdened Albertans.

Alberta—Now!, 1935 to 1945: A Record of 10 Years of Government Without Borrowing, published by Social Credit supporters in the State of South

Australia, proclaimed Alberta's Social Credit experiment a bold success. It called young Manning a visionary who dared to challenge the 'old boys' controlling the banks and the courts. And the authors urged voters in the state of South Australia to elect a Social Credit Government, like Manning's.

According the Australian activists, Manning's party had been persecuted by the Lieutenant Governor, the Governor General, the courts, and the media.

In fact, Social Credit bills to censor the media and to tax and license banks had been declared unconstitutional by the Alberta Courts, the Supreme Court of Canada and the Judicial Committee of the Privy Council at Westminster, England.[135]

The Australians insisted that before Aberhart came to power 'people were starving, though the granaries were full the treasury was empty'. According to the writer, overwhelmed by debt and poverty in 1935, the Albertans hitched their wagon[136] to Social Credit and elected the world's first Social Credit Government, led by William Aberhart. "Starting with an empty treasury, here are the government's achievements: reduced national debt, reduced income tax, abolished sales tax, increased old age pensions, increased mineral production, rehabilitated farmers, making them prosperous," the pamphleteer declares.

Other achievements claimed by Social Credit included mother's allowances for both deserted wives and widows, public health units, public health nurses, mother and child care, free treatment of tuberculosis and polio, cancer clinics and research, maternity benefits to allow poor mothers to give birth hospitals, hospitalization regardless of finances, and free hospital and medical care for senior citizens. The pamphlet declared that the Social Credit government claimed to have reduced the provincial death rate by 12%. (The fact that many of these policies had also been advocated by the former United Farmers of Alberta government didn't get much ink.)

Manning's Appeals to Youth and Social Reformers

The young premier capitalized on his appeal to younger Albertans, who, like him, looked forward to making massive political and economic changes that would increase Alberta's economic power in Canada when WWII ended. He did not promise to take Albertans to the Promised Land as his mentor had, only to join in their march to get there.

Ernest Manning's first speech as Premier challenged young Albertans.

"I want your help to make Alberta a province in which every young man and woman will have a successful future. Let no one forget that upon the shoulders of those who our young people today will now rest the responsibility of coping successfully with the common problems of the post war era. And I so earnestly appeal to every citizen of this province, both young and old, to broaden their horizons, to rise above all the petty bickering of party politics, and to unite together for the purpose of attaining the results which collectively you desire from this administration of your affairs, Only then can we hope to establish a truly effective democracy," Manning said.[137]

The new premier's popularity with the press contrasted with that of his mentor. Aberhart had been a favourite target of political cartoonists and editorialists who mocked his economic policies, constitutional wars and utopian daydreams of paying Albertans dividends gleaned from unproven oil riches:

> If the people of Alberta believe that affluence for all will be the natural result of any sort of control of the banks by the province, they are due for certain disappointment. Tar Sands, oil and gasoline have now become the playthings of our premier. The fountain pen has been thrown aside. It won the last election and will not win the next. He turns to natural resources, especially to those Alberta does not own and which he declares shall not own since he refuses to take away our public property from the private corporations which now own it. Premier Aberhart cannot be trusted to quote figures. He is entirely undependable when he makes estimates of the province's capacity to produce wealth. For instance, he said on Sunday from his Calgary pulpit that the potential productive resources of the province was $7,409,000,000. He goes on to say that there are 100,000,000,000 barrels of oil in the tar sands. That's a lot of oil. Also he says that there is 35,000,000,000 barrels of gasoline there or enough to keep the world in gasoline for 100 years. Out of all this he proposes to give 13600 per month to every adult.[138]

It seemed like the new premier had a Midas touch when Aberhart's once-mocked dream of the province striking it oil rich came true in 1948. With oil money flowing into the coffers and fuelling industry, Albertans soon forgot that the Socreds never did pay up on their promise to give every adult in the province $25 a month. And the bankers continued to work undisturbed by Social Credit reforms.

Back to the Bible

Manning also took the helm of the *Back to the Bible Hour*. Not only did he give the show a quieter tone, he changed his definition of what Aberhart used to call 'Sons of Satan'.

While Aberhart fought to release Albertans from the chains of bankers and financiers, Manning warned of atheistic Communism. His focus deepened after World War II, as Cold War between the United States and Russia intensified. Manning's sermons on 'end time' prophecy had more than a little Cold War politics subtly inserted to liven up the scripture and moral instruction. It wasn't just the godlessness of the Communists that inspired Manning's sermons. As the British Empire transformed itself into the less influential Commonwealth of Nations, Alberta had become dependent on oil companies, mostly from the United States, to develop its oil and gas sector. [139]

When Manning came home empty-handed from Ottawa, where he tried to convince Prime Minister John Diefenbaker that Canadians should buy Alberta oil, Albertans were disappointed. When Toronto and Montreal moneymen failed to invest in Alberta oil and bought cheap foreign oil, their feeling of betrayal were soothed as Americans had moved into Calgary and turned the province into a source of fuel for U.S. industry.

Manning was much like Aberhart in his paternalistic approach to his radio congregation. He told them to simplify their lives by following the safe course laid out for them in scripture. And he didn't have to remind viewers that he was Premier of Alberta, the announcer did it for him.

> This is Ernest C. Manning greeting you from Edmonton, Alberta. I'm sure many of you find life complicated and often difficult. Some fixed guideposts can help you chart a safe course, give you confidence amid the storms that often obscure your path. Not only do the scriptures provide you with such guideposts, they tell you of one who wants to be your saviour, your pilot and your friend. We invite you to commit your soul, your life, your all to him today.[140]

Ernest Manning didn't like critics any more than Aberhart did. As Provincial Secretary, he had worked with Aberhart to bring in the *Act to Ensure Publication of Accurate News and Information* because he viewed the press as all too willing to distort news and misrepresent facts.

Like Aberhart, he often blamed the media, not government policies, for giving Social Credit a bad image outside Alberta.

"It has been very, very grossly misrepresented to the Canadian public by the media particularly and a few political opponents. This means you have prejudices to bring down. I, for example, I've been out in Eastern Canada and if you mention Social Credit, the first thing that comes to mind and somebody says 'Oh, it's that funny money scheme that comes out of the West,'" said Manning.[141]

He went on: "Well, no responsible adherent to Social Credit would ever advocate printing press money or this kind of stuff that couldn't be further from the truth or more ridiculous." (In fact the Social Credit government did attempt to issue scrip as a means of monetary exchange in the province. The plan failed.)

Sept 1910, Lethbridge crowds listen as PM Sir Wilfrid Laurier praises the city's co-founder and Father of Confederation, Sir Alexander Tilloch Galt's vision of Western Canadian Economic Expansion and immigration.

WCTU member, Louise McKinney of Claresholm, was one of two women elected to AB Legislature in 1917. She and Nursing sister, Lt. Roberta McAdams, were the first women elected to any legislature in the British Empire.

NOTICE OF EVICTION

Then spake the Consul Aulus,
He spake a bitter jest:
"Once the jay sent a message
Unto the eagle's nest:—
Now yield thou up thine eyrie
Unto the carrion-kite,

Or come forth valiantly, and face
The jays in deadly fight.—
Forth looked in wrath the eagle;
And carrion-kite and jay,
Soon as they saw his beak and claw,
Fled screaming far away."

—*From Macaulay's "Battle of Lake Regillus."*

THE Federal Government, guardian of the civil liberties of all Canadians, soon realized the dictatorial import of the new "Social Credit" legislation. The Ottawa government requested the provincial government to delay action until validity of the acts could be determined. This was construed as hostility by the Premier and his followers were urged to "bombard" Ottawa with telegrams, protesting against Federal "interference." (August 14, 1937.)

Premier William Aberhart's attempts to pass outlaw bills by claiming the British North America Act didn't apply in Alberta were lampooned by *Calgary Herald* Cartoonist Stewart Cameron.

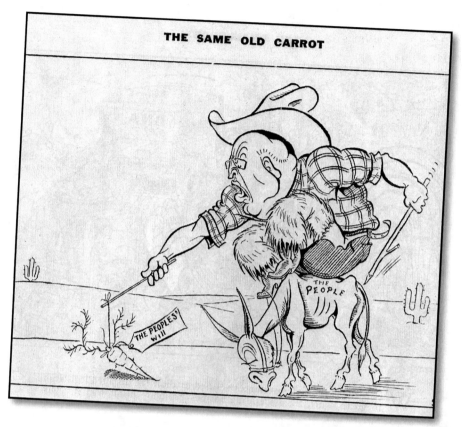

Calgary Herald Cartoonist Stewart Cameron accuses Aberhart of riding on the backs of depression wearing ABs in his fight over provincial rights. Aberhart sought to 'even the score' by making the press subject to Social Credit control through the *Accurate News and Information Act.*

Mounties threaten to bring down the Social Credit Puppet Show as Activists and MLAs are charged with behaviour unbefitting 'honourable members' of the Legislature including libel and attempted murder.

Socred revamping of the *Sexual Sterilization Act* let the Eugenics Board travel Alberta searching for defectives. Even the Lethbridge Nursing Mission, usually a site of baby weigh-in like this one, played host to the eugenics board.

Premier Ernest Manning preferred to think of himself as a 'folksy, progressive, populist leader and pastor. He's seen here with a group of Southern Alberta seniors.

More welcome than others? Children of Northern Europeans, British, and native born Canadians were sterilized in lesser proportions than Eastern Europeans and aboriginals.

Burdett area farmer turned politician, Harry Strom, seen here with his wife, Ruth, may have wished he'd stayed on the farm as he tried to move the Social Credit Party's Human Rights and Mental Health agenda into the 1970s.

Third generation Swedish Albertan, Harry Strom, became Alberta's First Native Born, non-Anglo Saxon Premier in 1968. But he couldn't stem the Progressive Conservative Tide led by Peter Lougheed.

Albertans eye the future as Peter Lougheed, seen here receiving the Kainai Chieftanship on the Blood Reserve, becomes Premier. His gov. rewrites the *Mental Health Act*, upgrades Human Rights leg. and abolishes the Alberta'sEugenics Board.

XVI: MANNING'S VIEWS ON PATIENT RIGHTS AND MENTAL HEALTH

In 1947, Ernest Manning asked Dr Claire Hincks, founder of the Canadian National Committee for Mental Hygiene (an organization that has survived into the 21st century as the Canadian Mental Health Association) to study conditions in Alberta's mental hospitals, training schools, and mental health clinics.

The premier suspected Depression cuts had left the province's mental hospitals, training schools, and mental health clinics in a poor state. The patients lived in near poverty; but Manning needed to know just how poor those conditions were. He had good reason to be concerned. His seven year-old, Keith, had cerebral palsy and epilepsy and would soon need full-time care.

Hincks had two months to investigate before delivering a report praising the efforts of the staff and noting that, given the tight budgets, the facilities provided a 'credible standard of humanitarian care'.[142]

Premier Ernest Manning was pleased by Dr Hincks' report. But the report was not the glowing endorsement Manning thought it was. While Hincks did not have time to provide in-depth assessments of individual institutions, he did note that the institutions were understaffed and the budgets did not allow for more than a minimum standard of care. The rights of patients and the province's eugenics policy were not mentioned in the report. Hincks, a eugenicist, was also unlikely to look too closely at the way the *Sexual Sterilization Act* was being enforced.

Manning had no intention of rejecting William Aberhart's legacy, including the expanded definition of 'mental defectives' or the Aberhart government's broadening of the Act to include sexual sterilization of patients with sexually transmitted diseases and chronic illnesses. Nor was he about to revoke the changes that removed the need for patient or family consent to sterilize mental defectives or Huntington's chorea patients.

Manning's government made few legislative changes to the *Mental Diseases Act* or the *Sexual Diseases Act*. The 1955 Amendment to the *Sexual Sterilization Act* were administrative: the residence of mental defectives was deemed to be that of his married parents, custodial parents in case of divorce

or widowhood, or guardian. In 1959, the Act ensured that the estate of mentally defective patients could be forced to pay patient expenses that were not
payable by a city, town, village, municipal district, country, improvement district, or special area. Whether or not the government proceeded to confiscate
the estate was at the Minister's discretion.

In 1959, changes in the *Mental Diseases Act* created emotionally dis-
turbed children's wards in Alberta's municipal hospitals. If children needed
treatment for more than six consecutive weeks, the Superintendent could
order them sent to a mental hospital. The superintendent could also demand
that parents pick up their child. Parents who refused could be fined $50 or
sentenced to a week in jail.[143]

The Premier's attitude to critics of either the *Sexual Sterilization Act* or
the mental health system was hostile. On at least one occasion, critics of
the system were sued by the Province. In 1980, Manning still believed the
system he presided over was good, lamenting the move to an emphasis on
the rights of patients.

> Over the years, supervision has shifted from medical people to social work-
> ers. And no matter how well trained they are, they are not psychiatrists or
> medical doctors. The trend goes hand in hand with the recent emphasis on
> 'individual rights'. (Ernest Manning, University of Alberta archives, EC
> Manning, Fonds, Access no. 81-32)

Despite his paternalistic attitude, it would be unfair to cast Premier Manning as a heartless politician. Many of his ideas about mental health were
progressive. In archived interviews, the elderly Manning outlined a holistic
approach to both physical and mental health. And a belief that small institutions, cottages, were beneficial to the child.

This is exactly the kind of care his son Keith received at the Red Deer
Training School after he became a resident in 1960. Suffering both rages
and seizures, Keith Manning required more care than the Mannings, or any
family, were able to provide at home. At first, they scraped together money
to send him to a private sanatorium in New York State, U.S.A., but the
cost of private care quickly moved beyond limits of the Premier's salary. The
training school became a haven for Keith.

Life for Alberta's Mentally 'Defective'

Keith Manning had only one roommate, whom he chose from among the other patients at the Red Deer Training School. His parents were encouraged to visit him. And they did so, eagerly, stopping at Keith's cottage every weekend on their weekly commutes between Calgary and Edmonton. Keith was not slapped or restrained when his frustration drew him into rages, and he was never threatened with sterilization if he did not behave. Instead, he was comforted and taken for a walk by handpicked staff who spent hours talking to him. As a teenager, Keith was never threatened with an appearance before the Eugenics Board if he did not behave. The Premier and his wife were satisfied that their son and the young relatives of other political families in the province got good care.

Children from prominent political families were well cared for by the provincial employees at the Training School. They did not experience crowded wards, forced labour, or threats of sexual sterilization if they did not conform to the strict discipline of the school.

Daily life for children from less notable parents, like Leilani Muir, who later was awarded $750,000 in damages by the provincial courts, included clean-up of excrement from other patients, life in austere wards, and sexual sterilization under the guise of appendectomies. Some patients were beaten and used as guinea pigs in drug trials and laboratory experiments. Disobedient youths were often threatened with sterilization by the training school director, Dr L.J. Vann.[144]

XVII: MOST PROGRESSIVE PUBLIC HEALTH IN CANADA

No one shared the Premier's pride in Alberta's health and public welfare system more than the Minister in charge of the portfolio, Dr William Wallace Cross[145] Minister of Health and Public Welfare (1935-1957). As part of his immense portfolio, Cross oversaw the province's mental hospitals, mental hygiene clinics, and the Province's Eugenics Board. Training Schools for the Mentally Defective were partly in the Minister of Education's portfolio, but in practice Cross shared responsibility for them because the training schools provided mental health and medical treatments, including sterilization.

Alberta's Health and Public Welfare system was born during the Liberal and UFA eras, but it was the Social Crediters who turned it from a starving infant into a robust, modern system. And they did it while Alberta was still the poor sister of Confederation.

Banished to history were the days when Albertans, including those in Cross's own riding of Hand Hills, died from lack of a public hospital, lost children because they couldn't pay for a doctor, got sick from drinking contaminated water, or had no access to mental health care.

Social Credit didn't give Albertans the promised dividends, but it delivered on its public health promise in spades with mental hygiene clinics, maternity care, polio clinics, free immunization, public health units, cancer clinics, baby clinics, and TB clinics—all designed to reach the remotest farm family. Most services were free to anyone who needed them.

Manning, Aberhart and Cross were determined that there would be no more tragic stories of homesteaders going in the face of endless work and poverty.

> This is one of the saddest cases of its kind ever brought to the attention
> of the citizens of this vicinity, but is only an example of many such cases
> that are taking place in Western Canada frequently among the pioneers of
> the prairie who have to suffer the hardships so common to a new country,
> namely: solitude, overwork and lack of proper personal attention in the
> way of nourishment. Many a lonely homesteader puts in his hard days toil

and retires at night on a meal made by his own hands and scant, because after working in the fields he has not the initiative to go to the trouble to prepare a better one.

—*The Hanna Herald*, Vol. 1, No 24, June 5, 1913[146]

Cross, who as a country doctor in Youngstown and Hanna, did surgery on kitchen tables and delivered babies in farm houses, was so pleased with Alberta's public health system that he wrote an overview of what Alberta offered its citizens in 1947. It appeared in provincial newspapers.[147]

Alberta Public Health Services By HON. W.W. CROSS began with a vision of health care for the province personified best in its district nurses and rural health units.

That all Alberta citizens may have the incentive to health and the knowledge of how to achieve it and retain it is he reason for existence of the health education division of the Alberta department of public health. Unsung heroines of the Alberta public service are the district nurses. Their life is necessarily a selfless one. She lives alone in a cottage which is also her office where she receives emergency cases or sick people not quite ill enough to need hospital treatment, or from where she goes forth, by horse or dog team, to tend the sick in their homes or supervise the care of newly born children, a vital service since upon it depends the future health of the community. Most of their work lies beyond the reach of doctors.

Besides the rural service, there are other nurses who carry on baby and pre-school clinics and general educational work concerned with the health of the child.

Giving a purely preventive service but on a broader scale than the child hygiene clinics are the staffs of rural 'health units'. At each of these a public health laboratory is established besides the minimum staff of medical health officer, at least two nurses and a sanitary inspector.

Cross, for whom the Alberta Health Services' Cross Cancer Institute in Edmonton, Alberta, is named, was the driving force behind providing free care to Alberta's cancer patients.

"An unrelenting fight against cancer is carried on through the medium of two cancer clinics where patients can be examined and obtain authority for further diagnostic and treatment services at no direct cost to themselves. Diagnostic services include examination, X-ray examination and, when authorized by the clinic, surgery. Treatment may consist of X-ray therapy, radium therapy and surgery. The clinic pays for hospitalization up to two weeks if this time is required to make a diagnosis. Admission to the clinic is on the recommendation of the patient's own physician," Cross wrote.

Cross noted that polio patients could expect 'free treatment regardless of the patient's financial resources' once the acute stage of the disease ended.[148] "Care of the sufferer does not end there, his case continues to be supervised at outpatient clinics, and he is assisted with orthopaedic appliances if they are required," wrote the Minister.

As part of its war on communicable diseases and infant mortality, the province also provided free tuberculosis treatment to Albertans.

> Tuberculosis, the dreaded 'white plague' of yesteryear, is no longer a hope-less disease though it requires a long and rather tedious treatment. But because the earlier it is discovered the sooner it can be cured it gets no quarter in Alberta. Diagnosis and sanatorium treatment are free to all Alberta residents. Two mobile X-ray units were made possible by the generosity of the Alberta Tuberculosis Association from the proceeds of Christmas Seal sales. Up to September, 1946, these units had made pos-sible the X-ray examination of 226,987 people. But besides these, clinics are held at specified centres.

The disease-fighting crusade led Cross' department to instruct the Royal Canadian Mounted Police to shut down red light districts, like the Point in Lethbridge, which had been in operation without threat of prosecution since the 1880s.

> As a result of the department's war on venereal disease, and with the co-operation of R.C.M. Police and local police forces, houses of prosti-tution have been almost driven from Alberta. The anti-venereal war has been going on without pause for more than 25 years. Treatment is avail-able at free clinics in the larger cities, but if any phase of the work is to be emphasized it is the prevention and much of the success of this campaign is due to assistance rendered by police in finding the sources of infection and bringing them under control...

He went on... "unromantic though the work of the sanitary division may be, it has been justified by the decrease of disease ordinarily associated with poor sanitation, and most notably by the steady downward trend of infant mortality."

Cross insisted that Alberta's three provincial laboratories, and munici-pal hospital system, now rivalled other the public health systems in other

Canadian provinces. He was particularly proud of the fact that the integrated system cut infant mortality, communicable disease rates, and facilitated TB and cancer treatment.

> The municipal hospital plan in effect since 1918 has been a blessing to over one-third of the Alberta Canada is six hospital beds per thousand of population, in Alberta the percentage is over seven to assure that the highest standard is maintained, the hospital services division provides assistance advice and periodic inspection. A service especially appreciated is the free maternity hospital service. Co-operating with the hospitals, the medical profession and other branches of the health department the provincial laboratory, in two branches, the pathological and the bacteriological. A function of untold value is the free tissue examination provided to all physicians and hospitals and integrated into the war on cancer. The bacteriological branch of the laboratory is concerned with all those examinations which are of importance to public health in the control of communicable diseases and to the clinician in his search for the diagnosis of baffling infections…

Even the province's cattle could get their blood tested at the provincial laboratory, although it's not clear whether this service to farmers was free or not: "But the work of this laboratory is not restricted to the human species. Blood of cattle is examined for evidence of contagious abortion. Anyone may ask for an analysis of his local water supply," wrote Cross.

With infant mortality dropping and communicable diseases under attack, Cross had no reason to doubt that the province's mental health system was not working just as well as the services designed to fight physical illness. The province's mental hygiene clinics which treated patients with emotional issues not severe enough to place them in the hospital were largely viewed as successes.

He had even less reason to doubt the validity of the *Sexual Sterilization Act*. A graduate of the University of Toronto, he had been well schooled in eugenics. One of faculty in the Medical School was none other than noted eugenicist Dr C.K. Clarke, co-founder of the Canadian National Committee for Mental Hygiene.[149]

"Eugenics also comes within the purview of the program and is the care of a board which examines all cases referred for consideration and sterilization. Sterilization of mental defectives, upon recommendation of the eugenics board, is provided for by law, as also is sterilization by their own consent of former mental patients," wrote Cross.

XVII: THE CRITICS MUST BE WRONG

E rnest Manning loved reminding voters of the progress they had made
together under Social Credit, especially when the critics suggested it
was time to give way to newer ideas and upstart opposition parties.

> You men who are in the business of farming know that when you first
> hire a fellow to help out on the farm, he's more a nuisance to you some-
> times then he's good. He doesn't know the equipment, he doesn't know
> where the fields are and he doesn't know how you want it done. When
> he gets a little experience, he becomes valuable. Why? I've never heard
> of a businessman and I've never heard of a farmer using as an excuse for
> the firing a man the fact that he's been with him too long and he's gained
> too much experience. The only place where people talk that way is in the
> field of politics.[150]

Manning did not take kindly to accusations that Albertans were not well
served by their provincial government. In 1947, social worker Dr Charlotte
Whitton wrote a report "Welfare In Alberta",[151] written for the IODE[152]
that alleged mistreatment of the poor, including forcing single mothers
and poor families to sign away custody of their babies before birth to fuel a
profitable export operation of unwanted babies to the United States. When
Whitton was quoted in a *New Liberty* magazine article comparing Alberta's
welfare system to Hitler's Germany, the government of Alberta sued her, the
writer, and the IODE for libel. The government's charges were eventually
dropped. And while the allegations of selling babies were never proven in
court, foreign adoptions were quickly halted.[153]

A few years later, there were rumblings that the Eugenics Board had
sterilized at least 10 people illegally. The government did not respond to the
allegations. Instead, a board member was quietly replaced.[154]

Sometimes trouble just won't go away no matter how much you want it
to. The 1960s brought charges that Alberta's Social Credit government did
not respect the rights of the mentally handicapped or mental patients.

In 1963, David Gravels, president of the Calgary West New Democratic Party, claimed that most of the children at the provincial training school have been sterilized and that a psychiatrist had resigned in protest.

The Calgary West NDP Association wanted an investigation of the act. The Alberta Catholic Welfare Association voted to ask the province to rescind the *Sexual Sterilization Act* because the legislation allowed sterilizations to proceed without consent.

The new Health Minister, Dr Donovan Ross, a physician like his predecessor, vigorously defended the Social Credit record. "Those who have undergone surgery have done so with parental consent wherever possible," Ross claimed, insisting there had been no mistakes by the Eugenics Board. "The board only recommends sterilization when it is obvious that the persons involved are psychotic or so mentally retarded that they would, not be capable of looking after their progeny," he said. He rejected any suggestions that the Board did not look out for the patient's interests. "The operations, are performed for the protection of the person involved, for the protection of any children that could born, and for the protection of society," he insisted.[155]

Ross' rebuttal was unlikely to silence the critics. A reading of the Act should have made it clear to the minister that family or patient consent was not required for the mentally defective, many patients with Huntington's chorea, or wards of the court. Ultimately, Ross was proven wrong as patients, such as Leilani Muir, who sued the Province of Alberta for wrongful sterilization, were shown to have normal intelligence and not suffering from any genetic defect that could be passed on to their children. Many were tricked into the operation under the guise of supposedly needed appendectomies.

Ross vastly underestimated the number of patients being approved for sexual sterilization. He said that Department of Health records showed that 2,103 people had been sterilized between 1928, when the *Sexual Sterilization Act* was passed, and January 1963. Ross went on to add that 139 were presented to the board each year and that the number of sterilizations annually was 78.[156]

In fact, contemporary news reports alerted the public to the fact that the board rarely decided against sterilizing a patient brought before them.

> In 1961, surgery was recommended for 119 of 121 mental defectives studied. The act, under which 893 males and 1,210 females been sterilized, until the end of 1962, is aimed at deterring transmission of mental disabilities or deficiencies.[157]

The Eugenics Board in the only other Canadian province with a *Sexual Sterilization Act*, British Columbia, averaged five operations a year. But Ross was annoyed by the controversy. He refused to consider any changes to the 'useful' Act. Furthermore he told reporters that had been 'plagued by calls to his office' thanks to the NDP and Alberta Catholic Welfare Association questioning of government policy. He added that other provinces only shirked from sterilizing mental patients and the mentally retarded because they had 'not enough guts'.

The Minister's tough stance against the critics got the support of many Albertans including the editorial staff of provincial newspapers like the *Lethbridge Herald*.

SOME FACTS ON STERILIZATION

Before the public gets too worked up over the sterilization program at the institution for mentally defective persons at Red Deer, some facts should be kept in mind. These are not otherwise normal persons suffering from mental illness. They were born mentally subnormal and can never be anything else. They are defective in different degrees, some of them no more than animals, some even little more than vegetables. Whereas the so-called 'retarded' child or person can usually be fitted into home and community life to some extent, these cannot. Without the best of care and attention, most or all of these persons would long since have died. Nature would have dealt with the problem that way. Contemporary society demands that they be cared for. They cannot be permitted to die through neglect. Some day society may subscribe to euthanasia (mercy-killing), but at present it does not. In most cases their mental defectiveness is inheritable. They are not capable of reproducing normal children. The mating of two such persons would likely produce little 'more than a blob of living matter'. Sterilization does not affect sexual powers; it only eliminates the capacity to reproduce. Sterilization is not undertaken at the Red Deer Institution without the unanimous recommendation of a four-man panel of eugenics experts. Parental consent is also obtained wherever possible. This is a distasteful situation at best. Whoever opposes sterilization must take responsibility for perpetuating the consequences of the lack of it. Alberta has one of the best set-ups in the whole world for the care of mental defectives. She is indebted to those dedicated persons in charge of the facilities.

—Editorial, *Lethbridge Herald,* December 12, 1963[158]

XIX: CANADIAN POLITICS 101: IF YOU CAN'T SHUT UP THE CRITICS, COMMISSION AN ENQUIRY

Not everyone agreed with Minister Donovan Ross' contention that there were no problems with the operation of the Eugenics Board. Stories also began appearing in newspapers of alleged abuse of patients in Alberta mental hospitals. In late 1967, journalist Torey Salter faked schizophrenia and got into the Alberta Hospital at Edmonton (better known as Oliver) to find out if the conditions there were as bad as reputed. Her article in *Canadian Magazine* in February 1968 outlined 'five days of degradation' that horrified readers coast to coast.[159]

The onslaught of newspaper stories and growing public cries for change prompted Premier Manning to ask University of Calgary professor Buck Blair to study Alberta's mental health system. Manning himself was preparing for retirement and would be out of office by the time Blair's 340-page report was tabled 11 April 1969.

The portion of the report dealing with the *Sexual Sterilization Act* was written by a eugenicist named Dr David Gibson, who claimed that "eugenics programs are supportable in terms of biological and social sciences and that board members adequately and justly implement the act."[160]

In fact, many scientists no longer supported the way Alberta's eugenics program was run. In 1974, Tim Christian, assistant law professor at the University of Alberta, with funding from the Alberta Law Foundation and the Department of Justice Canada, studied a random sampling of 430 files of patients sterilized under Alberta's *Sexual Sterilization Act*. The files listed each patient's sex, age, occupation, religion, race, sex reactions, social and moral reactions, and IQ. Christian concluded that the Eugenics Board "was given authority to impose its self-righteous, waspish notions of normalcy on those persons least able to defend themselves."

"Persons presented to and approved for sterilization by the board occupied socially vulnerable positions in Alberta. They tended to be female, young, inexperienced, unemployed or employed in low status jobs, from small towns, ethnic minorities, single, and many were labelled 'sexual deviants'," said

Christian. He theorised that the reason members of some ethnic groups were sterilized disproportionately was because they fared worse on IQ tests than British or West European ethnicities. Language and cultural barriers inherent in the tests backed up prejudices about inferiority of these groups.

Alberta's Indian, Métis, Ukrainian, Polish and Russian populations were more vulnerable to sterilization than other ethnicities. "In the time periods 1939-1943, 1959-1963 and 1969-1972, a disproportionately high number of Catholics were dealt with by the board," said Christian. He added that the most extreme discrepancy occurred between 1969 and 1972, Indian or Métis Albertans were 3.4 percent of the Alberta population, but those ethnicities were 25.7 percent of the patients sterilized during that time period.

While the Act was meant to prevent transmission of inherited mentally illness or mental defect, it was not the reason many patients were sterilized. Especially in its early years, the Eugenics Board tried to prevent 'abnormal sex reactions' in patients. Castrations were done instead of vasectomies when behaviour modification was the goal.[161]

XX: ERNEST MANNING, SOCIAL CREDIT AND CHANGE

The man most historians would consider one of the grandfathers of 21st-century Western Canadian conservatism never considered himself or his party anything but progressive. Ernest Manning was the co-architect, with William Aberhart, of Alberta's 1935 Social Credit revolution.

He began his career as the devoted disciple of the man who vowed to rid Canada of the 'Sons of Satan': the bankers, the financiers, the political old boys. Yet, by the time he died, Senator Ernest Manning, had spent a decade sitting in Canada's Upper House as part of Canada's consummate 'old boy' assembly.

The young firebrand who wanted to give Albertans dividends from their own oil, didn't start out to curry favour with the multi-national oil companies who today exert paralysing control over Alberta's political agenda. This control was shown as Premier Stelmach retreated from his government commitment to raise oil royalties in 2010. The fact that the Conservatives opted to raise the royalties after a province-wide consultation with Albertans has been largely forgotten by the Premier's critics, who accused him of putting the provincial economy at risk by angering oil companies in the province.[162]

Alberta's 21st-century economic masters are the kind of men and women Aberhart detested. And while his successor, Ernest Manning, became more tolerant of money interests, Manning remained the man who had listened intently and approvingly as Aberhart stirred the radio waves and prophesied the downfall of the rich at the hands of the God-inspired people of Alberta. Like his mentor, Manning, the preacher politician, demanded submission from his congregation of voters.[163] His paternalistic regime wound up creating the kind of peaceful, compliant political climate the multinational conglomerates loved. But there is much to suggest that Ernest Manning, even as a member of the Canadian Senate, never did become the ultimate old boy that the pundits at the *National Post* and the guys at the Fraser Institute wished he was.

Manning was a paradox. He made the province 'good for business', but earthly wealth wasn't his number one priority, nor was his highest priority to make Alberta 'good for investors'. Sure, he wanted individual Albertans prosper in this life, but he was more interested in preparing his flock for the Second Coming of Christ and eternal life.

Another paradox, Manning, who insisted on keeping the provincial Eugenics Board in place even after the most scientists believed it was based on false science, also oversaw the creation of the *Alberta Human Rights Act*, which received Royal Assent April 15, 1966.

What can explain the contradictions between Manning's professed belief in preserving human dignity and his willingness to ignore rights of Alberta's most vulnerable citizens? Was his devotion to his mentor, his religion, his personality, or the ideology he espoused? Or all of the above?

Manning was labelled a conservative, but he revealed himself a radical, lifelong disciple of William Aberhart, who remained true to the gospel of Social Credit, on the night of his retirement as Premier. Manning eloquently defended the Social Credit record in his December 1968 retirement speech. Manning still saw himself and his mentor as part of a progressive movement not understood by its backward thinking critics.

> The great founder of our movement, William Aberhart was a man whose thinking was 20 years ahead of his time. That's why, by many, he was not understood. It was from him that I learned the folly of living in the past. If he were alive today he would not be reliving the grim battles of 1935. His keen and penetrating mind would be probing into the 1970s and 1980s and reaching out to the problems which must be solved to avoid the dangerous pitfalls which otherwise that future holds in store.

Pointing to the province's economic successes, Manning urged the citizens of 'this progressive province' to lead Canada's way as William Aberhart envisioned. But his self-proclaimed progressive was a person uncomfortable with change. He likened 1960s Canada to a rebellious, often unreasonable teenager.

> I am and will be identified with the past. Today's 40 year olds were 7 year olds when I entered the cabinet. Society collectively is undergoing change, the majority has abandoned the bright perspective. In its place, an endless parade of disaffected people and organizations, complaints about living standards. In today's society people march only for the purpose of protesting. Trying to solve problems with your feet instead of your head.

Here in our province of Alberta, in 1969, the total bill for education public high schools, technical college, and university, is at $425,000,000s of dollars. Now Ladies and Gentlemen, that is greater than the total provincial budget of only five years ago, by 1974, projections will be $75 million more than the budget of two years ago.

Fundamental change in our whole system of federalism is unavoidable. Now in this era of fundamental change we have to be concerned for role of the individual citizen. He is increasingly to become a pawn of an all powerful collectivist state. The answer depends on the decisive battle for the minds of men that is now being waged in every sphere of life.

It is my unshaken conviction that every man without regard to his colour, race, or creed has an unalienable right to personal freedom to develop himself as he chooses and to the degree to which he is capable and that the role and the responsibility of the state is not to circumscribe his initiative or prescribe his course but rather to encourage and assist him to obtain his own desired goals as a free and creative individual.

The recognition of the dignity and supremacy of the individual has always been the basic premise of the Social Credit philosophy of enlightened government. It has been our guiding principle throughout 33 years of public administration. (Ernest C. Manning, Premier of Alberta, 04 December 1968)

Manning retained a progressive vision to reform society but he held on to that vision as only an inherently conservative personality could. Manning's own personality, as well as the authoritarian nature of his political and religious apprenticeship with William Aberhart, made Manning, the self-proclaimed progressive, uncomfortable with both change and critics.

His tendency to shut down debate, first shown by his support of Aberhart's *Accurate News and Information Act* of 1937 and, later, by his own government's lawsuit against Charlotte Whitton and her co-defendants, may have been the root of Social Credit's failure to deal with flaws in Alberta's Health and Welfare systems.

Perhaps that explains why both Canada's 21st-century left- and right-wing political establishments mistake Ernest Manning for a pro-corporate reactionary conservative. Manning's belief that he was part of a prophetic mission made it difficult to see opposition criticisms as valid observations. That same tendency in Manning's political heirs, may still present a great danger to Canadian social policy.

XXI: PUBLIC REVOLT AGAINST PATERNALISM

C omplaining started almost soon as the volunteers began sweeping up the confetti left on the floor by jubilant Social Crediters celebrating Harry Strom's winning campaign for the Social Credit leadership in December 1968. As the cries for change grew louder, the farmer/politician from Burdett probably wished he was back home riding the tractor. He faced a barrage of allegations that Social Credit was an out-of-date relic of Alberta's past. The cry was loudest in Alberta's two largest cities: Edmonton and Calgary.

The demands for change included calls that Strom's government bring in legislation to rescind the *Sexual Sterilization Act* and update Alberta's paternalistic mental health system.

The Canadian Mental Health Association, an early supporter of eugenics, announced that they now opposed it. In 1970, the Alberta branch of the CMHA followed suit by asking its professional advisory committee to investigate Alberta laws on compulsory sterilization.

The philosophy behind Alberta's mental hospitals was under attack. George Kohn, National Director of Administration for the Canadian Mental Health Association told members of Alberta's CMHA that 'banishment' in mental hospitals put patients 'at a great distance' from their families, friends, university resource material, and job opportunities. "We are entering an exciting era when we are building services for the mentally ill into the very fabric of the community," said Kohn.

A year earlier, obstetrician-gynaecologist Dr James Goodwan, backed up the claims of two University of Alberta geneticists, that Alberta's Eugenics Board approved sterilization of patients of provincial mental hospitals and mental hygiene clinics on 'very sketchy evidence' of mental deficiency. The geneticists, Drs Kennedy G. McWhirter and Jan Weiger, called Alberta's sterilization record a 'gross' violation of human rights 'legalized mayhem' that was 'reminiscent' of the sterilization laws of (Nazi) Germany. Weiger also alleged that Eugenics Board was made up of "people with a questionable knowledge of genetics." Godwin added that at least 10 people of normal intelligence had been sterilized as mental defectives and that alleged promiscuity, not the possibility of passing on a mental disorder to offspring, influenced the Board to sterilize patients. In one case, a supposedly mentally handicapped girl, who had been sterilized with her parents' consent, passed her Grade 12 exams.[164]

Premier Strom tried to answer the demands for change in Alberta's mental health system, commissioning his own policy paper to set out a new direction for Alberta's mental health and social services: *Social Futures for Alberta 1970-2000*. He also created the Alberta Alcoholism and Drug Abuse Commission in 1970, and a new Department of Health and Social Development, in 1971. The Strom Government amended the *Alberta Human Rights Act* to add protection against sex, age, and marital status to the existing prohibitions against discrimination based on race, religion, beliefs and colour. Strom was building on the "progressive" nature of the Social Credit policies.[165]

Ernest Manning had always professed belief in the equality of race, religion and beliefs. Indeed Manning purged anti-Semites from his own party in the 1940s. Sadly, he failed to purge Alberta's Social Credit of its anti-French, anti-Catholic elements. It was a move that doomed Social Credit to failure in the House of Commons and the party disappearance as a force in Canadian politics. His 1962 refusal to accept Quebecois Réal Caouette as national leader of the Social Credit split the party into the English-speaking Social Credit and Francophone Ralliement des Creditiste. The last Creditistes disappeared from Parliament in 1980. Manning's decision ensured that Social Credit died an even quicker death in Alberta. Just months prior to Manning's retirement in 1968, the last remaining Alberta Social Credit Members of Parliament were replaced by Progressive Conservative Members of Parliament in Ottawa. The Creditistes and Social Credit reunited in 1971, but it was too little, too late.

Albertans now saw Social Credit as a dying relic tied to outdated moralistic policies—especially when it came to mental health policies.[166, 167, 168, 169]

In the Province of Alberta, the Conservative Opposition had opposed the existence of the Provincial Eugenics board since it was created in 1928. Now re-invigorated, with the word 'progressive' added to their name, they came up with their own plan for Alberta Mental Health Services: "New Directions for

Albertans" in the 1970s. Once elected, they intended to modernize Alberta's mental health system and abolish the provincial eugenics board.

The leader of the Progressive Conservative Party, was a former Edmonton Eskimo with a Harvard Law Degree and deep roots in Alberta. Peter Lougheed was the grandson of Alberta's first federal cabinet minister, Sir James Lougheed.

XXII: THE SUN SETS ON ALBERTA'S EUGENICS BOARD

August 1971 didn't look much like the last days of an Alberta political dynasty. As the candidates in the provincial election went door knocking, they found voters busy organizing camping trips, picnics, and backyard barbeques.

Peter Lougheed's Progressive Conservatives wanted to give Albertans more community centres, old folks homes, and $1000 to any family wanting to purchase their first home. They also promised to dust off the musty old political culture of Alberta with an *Individual Rights Protection Act*, write a new *Mental Health Act* and rescind the *Sexual Sterilization Act*.

As the election results rolled in, it was clear the voters had more than summer on their mind. They had decided to end the paternalist rule of the Social Credit Party and they chose Peter Lougheed to lead them into the new Alberta.

Lougheed was true to his promise: *The Individual Rights Protection Act* and *The Mental Health Act, 1972* were among the government's first pieces of legislation, both receiving Royal Assent 22 Nov 1972. The *Sexual Sterilization Repeal Act* received Royal Assent 02 June 1972.

It took less than 50 words to abolish the Province's Eugenics Board.

Her Majesty, by and with the advice and consent of the Legislative Assembly of the Province of Alberta, enacts as follows.

The Sexual Sterilization Act is hereby repealed.

This Act comes into force on the day it receives Royal Assent.[170]

James Henderson, Minister of Hospitals under the Strom administration, protested the move, saying there was no need to repeal the Act because all the sterilizations were voluntary. He also insisted that the sterilizations were 'nearly all' initiated by a doctor and that the patient or a family member gave their consent. (Henderson either had misread or misunderstood the *Sexual Sterilization Act* because no consent was required to sterilize mental defectives. Other patients were wards of the government. Many of those operated on were not even told they had been sterilized.[171])

As the new decentralized mental health system returned former patients into Alberta's communities, the mentally ill and mentally handicapped were visible in Alberta communities for the first time in decades. Many former patients had problems integrating into society. Some wound up homeless, addicted, or victims of assault.

Repeal of the *Sexual Sterilization Act* did not end sterilization of the 'unfit'. Some families insisted that their disabled children be sterilized and many physicians complied.

INVOLUNTARY STERILIZATION UP IN ALBERTA

CALGARY (CP)—Involuntary sterilization of Alberta's mentally retarded has increased since the *Sexual Sterilization Act* was repealed in 1972, a seminar on the law and mental retardation was told Wednesday.

"The repeal of the act hasn't prevented involuntary sterilizations, it's just removed the last barrier," seminar co-ordinator Nancy Gibson told delegates.

Gibson said the last barrier was the eugenics board which, after examining an individual's situation, was empowered under the former act to order the sterilization of people who were deemed to be mentally deficient.

She said in an interview that the increase in sterilization stems in part from policy changes aimed at removing retarded persons from institutions and integrating them into society.[172]

Many Albertans still thought it was morally wrong for the mentally handicapped to form romantic relationships. In a 1974 newspaper article, the public was assured that both the mentally handicapped man and woman living together in one of the government's group homes had been sterilized.

GOV'T FORCES COUPLE TO SEPARATE

EDMONTON (CP)—Rob and Bea are two moderately retarded adults who talk in terms of 'we' and a shared affection.(3) They share a suite in a government-sponsored apartment project designed to give the retarded a taste of near-normal life and teach them how to meet the problem. But for Rob, 31, and Bea, 32, who assured program administrators they hug and kiss but don't 'sleep together', that almost intimate relationship is ending.

The Alberta government recently decreed the couple must separate after it learned of the relationship from a film, made at Hillside where they live, containing a segment on Rob and Bea.

Because they provide them with a place to live, officials fear it might appear that they condone the arrangement. The fear is that a public backlash about the relationship could lead to cancellation of the project, which moves the retarded from large, impersonal institutions into community life with the help of special counsellors and friends.

"We take turns cooking," says Bea. They go shopping and to church together. They haven't had sexual intercourse and both have been sterilized, they told their counsellors when asked on the videotape film about their relationship. "Maybe someday", was their reply.

When counsellors were told to end the living arrangement their first thought was how to tell two simple-minded people that politics won't let them stay with a caring, close companion. The government has spent thousands of dollars in the unique project and doesn't want to see it jeopardized.

Bruce Rawson, deputy minister of health and social development, who made the decision to separate the couple, said: "It is important to remember that these two people are just acclimatizing themselves, with help, to a new way of life, and they should not be making decisions that may be difficult to undo later." He explained that "though we've said they shouldn't be sharing the same room, that's not to say we aren't encouraging them to act in a close support relationship to one another."

Last year, the government repealed the *Sexual Sterilization Act* of 1928, because, said Premier Peter Lougheed, it offended basic human rights.

What about the right to make the natural decision to live with another person?

Rob and Bea have the same legal status as any other adults. They have been friends since their years in a Red Deer institution, for at least two or three years, said a counsellor.

Rob and Bea's living together was one of the "beautiful things" cited by Sam Lamendola, program supervisor, "that have happened since the project opened in March."[173]

XXIII: ABERHART'S GHOST: OIL AND THE FIFTY BIG SHOTS

Mental health didn't remain at the top of the agenda for long. Peter Lougheed's energies were focused on defending the province's oil and gas industry from perceived federal incursions that culminated in the National Energy Program of 1980.[174]

The lack of federal support Premier Manning had received when he canvassed the federal government and central Canadian business for support in developing Alberta's oil industry not only forced Alberta to accept American investment, it created a residue of anger in Albertans. "So there is a lot of bitterness, I think in some cases, it's now become more of a kind of an attitude that well, now it's our turn. Bitterness has kind of turned into, in some respects, revenge, I think but I wouldn't say that's endemic in Calgary. When people say well, there's too much American ownership here, they'll turn around and say well where the hell were you? Where was Bay Street? Where was Montreal, when we needed them? Where was the federal government for that matter?" University of Alberta Professor Larry Pratt told the CBC in the 1990s.[175]

Lougheed's stance against the federal government, along with the decline of the Social Credit Party federally and provincially, brought the populist supporters of Ernest Manning into Alberta's Provincial Progressive Conservative Party. Some Albertans still remembered how William Aberhart promised to save Alberta from the hands of Canada's 50 big shots. They remembered Alberhart's prophecy that Albertans would be wealthy thanks to oil.

Lougheed, grandson of a knighted Canadian senator, now carried the hopes of Aberhart's old constituency of shopkeepers, farmers, housewives and miners.

The blue-blooded lawyer from Calgary was Alberta's new populist hero. That political alliance of blue-blooded conservatives and working class populists brought profound changes to both the federal and provincial Progressive Conservative Parties in Alberta, and it set the stage for 'The West Wants In' cry in federal politics.

XXIV: A NIGHTMARE REVISITED

B y 1992, the few Albertans that remembered Alberta's *Sexual Steriliza-tion Act* thought it a relic of the past.[176] The Conservative Government of Alberta, now led by Premier Don Getty,[177] knew it wasn't. They also knew the provincial Eugenics Board the Lougheed Conservatives had abolished had violated the law. The province quietly settled a civil case brought by a woman who, at 15, was sterilized because she was the illegitimate child of a mentally handicapped woman. This unnamed victim later graduated with honours from a social work program.

In 1995, a part-time waitress named Leilani Muir woke the rest of Alberta up. Muir did something somebody who had been labelled 'mental defective' wasn't supposed to do.

Leilani Muir had been brought to the school by her mother and labelled a moron by the school staff after one intelligence test, that did not take into account her deprived childhood prior to being admitted to the school, rated her IQ as 64. At fourteen, after telling the Eugenics Board that she would like to have children someday, she was led into the room for what she thought was an appendectomy. In her late teens, she ran away from the school.

As an adult Muir married, supported herself, and later was found to have an IQ of 101. After she tried for years to have children, her doctor found the reason she could not conceive: her fallopian tubes had been removed during her supposed appendectomy. Muir's marriage dissolved soon after. When Leilani Muir asked the Province of Alberta to explain why the operation had been done, government staff refused to acknowledge the sterilization had been performed. So Leilani sued the government of Alberta.[178] To the government's horror, she insisted the trial be held in public. She wanted all Canadians to know what had happened in Alberta between 1928 and 1972.

When it was her turn to testify, Muir quietly counted her rosary beads and answered lawyers' questions about her childhood. But tears welled in her eyes as her lawyer talked about the school application with her name on it. It had 'mental defective-moron' scrawled across it, but nobody had bothered to write in any of the 'required evidence' about what her mental defect was supposed to be. Faulds informed the court that Ms Muir had taken another IQ test. As everyone in the courtroom already suspected, she had normal intelligence.[179]

"Here is a bright, responsive lady. There was sharpness to her. She picked up on issues quickly. That isn't a description of someone of low intelligence," educational psychologist Peter Calder told the court as he discussed the shocking changes in Muir's test results between 1957 and 1987. Muir scored a 64 on her test at the Provincial Training School for Mental Defectives in Red Deer in 1957. She scored 87 at a mental health clinic in Victoria, B.C., in 1987. In 1989, her results were 101 when she was tested at the educational psychology clinic at the University of Alberta.[180]

As the case proceeded, University of Alberta Law Professor Gerald Robertson was called to the stand. He told the court that, as he studied the minutes of the Eugenics Board along with 145 patient files, it became clear the Eugenics Board felt entitled to ignore the law in order keep their sterilization assembly line on track. The situation got worse as time progressed. Instead of carefully reviewing each file and following up on each patient after surgery, in 1935, the Board began rubber stamping recommendations in five minutes or less. "The board frequently did not appear to have regard for its policy and procedures. I got the impression that the board did not seem to attach much significance to how serious the issue of sterilization was," Robertson told the court.[181]

The testimony took a bizarre twist when Dr Margaret Thompson, a former member of the Eugenics Board, took the stand.[182] She admitted that the Board had a policy of approving sterilizations for boys with Down's syndrome, even though Board members knew males with Down's syndrome are sterile. "Nothing would be lost by sterilizing such an individual to make assurances doubly sure, as it were," she explained.

She also admitted that mentally disabled boys had their testicles removed with the Board's approval. Dr Thompson also admitted that she approved the 'testicular biopsies' even though she wasn't sure why the boys had their testicles removed in addition to their vasectomies.

"There were probably strong medical reasons," she insisted. The court learned that there were no 'strong medical reasons'. The boys had their testicles removed so Training School Director Dr Jan Le Vann could obtain testicular tissue for his experiments.

By December, the government of Alberta hoped Muir would save them some money by settling her $2 million civil lawsuit in the Provincial Court of Queen's Bench for about $60,000. They claimed that their offer was fair because it was to similar amounts awarded in Canadian courts to adult victims of incest. "An analogy may be drawn to the types of injuries suffered by plaintiffs in sexual assault cases," the province said.[183]

Leilani Muir did not settle.

In January 1996, she was awarded $740,000 Canadian plus $230,000 in legal costs in a judgment by Court of Queen's Bench Judge Madam Justice Joanne Veit.[184] This judgment was for damages for her wrongful incarceration at the Red Deer Training School for Mental Defectives[185] and her subsequent sterilization at the hands of the Alberta Eugenics Board.

Veit said the Eugenics Board actions were high-handed, outrageous and offensive. She added that, in addition to having been wrongfully sterilized, Muir, had been wrongly confined because the government's intelligence tests did not take into account her abusive upbringing.[186]

"They've got to compensate all the other people who've gone through this," Muir told reporters. The Premier, Ralph Klein, told reporters that the province was open to at least considering offering compensation to the victims.[187]

XXV: ALBERTA POLITICS 101:
NEVER SAY YOU'RE SORRY

After reading the judgment, the Klein government decided not to appeal the case. Instead, they wrote out a cheque and delivered it to Leilani's lawyer. It was a good sign: Muir, then 51, hoped the province would apologize for putting her through their high-handed, outrageous and offensive ordeal. They didn't.

"If there's an apology outstanding for Leilani Muir, it should be rendered by those who were in a position of authority at the time. For us to apologize for something that happened when the Progressive Conservative government was not the government, I don't think it appropriate. We have done what I believe is reasonable and prudent and compassionate in the circumstances," said Brian Evans, the Justice Minister.[188] Perhaps, Evans, brusqueness was due to the fact that he knew the government was facing a torrent of lawsuits launched by people sterilized under the *Sexual Sterilization Act*.

The Government of Alberta's Statement of Defence, in the Muir case, had been that she was sterilized before the *Canadian Charter of Rights and Freedoms* or the *Alberta Bill of Rights* became law. It wasn't much of a defence because the judgment made it clear that Muir's sterilization violated existing laws at the time of her sterilization.[189]

Muir's sterilization, like dozens of other sterilizations, did not even adhere to the draconian provisions the *Sexual Sterilization Act*. First, sexual sterilizations were only to be performed when a patient was about to be released and only then if the patient had a mental defect which children could inherit or which would cause the patient or his or her children harm.

Muir was never actually released. She ran away from the Provincial Training School in her late teens. A woman of normal intelligence, she had no mental defect that she could pass on to her children.

Even before the trial began, it was clear that the Alberta Government did not follow the law when Leilani was sterilized in 1959. The Alberta government's legal team admitted that Muir was entitled to financial damages in its Opening Statement when the trial began in mid-June 1995. "The sterilization should not have occurred to this woman in this case," said Bill Olthuis, a lawyer who represented the Province of Alberta in the civil trial.

The trial found evidence that many sterilizations violated the law at the time they were performed. "People were lied to and deceived at the time it happened and they were lied to after the fact," said Edmonton lawyer Allan Garber, who added that many patients were told they were having their appendix out.[190] Leilani Muir was only one of many patients who found Alberta bureaucrats unwilling to confirm that they had been sterilized.

When Faceless Victims Start Talking to Reporters

At 15, Wayne Ruston had been wheeled into the operating room to have an appendectomy that turned out to be a vasectomy.

He wondered why they gave him an enema and shaved his pubic area if he was just getting his appendix removed. "I went along with it because… I didn't know any better," Ruston told a *Lethbridge Herald* reporter in 1995. "They never approached me to see if I wanted this done. They never explained to me, they never sat down and told me what this was all about. Nothing," he said.[191]

Ruston was born in Hamilton, Ont. He wound up in the foster care system for a while after his parents separated. Hoping to find a refuge in his dad's new home in Red Deer, he came to Alberta. But Wayne got himself into some minor legal scrapes. His dad thought the Deer Home, part of the Provincial Training School, might be a safe place for a kid who was on the verge of becoming a juvenile delinquent. (It was actually a home for the mentally handicapped.)

Five years after his operation, Ruston found freedom the same way Muir did: he checked himself out of the institution and headed to Ontario to work on a dairy farm, the first of many farm and maintenance jobs in Ontario and Alberta.

Ken Nelson, was a cerebral palsy patient who was sent to the school by his parents at age seven and labelled 'mentally retarded'. He too was sterilized at the Provincial Training School in Red Deer, at age 14. They said, "This happens to everybody."

"You have no say whatsoever in the matter," said Nelson.

According to Nelson, any sort of defiance was put down swiftly. When he refused to wash a mess off the floor, staff pushed his nose into the floor.

He also said that patients were kept in solitary confinement for up to three weeks at a time. "Can you imagine what would have happened to us if we challenged that board when we were in there?"

According to Nelson, he lost his right index finger when staff at the Provincial Training School for Mental Defectives in Red Deer slammed it in a door.[192]

Another victim, Loraine Bigelow, was a ward of the province when she was sterilized. She had no mental disability. "They sterilized me because of my hands, because of my physical handicap, if you want to call it that," she told reporters who interviewed her in Ontario. She had an inherited defect which left her with only one finger on each hand and two toes, one on each foot.

Abused by her own family, she lived in the Alberta Hospital for Crippled Children and when she didn't need hospitalization, she spent time in an orphanage. In 1965, she also stood before a panel that asked her if she ever hoped to have children. Like most young girls would, she answered, 'yes'. Within weeks, she was sterilized.[193]

XXVI: LAWSUITS

In July 1995, as the Muir trial got going, Donna Marie Whittaker, 38, launched her own wrongful sterilization lawsuit in the Court of Queen's Bench. As a fourteen-year-old, she was sterilized in 1971, at Alberta School hospital in Red Deer. (Also called the Provincial Training School for Mental Defectives, and later, Michener Centre.[194])

The child of an unwed mother, she had been admitted to the training school as an 11-year-old in 1968 after being bounced between relatives. At age 4, she became a ward of the province. Like Muir, Whittaker had had her Fallopian tubes removed. The court statement read: she did not become aware of the sterilization until years later when she consulted her physician about her seeming difficulty to have a child.[195]

As the government of Alberta announced they would pay Leilani Muir's $740,000 plus legal costs without appealing her case, a common suit was readied for filing by lawyers representing victims of the Eugenics Board.

In March 1996, 30 former patients of the provincial training school launched a lawsuit seeking $1 million each from Alberta government.

Both victims and lawyers representing them expected the government would settle the issue before going to trial. "I think it's likely in everybody's best interests that we try and find a way of dealing with these claims that doesn't involve the immense amount of time and effort that went into Leilani Muir's case," said Jon Faulds, who represented the claimants as well as Muir.[196]

Allan Garber, who had already filed suits on behalf of 25 people, was preparing several more. "I know there are political concerns and they want to be seen as rectifying a wrong from the past... It's the right thing to do," said Garber.[197]

Signals from the government looked positive: Justice Minister Brian Evans told reporters that the government wanted to settle other lawsuits out of court on an individual basis. "The decision was we could live with the

(Muir) judgment and we would look at the other cases that may arise on their own merits," Evans said.[198]

Faulds was willing to settle each case on an individual basis. He recognized the complexity of the issues involved in the Muir suit would be repeated in the upcoming suit.

Muir's award was for damages arising, not only from the fact that she had been wrongly sterilized, but from the fact that she had also been mislabelled a moron and, therefore wrongly confined.

Like Muir, many of the patients had multiple claims against the province. Not only were patients alleging wrongful sterilization, many also sought damages for wrongful confinement and sexual abuse and there were varying circumstances related to their sterilizations. "Nobody wants to go to court if they are offered what they are entitled to," says Faulds.[199]

By the end of March 1996, the government faced $126 million in sterilization lawsuits by 200 former patients and residents of provincial institutions. Many of the 2400 people sterilized between 1972 and 1998 were still living. The government could be on the hook for hundreds of millions of dollars payable to as many as 700 people who were sterilized or abused. Five of these victims were dependent in adult institutions. Two hundred were well enough to live independently.[200]

Alberta Politics 101: When Redressing Wrongs Costs Too Much, Fight the Victims

With the number of lawsuits increasing and the cost of compensating victims skyrocketing, the government decided to slow down the steady traffic of process servers to government offices.

In June 1996 that province announced it would fight the *Sexual Sterilization* lawsuits rather than settle out of court. The province now insisted that sterilizations, other than Leilani Muir's, had been lawful and asked the courts to throw out the suits.

Even before the announcement, government lawyers filed statements of defence at Court of Queen's Bench in Edmonton insisting the sterilizations were 'in accordance with the laws of the day'. (Clearly this contradicted evidence at the Muir trial which showed the province had contravened its own laws.)

"At all times the government and its employees acted in good faith and in accordance with the medical and social standards," was the government's response to seven of the lawsuits. They also claimed that under the *Limitations of Actions Act,* the plaintiffs filed too late. They did not make any such claims in the Muir case and it seem odd that they would make the claim now.

Justice Joanne Veit ruled the eugenics board handling of the files were not lawful, but were done in an "outrageous, high-handed and offensive manner" and encouraged the government to "make up for past wrongs".

Justice Minister Brian Evans claimed the Muir case was unique. He also said cases would be looked at on their own merits. Lawyers for the defendants were appalled. "Madame Justice Veit found they routinely did not follow their own rules so to say this only applies to Leilani Muir is to ignore the conclusions of the judgement," said Sandra Anderson, acting for more than 70 of the plaintiffs.[201]

As the government argued that the wrongful sterilization cases should be thrown out because they filed too late under the statute of limitations, the plaintiff's lawyer filed documents showing 'fraudulent actions'.[202]

The wrangling continued for more than a year with no settlement in sight. In January 1998, Alberta Court of Queen's Bench Associate Chief Justice Alan Wachowich set January 12, 1999 as the day the government and its former patients would meet in court. The trial could last eight to 12 months according to lawyer Allan Garber. More than four dozen witnesses would be called as the court reviewed the practices of the Eugenics Board, the school, and reviewed the thousands of Eugenics Board files.[203]

Twenty-three former patients, now living across Canada, (mostly in Edmonton and Red Deer) were already selected to form a 'plaintiff pool' that would represent all the victims. The youngest plaintiff was a man in his forties; the oldest, a woman in her 80s. "This is not something they particularly want to do but are prepared to do it…We've extended to the province an invitation to settle these claims and they've indicated they don't want to," said Garber. He hoped that in the months before the court date, an out of court settlement might still spare the victims further trauma, save taxpayers millions of dollars in trial costs, and ensure the victims received a settlement before they died.[204]

The government lawyers appeared to agree. "We're working toward a resolution but it's very complicated," claimed Doug Graham of Macleod Dixon, the Calgary law firm hired to represent the Alberta government.[205]

XXVII: THAT'S WHAT THE NOTWITHSTANDING CLAUSE IS FOR, ISN'T IT?

In March 1998, Premier Ralph Klein announced that his government was proposing an out of court settlement to the victims of Alberta's Eugenics Board. "It deals with compensation, I can tell you that," Klein told curious reporters shortly before the bill was tabled March 10. "It's very delicate in light of pending court action, it is a sensitive issue and we're trying to deal with it as sensitively and fairly as we can." Klein added that the legislation would deal with the plaintiffs' arguments that the province exceeded its constitutional jurisdiction by allowing sterilizations at its institutions.

Bill 26, *The Institutional Confinement and Sexual Sterilization Compensation Act*, was tabled by Justice Minister John Havelock on March 10, 1998.[206] "On behalf of the government of Alberta, I want to express our profound regret to those who have suffered as a result of being sterilized under the *Sexual Sterilization Act*," Havelock told the legislature. "With this legislation in place, we'll be able to move forward to resolve these claims and bring this matter to a close."[207]

The Bill capped maximum compensation for $150,000 for sterilization and damages arising out of confinement in provincial institutions. The minimum settlement would be $50,000.[208] And the Klein government planned to use the Notwithstanding Clause in the Canadian *Constitution Act, 1982* to limit victims' rights to sue for damages.

Disappointment is one word that describes the feelings of victims like Wayne Ruston, when they heard what Havelock was offering them. Ruston was one of 23 plaintiffs selected for the plaintiff pool for the 1999 trial and he had been expected a much higher settlement in light of Muir's award which came to nearly $1 million when awarded costs were added in.

Sure it was nice that the province finally admitted even a tiny bit of regret for what happened to them, but the compensation seemed like a pittance for the suffering Ruston and the other victims had been through. The other word that described Ruston was hopeful that his ordeal would soon be over. "I think, speaking for a lot of people, it's been a long time coming and I'm just glad it's almost finally done," he said.

The lawyers for the plaintiffs were not as circumspect. "This law is outrageous and without precedent in this province," said Jon Faulds, the lawyer for Leilani Muir now representing several other victims of the *Sexual Sterilization Act*. Faulds considered the Act an attack on justice in the province. "The government is placing artificial and self-serving restrictions on the court and the court's traditional power to set compensation for those who have been wrongly injured. The government is changing the rules of the game in the middle of play. It is litigating through the legislature," he added.[209]

"We have not been consulted. There has been no input from us. They are trying to impose a unilateral settlement without any discussion at all. This is about as high-handed as you can get," agreed lawyer Allan Garber, also representing plaintiffs. "We have told the province we would be prepared to talk settlement for considerably less than what Leilani Muir was awarded in some cases," he added.[210]

The Premier, Ralph Klein, and Justice Minister Havelock insisted they could not consult with victims or their lawyers before introducing *The Institutional Confinement and Sexual Sterilization Compensation Act* because the cases were already before the court. Faulds disagreed. He said it was unusual for a lawyer not be consulted by government lawyers in the case of an out of court settlement.

The Day Angry Albertans Forced Ralph Klein's Retreat

March 11, 1998 Justice Minister, John Havelock, stood before the legislature, a humbled man. To a silent assembly he announced that the government was withdrawing Bill 26, *The Institutional Confinement and Sexual Sterilization Compensation Act* because so many Albertans opposed its use of the Notwithstanding Clause.[211]

In less than 24 hours, angry Albertans told the populist Klein government that even 'King Ralph' risked political oblivion if he messed with Canadians' Charter rights. Havelock, stunned by the public outcry over Bill 26, offered to resign, if Klein wanted him too. Not because the bill would have harmed victims, but because it caused political fallout.

"I accept full responsibility for that and if the premier feels that I can't do the job for him anymore, I'm sure he'll tell me," said Havelock. "I thought it was good legal advice—it was not good political advice on this issue... We have made a mistake with the Notwithstanding Clause," said Havelock.[212, 213]

Klein had no intention of asking for Havelock's resignation. "Why should I? If all of us resigned every time someone said resign, we would have no one left... If every lawyer who gave bad advice was fired, there would be no lawyers."

Bill 26, *The Institutional Confinement and Sexual Sterilization Compensation Act*, proved to be one of the few political missteps Ralph Klein ever made. Even international news coverage of the Premier's December 2002 alcohol-fuelled late night lecture to homeless men trying to get some sleep in a shelter got the premier more sympathy from Alberta voters.[214]

Hundreds of Albertans called their MLAs and the Premier's office demanding that the Government of Alberta not use Notwithstanding Clause to limit the compensation to victims of the Alberta *Sexual Sterilization Act*.

Klein and Havelock probably expected opposition to the government's planned use of the *Constitution Act*'s Notwithstanding Clause to override the Charter of Rights and Freedom. They could have brushed it aside if it only came from outraged lawyers, newspaper editors and the Liberals and New Democrats who taunted them daily from their benches on the other side of the Alberta Legislature. What he probably didn't expect was that the so-called 'real Albertans', who delighted in the brash working class persona of the audacious ex-news reporter turned Premier, would be outraged, too.

Perhaps, Klein's mistake was trying to do politics the way William Aberhart or Ernest Manning would have done it. In the '30s, '40s, '50s, and early '60s, the Alberta government would not have had to override individual rights in order to limit compensation to the victims. In the 'Socred'[215] heyday, Bill 26 might have withstood attacks from the Opposition and victims' lawyers, but ordinary Albertans would not have phoned the Premier's office to complain. (In fact, ordinary Albertans might not have had telephones.)

When Ernest Manning became Premier in 1943, there were no Alberta or Canadian Bills of Rights, no *Alberta* or *Federal Human Rights Acts*, and the idea of the Queen herself coming to Ottawa to proclaim a *Constitution Act* incorporating a "Charter of Rights and Freedoms" was not even a distant dream.

Klein's second mistake was thinking that most Alberta voters were the same parochial congregation Aberhart governed when the Social Credit government weakened consent provisions and denied legal redress to citizens sterilized at the order of the Eugenics Board. It's true that some members of the populist right wing in Alberta, including Ted Morton, who became the provincial finance minister early 2001, are on record as opposing the introduction of the Charter of Rights and Freedoms. Populist voters were also a powerful force in Klein's leadership campaign and his continued popularity in the province. It was a rare political misstep, but Ralph Klein didn't count on so many Albertans having affection for the Charter of Rights and Freedom.

Some Albertans did blame lawyers and the liberal media for the debacle and wished Klein had used the Notwithstanding Clause. As one man's letter to the *Lethbridge Herald* showed, some Albertans still believed that it was okay to deny some individuals redress to the courts if it saved the taxpayers from paying money to the victims.[216] He wrote:

> The lawyers will be working with contingency fees, which means the higher the settlement, the more money they suck out of the taxpayers/people of Alberta. Given free rein, these cases will grind on until the galaxy collapses. The lawyers of today got their reputation the old fashioned way—they earned it!

> The government hit the deck when the legal community and the liberal faction of the media went ballistic. "How dare this government attempt to save the people of this province millions of dollars? In this case the judiciary will be suing the government, but really they are suing you and me, because we end up paying for the settlement. My fear is the government will be in the bunker, and be fearful of using the Notwithstanding Clause. But really that clause is to protect the people against a non-elected, unaccountable and unresponsive court that makes many stare in disbelief at some of the judgments that come forth upon the land."

No doubt Klein hoped the perceived 'pack mentality' of Alberta voters would favour limiting provincial liability. After all, the Notwithstanding Clause had already been used by a provincial government. Quebeckers, irked that the *Constitution Act* had been proclaimed April 17, 1982 without Quebec's signature, let Premier Robert Bourassa override the Charter of Rights and Freedoms in order to pass Bill 23 and force Quebec businesses to post signs in French.[217] But Albertans would have none of it, especially if it was used to deny victims of the Alberta Government redress for harm done to their bodies. Albertans were not as politically motivated to save on taxes at the expense of justice as the Premier hoped they would be. Canada's Charter and Rights and Freedoms had just proven its worth to Alberta's mentally ill and mentally handicapped.

Dragging the Province to a Settlement and a Real Apology

Even after withdrawing the bill, the Province insisted that the $150,000 cap proposed in *The Institutional Confinement and Sexual Sterilization Compensation Act* would remain their top offer as negotiations proceeded.[218] "If settlements cannot be reached or individual claimants choose not to negotiate a settlement, they retain the right to take or continue with court action," said Justice Minister Havelock.

Within weeks, the two sides agreed to a $48 million settlement for 500 plaintiffs, those who were disabled and living in institutions or care facilities. Each person would receive $75,000. Those still living and who resided outside a hospital or Michener Centre in three years would receive another $25,000. While the offer was originally made to clients of Edmonton lawyer Jon Faulds, Court of Queen's Bench documents showed that the province agreed to extend the offer to other dependent adults who were suing if they met the following criteria: claimants must have been sterilized under *Sexual Sterilization Act*, have their affairs managed by Alberta's public trustee, and be identified within 180 days of the settlement date.[219]

By September, this partial settlement was in danger as the government inexplicably decided not to pay thirteen victims represented by Edmonton lawyer Allan Garber. "We're very disappointed," Allan Garber said. "Our clients are quite elderly. We have a settlement. The province has refused to tender the settlement money."[220]

In November 1999, the Province of Alberta came up with the final settlement to its victims. Although the $82 million settlement included approximately $2 million in legal disbursements, victims still had to cover legal fees out of their individual awards. Settlements varied between individual.[221]

And the Government of Alberta apology to the victims expressed 'profound regret to those who suffered as a result of being sterilized under this act.' "There is a closure before this millennium stops… We can go into a new one with a clear conscience knowing that we opened a dark door and put light through it all," said Leilani Muir.[222]

Ralph Klein didn't seem very sorry. "I guess we extend regrets for the actions of another government in another period of time," Klein said. "It's unfortunate. I won't say criminal— it was the law at that particular time and, unfortunately, it was a bad law," said Ralph Klein.[223]

The Premier of Alberta seemed oblivious to the fact that the Eugenics Board's high-handed behaviour didn't even conform to the bad law he was talking about. He made no mention of the fact that these patients had been abused, violated, falsely confined, and sometimes falsely labelled as mental defectives. Nor did he condemn the Eugenics Board for not even bothering to adhere to the *Sexual Sterilization Act*.

But Klein was not alone. After Muir won her case in 1996, Jim Henderson, Health Minister under Harry Strom's Social Credit regime, claimed his busy portfolio had kept him from paying much attention to the Eugenics Board until the Lougheed Conservatives tagged it as a human rights issue. "I wasn't knowledgeable and maybe I should have been but there were a hell of a lot of other things on the platter," Henderson said in 1996.[224]

Eighty-two year old Anders Aalborg seemed to have a much better memory than the sixty-something-year-old Henderson.[225] He remembered problems with the Eugenics Board that were serious enough to have one member of the board fired, when he was a member of the Social Credit Cabinet back in the 1950s. What was the problem back then? The Eugenics Board was sterilizing people who didn't meet criteria laid out in the Act. "There were some of these cases where apparently there had been errors made," he told reporters. Aalborg linked those mistakes to the mess of money the province had to pay out to the victims. "Of course, this then gave them grounds for saying they should not have been subjected to this," said Aalborg.[226] What was so hard to understand?

XXVIII: ALBERTA'S POLITICAL CULTURE

In July 2006, Premier Ralph Klein asked the speaker of the legislature to change a five-day sitting of the provincial legislature, intended to debate spending an extra $200 million dollars in health and education spending. He wanted to go on a fund-raising fishing trip with some businessmen.

The Alberta Liberal house leader Laurie Blakeman wondered how the Premier, who already had a reputation for skipping legislative sessions, was suddenly worried about missing the five-day sitting only weeks away from his retirement. "Seeing as he's very near the end of his term, I'm surprised he's willing to be there at all. And frankly, I don't know how much he has to contribute to the goings-on anymore, but it would be fun to have him there," she told reporters.[227]

No doubt about, Ralph Klein was colourful character, one even his political opponents were going to miss. Ralph Klein was comfortable in places his Progressive Conservative predecessors, Peter Lougheed and Don Getty, didn't fit into—the old style taverns and coffee shops where the working class rig workers, tradesmen, and farmers gathered. He was a master at making Albertans believe that the both Easterners and welfare bums were living off their hard work.

As Mayor of Calgary, the popular Ralph Klein made an entrance on the national stage as a brash tough-talking defender of Alberta. In January 1982, a rash of convenience store and bank robberies, a housing shortage and overflowing jails prompted Klein read the riot act to out-of-province migrants. As he issued a Wild West – style ultimatum, he targeted migrants from Central and Eastern Canada as the culprits. Ironically, the Mayor who held court with his buddies at a hotel bar captured the same sentiment William Aberhart's radio sermons did when they rallied impoverished farmers and struggling shopkeepers to rise up against Central Canada's 'Sons of Satan' and 'international finance' in the 1930s.

When Klein was asked to explain, he was blunt: "The word I used was 'kick ass and get the...out of town. You're welcome to stay here a couple of weeks at government expense, but if you can't make it after that particular time, then don't go out and rob our banks and our convenience stores and mug our senior citizens and snatch purses. Get the hell out of town," was Klein's unapologetic response.[228]

Klein suggested he didn't really mind if the rules got bent a little, just as long as it kept the out-of-province folks from abusing their hosts. "If some bank robber complains that a police officer has roughed him up a little, I'm not going to get too excited about it," added Klein.[229]

The television reporter turned mayor became Premier of Alberta December 5, 1992. With his blunt blue collar talk he let it be known that he didn't have time for people who didn't work or who thought Alberta wasn't providing everybody with a fair chance in life. He berated two AISH recipients who heckled him at a rally, telling the audience that they didn't look disabled to him.[230] Anyone who listened to Klein might think that Albertans were pseudo-American right-wingers that didn't have much taste for social programs.

Nothing was further from the truth. Beginning as soon as the Liberals took the reins in the new province, Albertans put what energy they didn't spend in building farms and businesses into building public hospitals, mental institutions, universities and schools. More often than not, those public institutions were governed by locally elected boards. That is, until Ralph Klein came to power and replaced elected local hospital trustees with Tory appointees. His regime also cut sitting days in the Province's Legislature. Teachers, public employees, seniors, and public health care activists hit the streets with placards to protest Klein's cuts to government services. Ralph wasn't cowed by people he thought must be a bunch of left-leaning Liberals and New Democrats. He took delight in the controversy.

Creating Alberta's Right Wing Persona

If they listen to the pundits, and Alberta Agenda – pushing political scientists, a lot of Canadians may think Albertans favour American style politics, culture and social policy. The oil industry's economic control of the provincial agenda along with taxpayer and corporately supported tourist draw, like the Calgary Stampede encourages the perception, but there is more to the story. In the 1940s, Albertans, including Premiere Manning, would have preferred British or Canadian investment in the oil industry. While some British investors did heed the call, it was mostly Americans who brought their money into the industry, setting up an American dominated neocolonial economy inside the Commonwealth. The American-led oil industry has impacted local culture, especially in the City of Calgary, which continues to have approximately 75,000 American citizens living in that municipality of 1 million.[231]

Ernest Manning, who tried desperately to convince the federal government to support development of Alberta's oil and gas industry, could not help but notice that Eastern Canada continued to buy cheap foreign oil and Bay Street and Montreal financiers didn't take a gamble on Alberta's future. In the 1950s, Ernest Manning's *Back to the Bible* sermons took on a Cold War tone where the Godless Communists were cast in a dark role as Israel's enemy as the world neared its final War between Good and Evil on the Plains of Armageddon in modern day Israel. The United States is the good guy in the kind of fundamentalist eschatology Manning taught. Manning, like many evangelicals, believed the Apocalypse and the return of Christ could be within his lifetime. Not surprisingly, Manning hated Marxist socialism.[232]

After Manning's retirement, as both the provincial and federal Social Credit parties sank into obscurity, Alberta voters turned to the Progressive Conservatives. Peter Lougheed's feud with Prime Minister Pierre Trudeau over the National Energy Program, along with his creation of Alberta Energy and the Alberta Heritage Savings Trust Fund were the closest thing to the fulfillment of Aberhart's promises Albertans had seen in 30 years. Even Social Crediters became Conservative voters. But the old style populist followers of Aberhart and Manning didn't quite fit into the party of Alberta boy turned city slicker Joe Clark, or Brian Mulroney's Conservative agenda. When the old Premier's son, Preston Manning, moved into federal politics, they were ready to try to make Aberhart's old dream a reality.

Stephen Harper's Victory and William Aberhart's Prophecy

CALGARY, March 2004—Stephen Harper's family stands before a cheering crowd as the stage is flooded in a cascade of confetti and balloons. The television camera scans the crowd to reveal a beaming face in the audience: Preston Manning. Alberta was finally on the inside of Canada's political power elite. The dream that began in the mind of William Aberhart, before Preston Manning was born, had just come true.

As leader of the Reform Party, Manning himself had come very near fulfilling Aberhart and Ernest's Manning's dream. But until the Reform Party (renamed the Canadian Alliance in 2000) merged with the Progressive

Conservative Party, it seemed unlikely that any one of Aberhart's political heirs would ever sit in the Prime Minister's desk.

Only three years before, Harper, apparently despairing that Alberta could ever influence Ottawa, signed an open letter to Ralph Klein. The letter urged Premier Klein to build 'firewalls' to protect the provincial government's power and stave off any growth in federal government authority in the province.[233]

Harper and Manning

In a more moderate way, Preston Manning's role in Stephen Harper's life was similar to the role William Aberhart played in Ernest Manning's life. Manning schooled the younger man, Harper, in politics and Reform Party ideology. As Chief Policy Officer of the Reform Party, Harper had been indispensable to Manning by writing the Reform Party Bluebook in 1990. While Aberhart tried to solve the problems of Alberta's poverty with the ideology of Social Credit, Manning and Harper became good students of the Calgary School of Political Science, based at the University of Calgary. They blended Alberta's populist political culture, incorporating democratic changes including senate reform, religiously based social conservatism, with the right wing economics of University of Calgary academics like Tom Flanagan, who served as the Reform Party's Director of Policy and Communications, and Ted Morton, who was narrowly defeated by Ed Stelmach in the 2008 race for the P.C. Leadership in Alberta.

Grassroots Ideas Created in an Ivory Tower

Both Flanagan and Morton were born and raised in the United States, where Republican politicians tend to equate public institutions with left wing ideologies such as Marxist socialism and Communism. Flanagan views social welfare as a "hypertrophic" welfare state dominated by a socio-distant progressive elite that wishes to remake society according to its own rationalistic vision.[234]

Not surprisingly, the co-writers of the Alberta Agenda supported a free market economy, privatization of public corporations and institutions, and decentralized federalism. The view, in my opinion, appears to be based on the American models that misunderstand the history and strength of Alberta's public health and educations systems, and disregards Albertans' attachment to parliamentary and national institutions such as the Crown and the Royal Canadian Mounted Police.

The Alberta Agenda attempted to rekindle the fortress mentality of Aberhart's fight with Mackenzie King and of Peter Lougheed's stand off with Pierre Trudeau over the National Energy Program. It was also a transparent attempt to dismantle federal institutions in the province and would have, if accepted, caused rifts between the federal government and Alberta over taxation and health care.

The Alberta Agenda co-signers were Stephen Harper, Tom Flanagan, Rainer Knopff, Ken Boessenkool and Ted Morton. The letter was published in the *National Post* 24 January 2001. It asked Premier Ralph Klein to adopt a so-called five point 'Alberta Agenda'.

> Withdraw from the Canada Pension Plan to create an Alberta Pension Plan offering the same benefits at lower cost while giving Alberta full control over the investment fund. Collect our own revenue from personal income tax, as we already do for corporate income tax. Start preparing to let the contract with the RCMP run out in 2012, and create an Alberta Provincial Police force, resume provincial responsibility for health care policy. If Ottawa objects to provincial policy, fight in the courts. If we lose, we can afford the financial penalties Ottawa might try to impose under the Canada Health Act. Use Section 88 of the Supreme Court's decision in the Quebec Secession Reference to force Senate reform back on the national agenda.

Not surprisingly, Alberta's Premier wasn't impressed by a bunch of academics telling him how to do his job.

XXIX: COMPARISONS (ALBERTA AND OTHER CANADIAN PROVINCES)

A lberta's approach to the victims of eugenics sheds an interesting light on the province's political culture and its relationship to that of other Canadian provinces and the other countries. Let's take a look.

Eugenics in Canadian Provinces

British Columbia and Alberta were the only Canadian provinces to pass a *Sexual Sterilization Act* or to set up provincial eugenics boards.

As their neighbours on the eastern slopes of the Rocky Mountains passed the British Empire's first *Sexual Sterilization Act*, British Columbians considered what to do with mental defectives and the mentally ill. British Columbia's Royal Commission on Mental Hygiene (1928) recommended establishing 'special classes for mentally deficient children in all school centres having a school population of 500 or more and the establishment of vocational schools'.[235] The Commission's most controversial proposal was that the B.C. legislature enact a law that would include 'carefully restricted and safeguarded measures of permissive sexual sterilization of certain suitable and definitely ascertained cases of mental abnormality with the object that such cases may be permitted safely to return to their normal place in the community'.[236]

In 1933, British Columbia's legislature, under the Premiership of Liberal Thomas Dufferin "Duff" Pattullo, passed its own *Sexual Sterilization Act*. While Pattullo, elected in the middle of the Depression was the Liberal Leader in the B.C. Legislature, his party shared few policies with the federal Liberals. Like Aberhart, Pattullo was sceptical of both capitalists and bankers. He was often at odds with the government in Ottawa.

At least two hundred British Columbians were sterilized between 1933 and 1973, the year the B.C. Act was rescinded.[237] It's impossible to pinpoint the exact number of sterilizations that took place in that province because the records of the B.C. Eugenics Board outlining which patients were approved for sterilization are missing. No one seems to know exactly what happened to the B.C. records: how they were lost, by whom, and when. Nor is anyone certain whether their loss was purely accidental or done to avoid lawsuits like those in Alberta.

We do know that, in 1963, the number of Albertans sterilized far surpassed those done in British Columbia.[238] When asked about the number of sexual sterilizations in that province, a British Columbia government spokesman told Canadian Press that the B.C. law was enforced in a limited way. "You couldn't describe its use as anything but sparing," said the unnamed spokesman. British Columbia averaged seven sterilization operations a year under the *Sexual Sterilization Act* in the late 1950 and early 1960s, according to this government official. The Eugenics Board in Alberta authorised 119 sterilizations in 1961.[239]

In British Columbia, patients were to be sterilized only if they 'would be likely to beget or bear children who by reason of inheritance would have a tendency to serious mental disease or mental deficiency'.[240] British Columbia's consent clauses were almost identical to the original 1928 wording of Alberta's *Sexual Sterilization Act*. In British Columbia, patients or their wife, husband, parent or guardian had to consent in writing. Patients unable to give informed consent, who did not have guardians, could be approved by the Provincial Secretary. Alberta removed the need for consent to sterilize mental defectives and some Huntington 's chorea patients in 1942. Despite the stricter rules, some British Columbians were sterilized without consent and many patients did not know they were sterilized.[241,242]

A verdict is still pending in a January 2001 lawsuit brought by the Public Guardian and Trustee of B.C. against the Province of B.C. on behalf of 13 mentally disabled women who were sterilized under the *Sexual Sterilization Act*. The women alleged that they did not consent to the operation and the sterilization violated government policy.

"I'm quite confident that there are people who are not our clients for whom the board of eugenics authorized sterilizations," said Jay Chalke, Public Guardian and Trustee. "Our primary issue is that these individuals were denied the opportunity from the point of sterilization forward to bear children."[243]

The sexual sterilization was carried out by or under the direction of the servants of the Crown for reasons which were knowingly foreign to the administration of the *Sexual Sterilization Act*, according to court documents. In some cases there was no evidence the women could pass on a mental defect. One woman's mental problems were caused by a car accident. The sterilizations were done as a means of birth control, because provincial staff viewed the women as promiscuous, amoral and unfit to be mothers.

Like Alberta, British Columbia set up a Board of Eugenics. But the three-member board included a judge, psychiatrist and a social worker as opposed to the two physicians and two members of the public in Alberta. Only inmates of provincial institutions could be sterilized in British Columbia. In Alberta, the eugenics board also visited mental hygiene out patient clinics across the province.

As in Alberta, sterilizations continued after the 1973 abolition of British Columbia's *Sterilization Act*, usually because a family member or guardian requested the operation. In 1997, a B.C. mother had her 21-year-old son castrated to control his aggression and prevent him from having children. The doctor was reprimanded for unprofessional conduct and forced to take a course on ethics and legal responsibilities by the B.C. College of Physicians and Surgeons.

The Public Guardian and Trustee of B.C. tried to remove the mother as the man's guardian and launched civil suits against the patient's mother and physicians in the case. The lawsuits are still unresolved. The Public Guardian's suit against the mother, doctors and Nanaimo General Hospital alleged that the operation disfigured AR, increased his risk of early aging, bone degeneration and fatigue.[244]

Saskatchewan

He was just a Baptist preacher in training from Saskatchewan. Why should he disagree with the leading clergymen, physicians and scientists on both sides of the Atlantic? Not surprisingly, Tommy Douglas, wrote a glowing master's thesis on eugenics for McMaster University. "Problems of the Sub-Normal Family" praised the 'sexual hygiene movement' and the idea of state-sponsored birth control including sterilization as things that would benefit both society and 'sub-normal' individuals.

But Douglas did not remain a fan of eugenic sterilization.

In 1936, he took a trip to Europe. Douglas was stunned by the brutality of the German eugenics program and rising Nazi German militarism that would soon pull the British Empire, including Canada, into a fight for survival. Worse, he saw the spectre of the coming holocaust that would kill the disabled, the mentally ill, the gypsies, homosexuals, political and religious dissidents and 6 million Jews.

Douglas realized that eugenics laws could be used to exterminate the mentally retarded. He became convinced that all mentally retarded people would be exterminated in Nazi Germany and he was horrified at the thought that the sexual hygiene movement might eventually lead to euthanasia of defectives, even in Canada.

When Douglas became Premier of Saskatchewan in 1944, he did not institute a sexual sterilization act in that province. In many other respects, his policies toward the mentally ill were similar to his Alberta counterparts. Both provinces considered themselves progressive and adopted "progressive" ideas of the time, both had large segregated asylums and training schools for the mentally ill.

Douglas is not the first person, nor will he be the last, to change ideas they wrote into a university paper. But in his case, that paper has been used after the student's death to suggest that Douglas was a proponent of eugenic sterilization and that it was part and parcel of his 'leftwing' belief system.[245] That notion under estimates the influence of eugenics on 20th-century thinking. The idea that the defective should not procreate was so widely accepted that it was well accepted across the political spectrum and even became part of Protestant Christianity.

In the 19th and early 20th centuries, eugenicists reached out to Protestant churches with promises of upgrading the moral and mental climate of society: reducing poverty, mental illness, addictions, and illegitimacy. Not surprisingly both mainline and conservative Protestants on both sides of the Atlantic liked what they heard. The outreach by eugenicists also deepened the Protestant disdain for Roman Catholics' who were ridiculed as superstitious and backward for not following the eugenics gospel. Evangelical Baptists, like Tommy Douglas, Ernest Manning, and William Aberhart, believed controlling the sexual energies and illegitimate births, particularly among the morally suspect and poor, was the Word of the Lord. While Douglas was scared out of his devotion to eugenics, William Aberhart and Ernest Manning not only continued to support eugenics, they expanded the definition of 'mentally defectives', removed the need for consent for many categories of patients, and increased the number of defectives who were sterilized by the Alberta Eugenics Board.

William Aberhart and Ernest Manning's *Back to the Bible Hour* broadcasts conditioned generations of Albertans to look uncritically at the agenda of politicians claiming to support Christian values. Aberhart called his political opponents "Sons of Satan". Ernest Manning explained the Book of Revelations to his radio listeners using the Soviet Union and the Cold War as evidence of the imminent return of Christ.[246] Listeners knew that to oppose them was to side with evil.

Throughout Canada and the United States, right-wing economists and political parties continue to target churchgoers successfully. In Alberta, the Reform Party, Canadian Alliance, federal Conservative Party, the right Wing of the Progressive Conservative Party, and Wildrose Alliance have all followed the example of Social Credit by targeting Evangelical Christians and Mormons, as party recruits.[247]

Other Provinces

Just because most other Canadian provinces didn't have a eugenics board, doesn't mean mentally handicapped or mentally ill patients weren't sterilized without their consent in those provinces.

Ontario doctors, for example, performed hundreds of sexual sterilization, even though that province never passed a sexual sterilization act and had no eugenics board. Many families requested sterilization of their mentally disabled family members. It has also been alleged that hospital abortion committees forced women seeking abortions to consent to sexual sterilization. After the *Sexual Sterilization Acts* in Alberta and British Columbia were abolished, doctors continued to sterilize mentally handicapped patients at the request of parents or guardians, as was done in Ontario.

That practice was declared illegal by the Supreme Court of Canada in 1986 in a judgment concerning a Prince Edward Island family in which a 60-year-old mother wanted her mentally handicapped daughter sterilized to prevent a grandchild being accidentally conceived that would she feared could become her responsibility. The 1986 Supreme Court of Canada decision in E. (Mrs) v. Eve (1986)[248] made it illegal for parents or guardians to consent to sterilizations of mentally disabled patients. In the judgment, handed down by Supreme Court Justice, The Honourable Mr. Justice Gérard Vincent La Forest, the Supreme Court of Canada declared that "Sterilization should never be authorized for non-therapeutic purposes under the *parens patriae* jurisdiction."[249]

The judgment also knocked holes in the rationale of the 1928 *Sexual Sterilization Act* in Alberta—that society would benefit by preventing the 'unfit' from becoming a burden on society.

The importance of maintaining the physical integrity of a human being ranks high in our scale of values, particularly as it affects the privilege of giving life. I cannot agree that a court can deprive a woman of that privilege for purely social or other non-therapeutic purposes without her consent. The fact that others may suffer inconvenience or hardship from failure to do so cannot be taken into account. The Crown's *parens patriae* jurisdiction exists for the benefit of those who cannot help themselves, not to relieve those who may have the burden of caring for them.[250]

XXX: COMPARISONS (ALBERTA, U.S., U.K., AND GERMANY)

Eugenics in Alberta, the United States and United Kingdom

Before World War I, eugenicists, especially English speaking ones, regularly crossed the Atlantic to share ideas. Back then it was hard to differentiate between the eugenics movement in Britain or the United States.

The mutual admiration between the cross-Atlantic cousins was comical in its intensity: Americans eugenicists, beset with rapid immigration and racial divisions, looked longingly at the order of the Old World, including its class system. Many British eugenicists envied the New World because it seemed so perfectly free from the encumbrances of landed gentry, political marriages, and inherited power.[251] Both the American and British Eugenics movements included Social Darwinists, conservatives, radicals and moderate social reformers.

In the English-speaking world, it was often harder to find an intellectual who didn't admire Galton and Malthus than one who did. Canadians, though proudly part of the British Empire, were eager to hear about the latest scientific advances from both sides of the Atlantic. Canadians tended to favour positive eugenics measure, including family allowances, education programs, but they liked the energetic lobbying style Americans excelled at. As a result Canadians adopted both the American social hygiene movement's lobbying style and the British vision of ensuring maximum fitness of all its citizens through education, health care, and social reforms.

American Style: Take an Idea and Make it Your Own

Canada is a constitutional monarchy, which remains part of the 21st-century incarnation of the British Empire (the Commonwealth of Nations). The United States of America is revolutionary republic, but both countries are bold experiments in civil society and both have had a long love affair with expanding their frontiers in the name of progress.

In the late 19th and early 20th centuries, the middle classes in both countries were growing uneasy at the cost of progress. Millions of immigrants came from countries that many native-born Americans and Canadians considered inferior. In Canada this unease was especially acute in the West, where immigrants from Eastern Europe were encouraged to settle on homesteads. Not surprisingly the only Canadian sexual sterilization acts were passed in Canada's most Western provinces: Alberta and British Columbia. But neither province went as far as some U.S. states did.

Nobody did eugenics better than the Americans. Sterilization laws were passed in 31 U.S. states covering a far wider range of defectives than in Canada. With characteristic energy, the American eugenicists spoke in churches, halls, and to men's and ladies' groups. They wrote books and pamphlets, sponsored Better Baby and Fitter Family Contests, and even made movies like *The Black Stork* (1917), which extolled both the virtue of eugenics and euthanasia of disabled babies.

At the urging of eugenicists, Americans states banned interracial marriage and the marriage of those unable to pass health exams and passed laws to sterilize prison inmates and the feeble-minded. They successfully lobbied for immigration restriction and IQ testing of all immigrants.

Americans combined old style Galtonian pedigree analysis with IQ testing to create comprehensive tool for judging fitness. Alfred Binet[252] and Théodore Simon created the Simon-Binet scale to help French children improve test performance. It was never intended to be a static score indicating intellectual ability.[253] As Binet wrote *Les Idees moderne sur les enfants*.

> Some recent philosophers seem to have given their moral approval to these deplorable verdicts that affirm that the intelligence of an individual is a fixed quantity, a quantity that cannot be augmented. "We must protest and react against this brutal pessimism; we will try to demonstrate that it is founded on nothing." Alfred Binet: *Les idées modernes sur les enfants*, 1909.[254]

Binet and Simon condemned attempts by American eugenicists, including Lewis Terman and H.H. Goddard to use intelligence tests as a measure of Galtonian fitness.

> Our purpose is to be able to measure the intellectual capacity of a child who is brought to us in order to know whether he is normal or retarded. We do not attempt to establish or prepare a prognosis and we leave unanswered the question of whether this retardation is curable, or even improvable. We shall limit ourselves to ascertaining the truth in regard to his

present mental state." Alfred Binet and Theodore Simon: 'New Methods for the Diagnosis of the Intellectual Level of Subnormals' in *The Development of Intelligence in Children*.[255]

Undaunted by the criticism, Lewis Terman and H.H. Goddard refined intelligence testing as a scientific way to weed out criminality, mental illness, low intelligence and moral decay from society. Goddard's pedigree analysis of the Kallikak family was used by American eugenicists to further their cause for eugenics legislation. As Goddard wrote in *Human Efficiency and Levels of Intelligence* in 1920.

> "...our thesis is that the chief determiner of human conduct is a unitary mental process which we call intelligence: that this process is conditioned by a nervous mechanism which is inborn: that the degree of efficiency to be attained by that nervous mechanism and the consequent grade of intelligence or mental level for each individual is determined by the kind of chromosomes that come together with the union of the germ cells. That it is but little affected by any later influences except such serious accidents as may destroy part of the mechanism." (Goddard, 1920, p. 1).
>
> —Goddard, H.H.(1920). *Human efficiency and levels of intelligence.* Princeton, NJ: Princeton University Press.[256]

Lewis Terman was blunter.

> But why do the feeble-minded tend so strongly to become delinquent? The answer may be stated in simple terms. Morality depends upon two things: (a) the ability to foresee and to weigh the possible consequences for self and others of different kinds of behaviour and, (b) upon the willingness and capacity to exercise self-restraint. That there are many intelligent criminals is due to the fact that (a) may exist without (b) On the other hand, (b) presupposes (a) In other words, not all criminals are feeble-minded, but all feeble-minded are at least potential criminals. That every feeble-minded woman is a potential prostitute would hardly be disputed by any one. Moral judgment, like business judgment, social judgment, or any other kind of higher thought process, is a function of intelligence. Morality cannot flower and fruit if intelligence remains infantile. Lewis M. Terman, "The Uses of Intelligence Tests" (from *The Measurement of Intelligence*, 1916).[257]

With a population of just over a million by 1969,[258] Alberta's sterilization rate was higher than that of many states in the U.S. 31 of 50 U.S. states that passed

Sexual Sterilization Acts sterilized 60-65,000[259] men, women and children. By 1944, 40,000 Americans had been sterilized under eugenics laws. 22,000 were sterilized by 1963, according to a study released in 2000, and funded by the United States Holocaust Memorial Museum and the Merck Co. Foundation.[260]

The first American sexual sterilization bill to become law was passed in Indiana in 1907. A similar Michigan Bill was voted down in the Michigan Legislature in 1897, while the Governor of Pennsylvania refused to sign a sexual sterilization bill passed in his state legislature in 1905.[261] In 1917, sixteen American states already had sexual sterilization laws aimed not just at the feeble-minded and the insane, but at prison inmates, and people with chronic illnesses such as epilepsy.

Many American eugenicists, including Margaret Sanger, founder of Planned Parenthood, thought the numbers of black Americans should be restricted. Sanger's birth control clinics were strategically placed in black neighbourhoods.[262] Not surprisingly, a disproportionate number of blacks were sterilized in the United States.[263]

In 1978, the National Centre of Health Statistics found that sterilizations in the U.S. rose 25 percent among married couples between 1973 and 1976. Sixty percent of those sterilizations were federally funded sterilizations. Such funding was often targeted at the poor. That same year, the Public Citizens' Health Group declared that 20.5 percent of hysterectomies were done for sterilization and that 44.4 percent of hysterectomies done for sterilization purposes were on black women.[264]

Blacks were not primary targets of eugenicists in Alberta, mostly because only the small number of blacks who lived in the province. But Aboriginals and Eastern Europeans were also more likely to be sterilized in both Alberta and the United States.

The American Sexual Hygiene Movement also lobbied for marriage laws forbidding racial intermarriage and marriage of the unfit, as well as for restricted immigration. By 1914, eugenicists had convinced thirty state legislatures to pass laws that disallowed the mentally handicapped, people with sexually transmitted (venereal) diseases and the feeble-minded to marry. Eugenicists also convinced legislators to stop the epidemic of defectives with stricter immigration laws and IQ testing of immigrants, schoolchildren and soldiers.

In 1927, the *Buck v. Bell* decision by United States Supreme Court Justice Oliver Wendell Holmes Jr. upheld the constitutionality of compulsory sterilization of mental defectives. Holmes' judgment contained the infamous words: "the principle that sustains compulsory vaccination of schoolchildren is broad enough to cover the cutting of the fallopian tubes. Three generations of imbeciles are enough."[265]

Holmes believed that allowing degenerate breeding would condemn the United States to poverty, criminality, and imbecility.

"It is better for all the world, instead of waiting to execute degenerate offspring for crime, or to let them starve for their imbecility society, can prevent those who are manifestly unfit from continuing their kind," U.S. Supreme Court Justice Oliver Wendell Holmes wrote.[266] It wasn't a shocking statement in the 1920s.

Buck v. Bell was a test case brought to the U.S. Supreme Court in 1924 by the Commonwealth of Virginia in order to test the constitutionality of the state's sterilization law. It concerned the case of a girl whose mother and grandmother were both labelled imbeciles. The judges ruled on the constitutionality of sterilizing the girl. In March 1980, new light was shed on the Commonwealth of Virginia's eugenic past. Thousands of patients had been sterilized in Virginia's state mental homes between 1924 and 1972. Many of the sterilized were not mentally retarded. Many were social misfits, prostitutes, incompetent persons, and others defined as incorrigible. In Virginia, parents who conceived a child outside of marriage were fined 10 percent of their salaries from the fourth month of pregnancy to nine months after the marriage.[267]

Eugenics died a hard death in the United States. In 1976, Dr Constance Uri, alleged that federal Indian hospitals in the United States forced aboriginal women to be sterilized and that as many as 50% of these women did not know they had been sterilized. Even worse, the patients were used as guinea pigs. She added that women were pressured to use birth control and to abort foetuses. "They tell Indian mothers to have an abortion because they can't afford more children. But all Indians are poor. No traditional Indian women would murder her unborn child," Uri told a Canadian audience of 60 people when she visited the University of Lethbridge.[268]

At the request of Senator James Abourzek, the General Accounting Office investigated the charges. The GAO reported that 3406 Native American women between the ages of fifteen and forty-four were sterilized between 1973 and 1976. While not confirming that some sterilizations were forced, the GAO report verified that many tribal women believed they would lose their government benefits, services, or have their children taken away from them by the government if they did not consent to sterilizations.[269] In 1978, the city of New York was sued for $12 million by a 22-year-old named Rosalind Johnson, who had been given an abortion and sterilized two years earlier, after she was picked up for vagrancy.[270]

The idea of sterilizing the poor and minority groups remained acceptable enough to appear in the U.S. media in 1987. Journalist Andy Rooney's eugenics views were clear in his June 1987 column "Moratorium on Multiplication". After attacking population growth in the Third World, he moved closer to home.

> It's a pain for those who feel strongly about the tragedy of the black condition in America to see so many blacks assuring themselves and their children a dismal future. The least responsible black people are having the most babies. Today 60 percent of all black babies are being born to unmarried women. Sixty percent! The men the black mothers slept with are gone with the wind…A large percentage of these mothers are on welfare because they can't take care of themselves, let alone an infant. There is no reason to believe if there is anything at all to eugenics that many of their children will be able to take care of themselves.[271]

Germany

> Young Children Within Range of Sterilization Plan
>
> BERLIN, Jan. 4.(A.P.)—Ten year-old children and women as old as 50, men even older than that are within the age range of Germany's sweeping new sterilization program. It was revealed today by Dr Arthur Guest, eugenics expert in the ministry of the interior. Dr Guest said that when the present 'waiting list' of incurables was disposed of, the work of the eugenics courts, set up under the national sterilization law which became effective January 1, would be confined mostly to children coming out of school.
>
> Only 'urgent' cases will be dealt with in the near future, he said, and added the interesting revelation that the 280,000 incurable inmates of Germany's public institutions would not be sterilized, only those who are at large.[272]

Eugenics was popular in Northern European countries, including Sweden and France. But nowhere were those ideas more forcefully employed than in Germany between 1933 and 1945.

Germans could be forgiven for not predicting the Holocaust when they read the 1933 *Law for the Prevention of Genetically Diseased Progeny*. Like Alberta's original 1928 *Sexual Sterilization Act*, Hitler's law had a provision for patient consent. It was also couched in language that made it appear to be concerned with the patient's best interest. But coupled with his 1939 edict on euthanasia and the Nuremberg Laws on citizenship and race, the 1933 law allowing the disabled to be sterilized helped concoct a toxic potion that made the German state the perpetrator of a holocaust inconceivable in a country that prided itself on its culture and civility.[273]

It All Seemed so Innocent

The first German sterilization court order was handed down in Goerlitz 05 January 1934. A 54-year-old labourer named George Peugner was ordered to be sterilized for contributing to the delinquency of a minor.[274] Not to be outdone, Berlin's Eugenics Court, presided over by Judge Hans Joachim Mate, issued three sterilization degrees in its first session 06 March 1934. The public was not allowed in the court due to a secrecy clause in the law.[275]

With the rest of the world, Albertans watched Germany put its sterilization and euthanasia laws into place. Even as the bombs began falling and the Nazi eugenics moved Jews, Gypsies, the disabled and anyone else the Hitler regime thought counter-productive to the Aryan dream, into concentration camps, 'racial purity' remained a respectable term in Alberta.[276] In addition to the six million Jews who died as a consequence of Hitler's eugenics legislation, another 5.5 million Gypsies, Poles, homosexuals, Jehovah's Witnesses and other religious dissenters, along with political criminals, died under these laws. Germany sterilized about 400,000 people and euthanized 70,000 individuals as feebleminded and unfit between 1933 and 1945.

As Canadians soldiers freed the few survivors from concentration camps that escaped from under the German vision of creating a 'master race of superior intellect, strength and beauty', Albertans were being wheeled into operating rooms without consent because they had been labelled 'defective' by a four-member board that offered them no chance of appeal.

Few Albertans, horrified by Germany's Nazi regime, drew any parallels between Alberta's *Sexual Sterilization Act* and the Nazi eugenic policies. But the two programs had a lot in common.

Common Roots

The 1928 version of Alberta's *Sexual Sterilization Act* had similar wording to Germany's 1933 sexual sterilization law: *Law for the Prevention of Genetically Diseased Progeny.*

That's no accident! Both the Germans and Canadian eugenicists gazed admiringly at U.S. legislation. Hitler based his law on model laws developed by the eugenicists in the United States, including the *Model Eugenical Sterilization Law* written in 1922 by Harry Hamilton Laughlin, an Assistant Director of the Eugenics Record Office at the Carnegie Institution and Eugenics Associate of the Psychopathic Laboratory of the Municipal Court of Chicago.

Laughlin was a great favourite of Hitler, who ensured he received an honorary degree, signed by Hitler himself, from the University of Heidelberg in Heidelberg, Germany for contributing to 'racial hygiene' in 1936.[277]

Adolf Hitler called American eugenicist Madison Grant's, *The Passing of the Great Race*, his 'bible'. Grant's other books included *The Conquest of the Continent, or The Expansion of Races in America*, London, New York, C. Scribner's Sons, published in 1933, *The Alien in Our Midst, or Selling our Birthright for a Mess of Pottage, these were the written views of a number of Americans (present and former) on immigration and its results*, published in New York, N. Y. by the Galton Publishing Co Inc. (1930). Finally, *The Founders of the Republic on Immigration, Naturalization and Aliens*, New York, C. Scribner's Sons, 1928.[278]

The Nazi racial hygiene program borrowed from American studies including Goddard's Kallikak *Pedigree Analysis*, and its U.S. eugenics policies, including compulsory sterilization of the unfit, anti-miscegenation (laws forbidding marriage between races) and immigration restrictions.

Many academics have likened the three Nuremberg Laws on Citizenship and Race: *The Reich Citizenship Law* of September 15, 1935 *First Supplementary Decree* of November 14, 1935; *Law for the Protection of German Blood and German Honour* September 15, 1935; and the *Law for the Protection of Hereditary Health: The Attempt to Improve the German Aryan Breed*, July 14, 1933 to the Jim Crow laws in the United Sates.

But Hitler took eugenics further than anyone thought was possible to go in a Western European country with strong Christian roots. Killing disabled patients was not acceptable in Germany and Hitler knew that. (Some sources suggest even Hitler didn't like the idea at first.) No German

Parliament would pass such a law. But in October 1939, Germany was at war and the Reichstag shut down. Hitler signed this one-page edict on his personal stationery and backdated it to the beginning of the war: 1 September 1939. Translated into English, it reads as follows.

ADOLF HITLER

Berlin, 1 September 1939

Reichsleiter Bouhler and Dr Brandt are instructed to broaden the powers of physicians designated by name, who will decide whether those who have—as far as can be humanly determined—incurable illnesses can, after the most careful evaluation, be granted a mercy death (signed Adolf Hitler).

Killing the disabled was now law in Germany.

Making Eugenics Politically Palatable

Germany also used 'positive' techniques employed in the United States, U.K., and Canada. The included education campaigns, pro-eugenics films, and promoting early marriage of the 'fit' to encourage some segments of society to have large families. In 1936, Hitler decreed that all German Army recruits would take four lectures on eugenics and race within one year of joining the German military.[279] By this time the brainwashing of Germans was well underway.

Three years earlier, in October 1933, readers of the *Lethbridge Daily Herald* had already glimpsed the militaristic goals behind Nazi eugenic Germany in the papers by a critic of Professor Ewald Banse's book *Wehrwissenschaft* (military science).

MILITARY EUGENICS

German children must also be taught, our masterpiece continues that warlike persons must be given more favourable conditions than others in which to live and breed, and it will be the duty of these warrior supermen to practice 'military eugenics' and thus graft their soldierly qualities into less warlike sections of the population.

"The dying warrior dies more easily," says Prof Banse, "when he knows his blood is flowing for the national God. The church must be patriotic and militaristic, for only thus can it give men the strength they need to risk their lives for their country…"

The book is *Wehrwissenschsft* (*Military Science*). It is written by Prof Braid Banse, who has just been appointed to the chair of military science in the Brunswick Technical High School. Incidentally, the German press has been instructed not to record such appointments; they look bad to a watching world. In the same way it is high treason for any German to describe the government's military preparations.

"Lamentations about the Treaty of Versailles," he says, "lead nowhere, and only make us ridiculous, if we do not take our fate in our own hands and concentrate before anything else on our psychological readiness for and knowledge of war. For nobody should be in doubt that only war can change our coming fortune."

Only eugenics, according to the Nazi professor, can create a race of super warriors able to survive the "bloody battle, and in particular, a war of materials; it is gas and plague, it is tank and aircraft horror, it is hunger and poverty, it is baseness and falsehood, it is deprivation and sacrifice. Only a nation can endure it whose every member has known for years, and is in his heart of hearts convinced that his life belongs to the state, and only to the state, which is the guardian of nationhood and mother tongue and all culture."[280]

The August 1935 International Eugenics Congress was held in Berlin and while at least one speaker, Dr Jean Dalsacre of France, said, "there was absolutely no evidence sterilization tended to cure sex and other aberrations," many speakers praised the German system.[281]

Professor Clarence Gordon Campbell of New York was convinced that Germany had the right system of raising babies. He told the congress that "selective breeding and encouragement of families were the conditions essential to survival of the fittest races." Campbell praised the Third Reich's comprehensive racial policy of population development and improvement. According to him, other 'races' would have to follow the German example to keep up their racial quality and accomplishments.[282]

CHAPTER XXXI: IS EUGENICS DEAD?

N o. The eugenics movement is not dead: not in Alberta, not in the rest of Canada, and certainly not internationally.

Despite the 1986 *E (Mrs) v. Eve* ruling by the Supreme Court of Canada, the debate over the sterilization of the mentally disabled, as well as other practices favoured by Galton and his followers, continues in Canada and internationally.

Eugenics and Canadian Society

If anything, the eugenics ideology may have expanded into everyday life, along with medical services such as prenatal genetic counselling with the intent of eliminating defective foetuses. It doesn't stop there.

Public discussion about limiting access to treatment for the physically disabled and chronically ill have expanded to include public support for physician-assisted suicide. Social Darwinist arguments that society is being pulled into debt and disarray by the 'unfit' can easily seep into the thinking of well-meaning politicians, economists and taxpayers, who fear the financial burden of caring for increasing numbers of the poor, sick, and aged, as their great-great-grandparents feared being drowned in a deluge of the 'unfit'.

The myth persists that the poor, sick and the elderly are about to burden the productive members of society beyond its ability to cope. At the Liberal Party of Canada – sponsored Canada At 150 Conference, held March 2010, one gloomy speaker after another fretted about how an aging society and a tide of dementia were about to drown Canadian taxpayers in debt. Even the level-headed David Dodge, former head of the Bank of Canada, seemed to have bought the gloomy predictions that we just won't be able to afford all the hospital beds and that we have three options: create a health-care tax to raise money to pay for it all, reduce services provided for free and let the private insurers into Canada, or reduce service and increase wait times for more ordinary Canadians while letting the rich buy what they need.[283] It appeared nobody thought to tell the speakers that the reason people live longer is that they are healthier and will be able to work longer. Nor did they seem to understand that 92% of seniors over 65 have no signs of dementia. Almost two-thirds of Canada's very elderly seniors (over 85) are free of dementia. Many elderly people live on their own, work part-time, pay taxes and volunteer. But those facts are lost in the message that, if we let them live too long, the elderly will send us to the poorhouse.[284] (Work is now underway to discover which genes predispose individuals to Alzheimer's disease. That may well lead to prenatal genetic testing to weed out carriers of genes, deemed to be the cause of it and other dementias.)

Families with disabled children are also seen as a burden. Rachel Barlagne's family immigrated from France to Montreal with enough money to start their own business, but in February 2010, they announced they would have to fight a Citizenship and Immigration Canada ruling ordering them to abandon their business and take Rachel back to France because her cerebral palsy would cost taxpayers an extra $5,259 per year.[285]

Brave New World

As the Leilani Muir trial got underway in 1996, Alberta scientists began mapping the genes of Albertans as part of the Canadian Genome Analysis and Technology Program in an effort to understand genetic disease.[286] Gregor Wolbring, then a spokesman for the Council of Canadians with Disabilities, worried that the mapping project would lead to more genetic tests and increase pressure on prospective parents to abort any less than perfect foetuses. The result could well increase societal attitudes that disabled people should not be part of society and, as politicians realized that taxes could be cut if services by cutting medical care for the disabled, people with disabilities would face increased discrimination.

In 1999, Tim Caulfield,[287] research director of the University of Alberta's Health Law Institute, sent out another warning. He pointed to a survey released earlier that year where 134 genetic counsellors and doctors were asked what medical options they would suggest if a foetus would develop a medical or genetic disease. Thirty to fifty-three percent of the study subjects said they would emphasize the negatives of the situation and counsel parents to abort a child that would be profoundly retarded or die young. Six to ten percent said they would counsel an abortion if they knew a child would have cystic fibrosis, sickle cell anaemia or Huntington's disease. Seven percent would counsel an abortion if the child would be born predisposed to Alzheimer's disease. Three percent would counsel abortion if a child was predisposed to alcoholism. Two percent would counsel that the parent abort a child pre-disposed to obesity. One percent favoured abortion of a child was to be born with cleft palate or was the 'wrong' sex.

"I think some of this is evidence of the potential for a subtle movement towards encouraging behaviour that could lead to a form of eugenics," said Caulfield.[288] He suggested that governments may want parents to abort foetuses who will add costs to provincial health care system. "It comes down to the idea that an individual with a disease will be a burden on the health care system. In the case of foetal diagnosis for Down's syndrome, about 89 percent of parents in Canada and 90 percent in the U.S. opt to terminate the pregnancy," said Tanis Doe, a blind wheelchair-using professor of social work at the University of Victoria. She told the University of Alberta in 1995, "Women are expected to, pressured to abort pregnancies when foetal disability is diagnosed."[289]

In the past five to fifteen years, the trend has not stopped. While genetic testing, genetic engineering, designer babies, amniocentesis and chorionic villus sampling detect genetic defects in the foetus, the physically disabled are more likely than able-bodied Canadians to be victims of violence, and more than 50% of Canadians admit that they discriminate against the mentally ill. Only 50% of Canadians would tell friends if a family member had a mental illness. But if that same family member had cancer, 72% would tell others. "In some ways, mental illness is the final frontier of socially-acceptable discrimination," said Dr. Brian Day, CMA President as the Review was announced. More than half of the respondents would not marry anyone with a mental illness.[290] The results also showed that only one in five Canadians would socialize with someone who has a drug or alcohol addiction.[291]

Warning Signs?

Robert Latimer, a Saskatchewan farmer who euthanized his daughter by rigging up a makeshift gas chamber in a pick-up 24 October 1993, received considerable public support for this 'mercy killing'. One group that does not consider Latimer a hero is the Council of Canadians with Disabilities. As they put it, "Mr. Latimer's view was that a parent has the right to kill a child with a disability if that parent decides the child's quality of life no longer warrants its continuation. CCD explained to the court and to the public how that view threatens the lives of people with disabilities and is deeply offensive to fundamental constitutional values."[292]

A February 2010 Angus Reid poll of 1000 Canadians found 67% of the respondents supported euthanasia.[293] Not surprisingly, eugenic arguments for ensuring humanity is not burdened by either the poor or the disabled are becoming less and less thinly veiled, while still couched in 'compassionate' language for ensuring humanity is not burdened with either the poor or the disabled.

Eugenics and Canadian Law

March 16, 2010 Bill C-384, a Private Member's Bill, was introduced into the Canadian House of Commons by Bloc Québécois MP Francine Lalonde. If passed and granted Royal Assent, Bill C-384 would legalize euthanasia and assisted suicide in Canada. Lalonde's bill would not restrict doctors to helping the terminally ill die a gentle death. It would make non-terminally ill patients suffering from either physical or mental illnesses, candidates for euthanasia. The Bill specifically mentioned mental patients, including people suffering from depression, as people that should be allowed to consider being 'put to sleep' permanently.

While Private Members' Bills that run contrary to government policy have little chance of becoming law, and this one proved to be no exception, the fact that Bill C-384 was discussed in the House of Commons in 2010 may indicate that, as memories of the Nazi eugenics program fade, the most abhorrent tools in the eugenicists' toolbox are becoming respectable.

The same month Lalonde's Bill was discussed by Canadian Parliamentarians, a *Canadian Medical Association Journal* editorial, "Time to Move on From the Euthanasia Debate," called for a discussion of the issue. The authors wrote: "We certainly live in a time when we have more potential control over our dying. But when it's needed, the discussion about that control—by whom and how much—seems to lead to enmeshed families at the bedside or to entrenched positions in public discourse."[294]

The authors doubted the intent of the doctors responding to a survey about euthanasia. Indeed, in Quebec last year, 81% of medical specialists surveyed said they had seen 'euthanasia' practised, and 48% said that palliative sedation 'can be likened to a form of euthanasia'. The editors of the *CMAJ* called for banishment of the value-laden word 'euthanasia' altogether.

As others have suggested, "Physicians can stop using the word euthanasia to describe the actions we might take to help dying patients and stop using such value laden terms as starve and kill to explain those medical actions".[295]

Not everyone thinks Canadian doctors should lead the debate. In light of the findings early in 2009 that 'locked in' patients were being misdiagnosed as vegetative, the national director of the Council of Canadians with Disabilities reacted strongly to a statement by the Manitoba College of Physicians and Surgeons that endorsed giving Manitoba doctors the authority to decide fate of disabled patients. Laurie Beachell, National Coordinator of the Council of Canadians with Disabilities, raised his concerns in a written statement dated November 30, 2009.

"Many of us in the disability community have heard the comment: I would rather be dead than live like you. We know that this cultural attitude comes into play during decision making at end of life. Thus, many of us with disabilities want people who know and care about us, first and foremost for our humanity, involved in the decision making that will occur at our end of life stage."[296]

Several jurisdictions, including the Netherlands, Switzerland and U.S. States of Washington and Oregon, already have euthanasia legislation. In 2009, the American euthanasia lobby group "Compassion and Choices", lost their case before the Montana Supreme Court. Their insistence that that Montana's State Constitution required that the state have 'Aid-in-Dying' legislation was shot down by the judges in a split decision. Had "Compassion and Choices" won their case, physician assisted suicide would have become law the State of Montana.

Few Canadians would link abortion rights to eugenics, but it appears that abortions are often performed for eugenic purposes. As delegates to the 1963 Canadian Medical Association Convention[297] discussed legalized abortion, the rationale touched on eugenics arguments. Three reasons were given as criteria for approving an abortion: health of the mother, sexual assault of the mother, and genetic defect of the foetus. No doubt, the doctors did not consider their arguments related to eugenics principles. But many activists for the disabled have expressed fears that pushing parents to abort abnormal foetuses may represent a rival of eugenics.[298] In Canada, the United States and Britain, most foetuses with Down's syndrome or other congenital abnormalities are now aborted at the recommendation of genetic counsellors.[299]

People who are judged incompetent to manage their own affairs are vulnerable to having their rights violated by the government. Even laws, like Alberta's *Dependent Adults Act*, that are meant to protect the mentally handicapped, mentally ill, and people with dementia, can be used to abuse vulnerable people. In 2008, an advocacy group, Elder Advocates of Alberta, took up the case of an elderly widow who had been stripped of her possessions and her right to make personal decisions by an unscrupulous lawyer, a physician, and a woman claiming to be her niece.[300]

Sometimes the disabled have to fight just to ensure that even their right to vote won't be obstructed. James Hughes, a Canadian with mobility issues, had to slide down a flight of stairs on his butt to exercise his right to vote in the March 2008 federal election. Things weren't any better when he tried to vote in October 2009. So he took his beef against Elections Canada to the Canadian Human Rights Commission. The Commission took Hughes' side in the case, noting that Elections Canada must "cease from situating polling stations in locations that do not provide barrier-free access". In their affidavit asking for interested party status at the hearing, the Council of Canadians with Disabilities told the Canadian Human Rights Commission that denying a disabled person access to vote is denying him or her most basic right to participate in democracy.

> Voting is an essential act by which all Canadians, including Canadians with disabilities, exercise their rights and obligations as citizens of this country. Given the fundamental importance of voting, barriers that people with disabilities encounter when they attempt to exercise their right to vote seriously undermine their status as equal citizens in Canadian society.[301]

Canadian activists like Ezra Levant have garnered considerable public support in their crusades to water down the powers of Canada's federal and provincial Human Rights Commissions to limit free speech. They raise valid concerns about the mandate of these Commissions. Unfortunately, they do little to support the role Human Rights Commissions play in ensuring vulnerable groups protect their civil rights. Nor do they offer practical alternatives. The disabled, the mentally ill, the homeless, the working poor in Canada often cannot pay legal fees necessary to protect their civil rights in Canadian courts.[302]

March 30, 2010, NDP Rachel Notley again took the Government of Alberta to task over its plans to follow the recommendations of a November

2009 review of the province's Legal Aid System. The review recommended that the government cover a $20 million shortfall in revenues from a trust account used to fund Legal Aid, by cutting eligibility for legal aid by at least 30%. "No Albertan is any less deserving of justice than another, and limiting access by 30% means 6,100 Albertans who need legal aid won't get it. Limiting eligibility sends a message that some Albertans aren't worthy of justice," Notley said. "A system that denies justice to marginalized people is unjust," said Notley.[303] And Legal Aid in Alberta usually only helps for clients facing criminal charges. Those Albertans who need to defend or launch "civil cases" but who do not have funds to pay legal and court costs are usually out of luck.

XXXII: SIGNS OF CHANGE

It's not all bad news: in March 2010, the Honourable Lawrence Cannon, Minister of Foreign Affairs, and the Honourable Diane Finley, Minister of Human Resources and Skills Development, confirmed that the Government of Canada ratified the Convention on the Rights of Persons with Disabilities at United Nations headquarters with full support of the provinces and territories.[304] Almost two years earlier, in 2008, the Harper-led government announced a $75 million campaign to de-stigmatize the mentally ill.

Clearly, the campaign was needed. As the funding for the federal campaign was announced, the Canadian Mental Health Association released their 2008 National Report Card, showing that 46% of Canadians think that mental illness is used as an excuse for bad behaviour. Twenty-seven percent of Canadians admitted they were afraid to be near the mentally ill. 61% Canadians would not have a family doctor with a mental illness. 58% wouldn't hire a lawyer with a mental illness.

More positive news: there are signs that Albertans are waking up from their political slumber. In 2009, as the world fell into a recession, oil prices dropped. The province quickly backed away from raising oil royalties and moved in another direction—cutting services to people who it viewed as non-contributors to the province. The move was criticized roundly by political parties and citizens' groups on both the right and left.

It looked like things were getting even worse when, in December 2009, the Province of Alberta cut nearly $12 million from its "Persons with Developmental Disabilities Program." While it represented only two percent of the Department of Seniors and Community Support's $604 million budget, the Alberta Association for Community Living insisted the cuts would hurt the mentally handicapped.

Bridget Pastoor, Alberta Liberal critic for Seniors and Community Supports, reacted angrily to the decision to cut $6 million from boards serving persons with developmental disabilities (PDD). She noted that the decision followed on the heels of a $10 million cut earlier in 2009. A few weeks earlier, Pastoor accused the minister, Mary Anne Jablonski, of using Question Period to gloss over hardship to vulnerable Albertans. Jablonski called the cuts an 'in-year adjustment'. In typical fashion, the cuts were made after the legislature took its Christmas break, avoiding the necessity of answering questions from opposition members.

Alberta Liberal finance critic Hugh MacDonald claimed his Party's alternative plan would save the provincial treasury nearly $600 million per year.

"There is absolutely no need to slash public health care, public education or crucially important programs like those serving people with developmental disabilities, not when there is so much wasteful spending," MacDonald said in a news release from the Alberta Liberals. "We'd far rather save over $7 million by combining the Ministries of Housing and Urban Affairs with Municipal Affairs, for example. Getting rid of the redundant Public Affairs Bureau would save nearly $15 million. Reducing travel and communications expenses would save $60 million, and the list goes on. There are savings to be had, but they shouldn't be made on the backs of people who have a legitimate need for help", said MacDonald in a party news release.

The Backlash and a Change of Policy

The Wildrose Alliance, Alberta Liberals and New Democrats all launched campaigns to fight the changes. As the opposition cashed in on voter anger, it proved a tough ride for the government MLAs. As hundreds of emails and letters poured in, the Speaker of the Alberta Legislature, Ken Kowalski, ordered the Alberta Liberals to take down a website they put up as part as their "Leipert Must Go Campaign" because, he claimed, it focused on an individual member of the legislature. Ken Liepert, Alberta's Health Minister, and Stephen Duckett, CEO of Alberta Health Services, were targets of much of the voter anger.

But the government appeared to get the message. In November 2009, Premier Ed Stelmach promised not to make the disabled targets of cuts. And Stelmach was true to his word. The March 2010 Provincial budget tabled by Finance Minister Ted Morton allotted $733 million towards Alberta Income Supports to the Severely Handicapped, an increase of $18 million, or 2.6 percent and he kept the 2009 Funding for Persons with Developmental Disabilities ($597 million) and Alberta Aids to Daily Living ($113 million) stable. The budget added $50 million to develop 500 new affordable supportive housing spaces. Health and Wellness received a $15 billion increase in spending. While the government's tuition allocations for academic upgrading were cut, the budget allotted $74 million for work training.[305]

XXXIII: LESSONS

Ralph Klein wasn't the only one who claimed not to understand that it wasn't just a 'bad law' that cost the Alberta treasury millions of dollars in damages to victims of the Alberta Eugenics Board and Alberta's mental health system. But the truth should have been obvious to everyone: The board was so devoid of oversight that it consistently broke even the meagre safeguards in the *Sexual Sterilization Act*.

Politicians knew there were problems with the Eugenics Board back when Klein was just a kid growing up in Calgary. But the Eugenics Board was nowhere near the top of the province's priorities: not when a burdening population, oil industry concerns, and fights with Ottawa were on the agenda.

Bad things happen when good people are too busy to ask questions. In Alberta's case it wasn't just the politicians who didn't ask questions ; most Albertans regarded criticism of the Eugenics Board as a distraction from the really important things, like turning Alberta into the economic and political powerhouse it now is in Canada's Confederation. Alberta's populist premiers were people with a sense of mission. They made a province of struggling farmers and shopkeepers believe they were the elect and that Alberta would soon be the Promised Land. And when Alberta struck it rich with oil in the 1948 Leduc Oil Strike, Albertans remembered the words of Aberhart and judged them to be true. Successive generation of Alberta politicians have used that identification of Albertans as a people set apart to sell their agenda to the public. And even Alberta's largely secular urban population still accepts the myth.

Even when policies like the *Accurate News and Information Act* and the *Sexual Sterilization Act* showed that the government intended to deprive Albertans of their civil rights, the politicians insisted that Ottawa was the villain for trampling on provincial rights.

Surely, Alberta's next great lesson must be that Alberta is not yet the Promised Land for everybody and that its politicians have used everything from provincial rights, to the promise of oil riches, to religious theology, to the tried and true 'we are being persecuted by the rest of Canada' rhetoric to convince Albertans to abandon the prairie love for non-partisan, practical community building. Instead they have asked Albertans to throw their common sense into the dust storm and blindly follow the fashionable ideologies of each generation like Social Credit, trickle-down free market economics and eugenics. Grinding poverty led voters to accept the promise of $25 a month as fair exchange for a installing a government that wanted to turn their province into a laboratory for an untested blend of religious and economic ideology. The fear of poverty still prompts Albertans to accept bottom of the barrel oil royalties from the multinational companies they think they are dependent on, ignore unsettling questions when their neighbour can't get legal aid or men in shelters receive midnight visits from an angry drunken premier, and believe rhetoric that the deluge of poverty and sickness is about to bankrupt them. It still prompts them to jump on political band-wagons without asking too many questions. Albertans must ask more uncomfortable questions of the ideologues and political theorists who try to mould Alberta to fit any ideology or economic interest.

The rest of Canada, for its part, has a few lessons to learn too. Canada as a whole needs to ensure that the concern for national unity or its evil twin, inter-provincial jealousy, do not prevent us from protesting when Charter rights in Alberta, Quebec or any other province, are denied by provincial legislatures. There are other lessons.

The Vulnerable Are Always at Risk

We all need to be aware how deeply the eugenics mindset has reached into Western Society and that every part of our knowledge base: science, history, social policy and economics now reflects the idea that children should be brighter, more beautiful, and more gifted with every passing generation and that the 'responsible' thing is to ensure the 'defective' are either not born or not allowed to reproduce themselves. History Professor John McLaren of the University of Victoria attributed sexual sterilization laws in Alberta and British Columbia to the transferring of Charles Darwin's Theory of Evolution to human society. Eugenicists believed that the unfit and immoral, feeble minded, criminals, the chronically unemployed, addicts, mentally ill, and sexually promiscuous, produced children like themselves. And that they reproduced more quickly than fit people did.[306]

Of the 2,822 people sterilized at the order of the Alberta Eugenics Board, 64 percent were women. Aboriginals and Métis represented 2.5 percent of the population, but they made up 25 percent of those ordered sterilized during the Strom Administration. Under UFA and earlier Social Credit premierships, Eastern European immigrants, particularly if they were Catholic, were more likely to be sterilized by the eugenics board.

Tim Christian, an assistant law professor at the University of Alberta, with funding from the Alberta Law Foundation and Department of Justice Canada, studied the files of eugenics patients in 1974. He concluded that "persons presented to and approved for sterilization by the board occupied socially vulnerable positions" in Alberta. They tended to be female rather than male, young, inexperienced, unemployed and dependent or employed in low-status jobs, residents of small towns, members of ethnic minorities, single rather than married, and were sometimes defined as "sexually deviant".[307]

Eugenics was good science in the 1920s. So it's not surprising that many progressively minded Albertans wanted their government to adopt policies that seemed humane and progressive. What makes less sense is that they continued to vote for a government that clung to the policy long after it knew there were abuses. Why did the Manning government insist that the *Sexual Sterilization Act* was a good law after scientists cast doubt on both the theories behind the law and the competence of the Eugenics Board to determine whether a disease was heritable?

The Social Credit government failed to adapt to changing ideas regarding the validity of eugenics and failed to oversee the Eugenics Board adequately. It also failed to investigate complaints about the Eugenics Board in the 1950s. Had they done so, Leilani Muir may never have been incarcerated at the Provincial Training School. Certainly she would never have had her fallopian tubes removed.

Instead, Alberta's Eugenics Board, with little supervision and the confidence of the provincial cabinet, simply expanded its jurisdiction beyond the law. The result: irreparable harm to thousands of Canadians residing in Alberta.

Democratic Disengagement

Years of massive majorities by the UFA, Social Credit, and Conservative governments, along with the well-honed fear that the rest of Canada 'has it in' for Alberta, have created a political culture that fosters the idea that the

Opposition is not necessary for democratic government and that, a vote for an opposition party is a wasted vote unless that party has potential to replace the government. Even then, most Albertans do not head to the polls.

Despite the province's populist reputation, political engagement remained low. According to Elections Alberta, 60% of Albertans didn't even show up at the polls during the 2008 general election. Speculating on the reasons, for the low turnout, Elections Alberta concluded that the conventional wisdom that Albertans are not showing up because the winner is a foregone conclusion is not backed up by the results.[308]

The voter turnout and plurality in the last 5 provincial elections was examined. The research suggests that, in Alberta, there is not a strong link between the closeness of the race (plurality) at the electoral division level and voter turnout. It was also found that while there is some consistency in the specific electoral divisions with high or low voter turnout, from election to election, this is not necessarily a function of the closeness of the race. There may be other factors that play a more significant role in determining the level of turnout than plurality.[309]

In the September 2009, Calgary Glenmore by-election, the Wildrose Alliance win was touted as a big endorsement for the Wildrose Alliance Party. But the truth was that most voters didn't show up to vote for the populist alternative or anyone else. Total voter turnout for the Glenmore by-election was only 39.1% and of that 39.1%, the WAC candidate, Paul Hinman, got 37%, while Alberta Liberal Avalon Roberts got 34% of the votes cast. Most voters appeared to boycott the by-election.[310]

Another worrying trend, during the Klein years, Alberta's locally elected hospital boards were replaced by regional boards appointed by the Conservatives. These boards have now been replaced by a super board of highly paid Conservative stalwarts.

Since the Conservatives became the federal government in 2006, Stephen Harper, an Ontario-born Calgarian, has been accused of a similar disdain for political opponents. His December 2008 and December 2009 requests that the Governor General prorogue parliament, were seen as worrying trend to many Canadians. While Canadians supported the Conservatives' 2008 request, which headed off a Constitutional crisis which could have forced the Governor General to choose a Prime Minister and support a coalition government that many Canadians opposed, the 2009 request was viewed with cynicism by many Canadians, as a way of evading opposition requested to hand over documents relating to the treatment of Afghan detainees.

Political Diversity

In Alberta, the Progressive Conservative Party now struggles to compete with their populist opponents. Wildrose Alliance and the Alberta Party are quickly gutting the old line Conservatives. Liberals and New Democrats hold their own, but do not rise in the polls. The new populist surge spans what political scientists like to call the left and right.

The province is far more diverse, urban and politically divided, than it was in 1935. Large corporations have replaced the farmer, family and shop-keeper as the constituency of the government. In March 2010, oil industry complaints forced Premier Ed Stelmach to roll back a new oil royalty regime that would have given a larger share in the province's oil revenues. Gone are the days when Alberta premiers stood up against the 'fifty big shots'.

Gone are the days when any Albertan could become premier by quoting scripture and promoting prohibition and "Christian Morality". Danielle Smith, a former journalist, is young, photogenic and the leader of pseudo-populist Wildrose Alliance Party. She knows enough about the "new Alberta" to stay away from 'divisive' moral issues, like abortion. The Wildrose Alliance policy of allowing the membership to choose its policy is reminiscent of the early UFA activists. But the party's emphasis on getting oil industry support for their ideas and its lack of coherent policy or moral issues would have been anathema to William Aberhart and the young Ernest Manning.

It's unlikely today's Alberta would be a place William Aberhart would have settled in. Albertans no longer rail at big shots because Albertans are proud of the fact that many of Canada's big shots live inside the province. While other provinces, such as Quebec, also insist they contribute more than they get out of Confederation, Alberta's role as a 'have province' means that it transfers millions each year to fund programs in other parts of Canada. Alberta is now a secular, materialistic province that both takes pride in and resents bankrolling of Confederation.[311]

Like other Canadians, Albertans are far more aware of their 'rights' than they were under the UFA and Social Credit regimes. In 1960, all Canadians got their own Bill of Rights. Alberta also passed its own Human Rights Act and Bill of Rights during the latter part of the Social Credit era.

In 1982, the Charter of Rights and Freedoms became part of the Canadian Constitution.

Ralph Klein's 1995 attempt to deny Charter rights to the victims of the Eugenics Board lasted less than a day thanks to public outrage. But people have to be paying attention to be outraged by rights abuses to insist those rights are protected.

In 1972, Albertans were paying attention. The MLA who brought in the Act to rescind the *Sexual Sterilization Act*, the Honourable Dave King, put it this way: "Our position was we were doing away with Legislation that was morally repugnant," said King, who served as education minister during the Lougheed years.[312]

On the 35th anniversary of the abolition of the Eugenics Board, King told a conference at the University of Alberta that the province had no right to take away the rights of the province's mentally handicapped and disabled citizens between 1928 and 1972, but he also said Albertans never had had a right to their decades of silent acceptance that allowed those abuses to take place. King told the conference that, if Albertans continue to allow the government to cut budgets at the expense of the vulnerable (the mentally ill, disabled, sick and elderly), then they have learned nothing from our eugenics disaster.

It's not only Albertans who must be wary. Many Canadians are so engaged in the business of living the good life that they don't bother to vote. The same complacency dominates many of the Western democracies.

If Alberta's eugenics disaster can teach us anything, let it be this: we have no right to disregard how the sick, poor and disenfranchised are treated by those in power. We have no right to be silent when the weakest among us become targets of politicians and ideologues. We are our brothers' and our sisters' keepers.

ENDNOTES

1. *Municipal Statistics.* Town of Ponoka. Website: http://www.ponoka.org/municipal/ponoka/ponoka-website.nsf/AllDoc/67B94B8FF3130DDE87256E3D00667D06? OpenDocument

2. *About Us. The Centennial Centre for Mental Health and Brain Injury.* http://www.mentalhealthexcellence.ca/about.php

3. From 1929 to 1972, the board approved 4725 of 4800 cases brought before it, of which 2822 were officially sterilized. Marsh, John H. "Eugenics: Keeping Canada Sane." *Canadian Encyclopedia.* Historica Dominion Institute. 2010 http://www.thecanadianencyclopedia.com/index.cfm? PgNm=ArchivedFeaturesandParams=A2126

4. Neurosyphilis is syphilis which spreads to affect the spinal column and brain.

5. King, David. "Looking Back, Looking Forward." Notes for Remarks to Open Conference. *Eugenics and Sterilization in Alberta: 35 Years Later.* Friday, April 27th, 2007.

6. The Act to rescind the *Sexual Sterilization Act* received Royal Assent June 2, 1972.

7. King, David. "Looking Back, Looking Forward." Notes for Remarks to Open Conference. *Eugenics and Sterilization in Alberta: 35 Years Later.* Friday, April 27th, 2007.

8. Section 33 of the Canadian Charter of Rights and Freedoms allows the federal House of Commons and Provincial Legislatures to override the Charter. The override expires after five years but can be renewed.

9. McMillan, Kate. "Let's Do it for Tommy." *Small Dead Animals.* 2 November 2007. http://www.smalldeadanimals.com/archives/007340.html

10. The Co-operative Commonwealth Federation was reorganized as the New Democratic Party in 1961.

11. Coren, Michael. Don't blame right-wing thugs for eugenics—Socialists made it fashionable," in the *National Post,* 16 June 2008.

12. *The Problems of the Sub-Normal Family,* Tommy Douglas's Master's Thesis from McMaster University, supported eugenics sterilization of the mentally disabled, but he rejected eugenics sterilization after a 1936 trip to Europe. He was convinced the Nazis would euthanize the mentally handicapped. As premier of Saskatchewan, he never allowed the passage of a sexual sterilization act in the province.

13. Galton, Francis F.R.S, *Hereditary Genius: An Inquiry into Its Laws and Consequences.* London and New York, MacMillan and Co. 1892. Page IV, Preface.

14. Bisset, Alex, ed. *Canadian Oxford Paperbook Dictionary.* Oxford University Press, Don Mills, On. 2000.

15. Darwin, Charles. *The Autobiography of Charles Darwin, 1809-1882* (1878.) With original omissions restored. Editor: Nora Barlow. Collins. St. James Palace, London. 1958 edition. Page 120.

16. Terman, Lewis M. (1916). "The Uses of Intelligence Tests." Chapter 1. *The Measurement of Intelligence.* Houghton Mifflin. Boston, 1916.

17. Gregor Mendel (1822-1884) was an Austrian monk who studied recessive genes in plants and animals. He never advocated human eugenics.

18. Hubbard, Ruth and Stuart Newman. Z Magazine, March 2002. McLaren, Angus. *Our Own Master Race: Eugenics in Canada, 1885-1945.* Toronto: McClelland and Stewart, 1990. Reprinted Toronto: Oxford University Press, 1997.

19. King and Hansen 1999. *British Journal of Political Science* 29. P. 77–107.

20. Helen McMurchy introduced Clarke to Hincks. McMurchy, appointed as Ontario's Director of the Feeble-minded in 1906, was Hincks' boss. Reference: LaJeunesse, Ron, *Political Asylums,* Muttart Foundation. 2002.

21. March, James H. "Keeping Canada Sane." *Canadian Encyclopedia.*

22. *Lethbridge Daily Herald,* 1912-08-05 page 7/10. (Lethbridge Baby Contest)

23. *Lethbridge Daily Herald,* 1914 (0908 P.3. (Lethbridge Baby Contest)

24. *Lethbridge Daily Herald,* 1914 08 September p.3.

25. Liberal-Conservative was the name members of the Great Coalition of Conservatives and Reformers used to describe themselves. The Coalition was formed to lobby the United Kingdom to support Confederation of British North America. By 1911, separate Liberal and Conservative parties re-emerged in Canada.

26. Den Otter, Andy A. *Civilizing the West: The Galts and the Development of Western Canada.* University of Alberta Press, 1982 and City of Lethbridge Archives.

27. Hall, David J. "Sir Clifford Sifton." *Canadian Encyclopedia.* Historica-Dominion, 2010 and "Sir Clifford Sifton". *Dictionary of Canadian Biography Online.* Copyright 2000 University of Toronto/Université Laval.

28. Den Otter, Andy A. *Civilizing the West: The Galts and the Development of Western Canada.* University of Alberta Press, 1982 and City of Lethbridge Archives.

29. Ellis, Greg. *The Stafford Family, Pioneer Community Builders.* City of Lethbridge Archives, Lethbridge, Alberta, Canada. 1995.

30. Magrath, Charles. *The Mortimer Press. 1910.* (30B) page 25 (30C) page 26.

31. CANSIM, table 075-0001 (persons). Estimated population of Canada, 1605 to present. Statistics Canada. http://www.statcan.gc.ca.

32. Creery Tim and Thomas Walkom. "Newspapers." *Canadian Encyclopedia.* Historica-Dominion. 2010.

33. Municipal Affairs, Government of Alberta. http://www.municipalaffairs.gov.ab.ca/documents/ms/population1913.pdf

34. Newspapers. *Our Future Our Past.* Alberta Historical Digitization Project. http://www.ourfutureourpast.ca/newspapr/date.sp?year=1913andSubmit=Look+up

35. "Lunacy Mostly Due to Drink. Cities Very Bad. The Insanity is Astounding." *Lethbridge Daily Herald,* 1912-08-05, p.7

36. "What the World Eugenics congress learned. Very few men of First Rank." *Lethbridge Daily Herald,* 29 July, page 17.

37. "It's Nice of them to have a Funeral." *Lethbridge Daily Herald,* 22 September, 1916. P.2

38. "Cause of the War." *Lethbridge Daily Herald,* 1916-05-11, p. 5/6

39. Hall, David. J. "World War I." *Canadian Encyclopedia.* Historica-Dominion. 2010.

40. "Lunacy Mostly Due to Drink. Cities Very Bad. The Insanity is Astounding." *Lethbridge Daily Herald,* 1921-05-09- 18 p. 1

41. "Clergy children." *Lethbridge Daily Herald,* 1930-02-1, page 21,

42. Canadian Press. "Discuss Social Hygiene." *Lethbridge Daily Herald,* p. 11, 28 August 1924.

43. "Letter to Miss Miller." *Lethbridge Daily Herald,* 12 January, 1914, page 10.

44. Taylor, Jeremy and Reginald Heber. "A Prayer on Behalf of Fools and Changelings and: A Prayer for Madmen." *The whole works of the Right Rev. Jeremy Taylor, Lord Bishop of Down, Connor and Dromore: with the life of the author and a critical examination of his writings by Reginald Heber, A. M.,* Volume 15. Duncan and Co., Richard Priestley, London. J. Parker Oxford, and Deighton and Son, Cambridge. Pages 355-356.

45. Taylor, Jeremy and Reginald Heber. "A Prayer on Behalf of Fools and Changelings and A Prayer for Madmen." *The whole works of the Right Rev. Jeremy Taylor, Lord Bishop of Down, Connor and Dromore: with the life of the author and a critical examination of his writings by Reginald Heber, A. M.,* Volume 15. Duncan and Co., Richard Priestley, London. J. Parker Oxford, and Deighton and Son, Cambridge. Pages 355-356.

46. (YMCA classes for girls.) *Lethbridge Daily Herald,* 12 January 1914.

47. "Traveller's Aid Does Godly Work." *Lethbridge Daily Herald.* 1913-12-19.

48. "Superintendent Chadwick Gives Interesting Information on the Subject." *Lethbridge Herald.* 1904 09 03 p. 3.

49. Mental defectives means mentally handicapped.

50. *Ordinance Respecting Insane Persons of the Northwest Territories,* Northwest Territories ordinances: 1888 (Revised 1889)

51. "Fears Racial Poisons Gaining Stronger Grip." *Lethbridge Herald,*1921-12, 22-p.10

52. Hannah (Annie Elizabeth Rolinson Gale City of Calgary Alderman, 1918 January 2 -1924 Jan 24. She may have been the first female alderman in the British Empire. Hannah Gale was a both a prison reformer and an advocate of free hospitals.) City of Calgary Archives.

53. Elizabeth Bailey Price, "Resume of Proceedings Of The Convention Of United Farm Women." *Lethbridge Daily Herald.* 28 January 1922. Page 12.

54. Alberta Journals, 1918, 4th Leg., 1st Sess. Alberta Sess. Sessions. Alberta Leg., 1st Sess. (March 21,1918

55. Alberta Journals, 1918, 4th Leg., 1st Sess. Alberta Sess. Sessions. Alberta Leg., 1st Sess. (March 21,1918

56. Alberta Journals, 1918, 4th Leg., 1st Sess. Alberta Sess. Sessions. Alberta Leg., 1st Sess. (March 21,1918

57. *An Act respecting Mentally Defective Persons* (*Mental Defectives Act*), Statutes of the Province of Alberta 1919, received Royal Assent 17 April 1919.

58. *An Act respecting Mentally Defective Persons* (*Mental Defectives Act*), Statutes of the Province of Alberta 1919, received Royal Assent 17 April 1919.

59. *An Act respecting Mentally Defective Persons (Mental Defectives Act)*, Statutes of the Province of Alberta 1919, received Royal Assent 17 April 1919.

60. Brett, Robert G. Lieutenant Governor of Alberta. Speech from the Throne. 15 February 1921.

61. Kilgour, David. *Uneasy Patriots: Western Canadians in Confederation*. Edmonton: Lone Pine Publishers, 1988. 'The Honourable Frederick Haultain 1897-1905." *Alberta Online Encyclopedia.*

62. The UFA was an amalgamation of farmer's groups including the Society of Equity and the Alberta Farm Association, Key organizer, Henry Wise Wood, was born in Missouri and encouraged the new organization to reflect his progressive and Christian beliefs. The Non-partisan League sent emissaries to Canada from the United States to encourage farmers to run candidates representing farmers' interests in elections. Sources: *Alberta Online Encyclopedia*, People and Places UFA http://www.abheritage.ca/abpolitics/people/influ_farmers.html

63. Elizabeth Bailey Price. "Resume of Proceedings Of The Convention Of United Farm Women." *Lethbridge Daily Herald*. 28 January 1922-01-28. Page 12.

64. *Sexual Sterilization Act*, Statutes of Alberta.1928.

65. "Reid Defends Minister." *Lethbridge Herald*, page 2. 1929-03-06.

66. "Reid Defends Minister." *Lethbridge Herald*, page 2. 1929-03-06.

67. 'Reid Defends Minister." *Lethbridge Herald*, page 2. 1929-03-06 .

68. Royal Assent to the Amendments given 11 April 1933.

69. *Act to Amend The Mental Defectives Act*, Statutes of Alberta 1933.

70. *Act to Amend The Mental Defectives Act*, Statutes of Alberta 1933.

71. Holloway, John, Letter, *Letters to the Lethbridge Daily Herald*. 05 April 1925 and Monday, 27 February 27, 1928 .

72. "Seen and Heard at the Herald." *Lethbridge Daily Herald*. 08 August 1923. Page 20. (Discussion of Mrs. Harrison's book on Soviet Russia)

73. *Lethbridge Herald*, Friday 23 September, 1921. Page 4.

74. *Lethbridge Herald*, October 3, 1920 and 17 February, 1926. Page 11. (Cardinal Bourne)

75. "World Needs Better Bred People Says G. B. S." *Lethbridge Herald.* 1928-02-11.

76. (Dr. Pusey) Associated Press. *Lethbridge Herald*, 19 June, 1924, Page 11.

77. (Dr. Pusey) Associated Press. *Lethbridge Herald*, 19 June, 1924, Page 11.

78. (Dr. Barnes) *Lethbridge Herald*, 31 March 1938 Page 2.

79. (Dr. Kerby) *Lethbridge Herald* 07 July 1936. Page. 4.

80. (Dr. Kerby) *Lethbridge Herald* 07 July 1936. Page. 4. s

81. (Dr. Kerby) *Lethbridge Herald* 07 July 1936. Page. 4.

82. In 1925, the Methodist, Presbyterian, and Congregational Churches in Canada merged to become the United Church of Canada after agreeing to a Basis of Union.

83. United Church Committee Reports In Favour of Birth Control and Sterilization. Report Submitted to General Council Now in Session in Ottawa But Not Yet Debated. *Lethbridge Herald*, 25 September 1936. Page 2.

84. The Eugenics Society of Canada at Toronto is urging legalized sterilization for certain classes in Canada. *Lethbridge Herald.* 18 February 1936. Page 4.

85. (David Tribe) 14 August 1925, *Lethbridge Herald*, Page 8.

86. Douglas, Major Cllfford Hugh, *Social Credit*, Preface and Introduction, 1924, www.mondopolitico.com/library/socialcredit/socialcredit.htm

87. Aberhart claimed to understand of 'the end time' prophecy. His Calvinist background grounded him well in teaching of the Elect (those predestined for Salvation) and the Damned (those predestined to go to hell).

88. Aberhart was a religious maverick who left a trail of theological wars behind him by the time he entered politics: Both his Prophetic Bible Institute and Bible Institute Baptist Church had split off from other congregations by 1929.

89. Ships of the British Navy—*HMS Dreadnought* (Battleship, 1906-1922). 5060. Online Library of Selected Images: United State Department of the Navy—Naval Historical Center 805 Kidder Breese SE—Washington Navy Yard, Washington, D.C. 20374

90. Canadian Broadcasting Corporation. William 'Bible Bill' Aberhart, Social Credit pioneer. The CBC Digital Archives Website. Last updated: 05 January 2009. [Page consulted 12 January 2010.] http://archives.cbc.ca/politics/provincial_territorial_politics/clips/13358/

91. Canadian Broadcasting Corporation. William 'Bible Bill' Aberhart, Social Credit pioneer. The CBC Digital Archives Website. Last updated: 05 January 2009. [Page consulted 12 January. 2010.] http://archives.cbc.ca/politics/provincial_territorial_politics/clips/13358/

92. Canadian Broadcasting Corporation. William 'Bible Bill' Aberhart, Social Credit pioneer. The CBC Digital Archives Website. Last updated: 05 January 2009. [Page consulted 12 January 2010.] http://archives.cbc.ca/politics/provincial_territorial_politics/clips/13358/

93. Canadian Broadcasting Corporation. William 'Bible Bill' Aberhart, Social Credit pioneer. The CBC Digital Archives Website. Last updated: 05 January 2009.

[Page consulted 12 January 2010.] http://archives.cbc.ca/politics/provincial_ territorial_politics/clips/13358/ and Canadian Broadcasting Corporation. 1935: The gospel of Social Credit. The CBC Digital Archives Website. Last updated. 05 January 2010. [Page consulted 12 January 2010.] http://archives.cbc.ca/politics/ provincial_territorial_politics/topics/1472/

94.   Canadian Broadcasting Corporation. William 'Bible Bill' Aberhart, Social Credit pioneer. The CBC Digital Archives Website. Last updated: 05 January 2009. [Page consulted 12 January 2010.] http://archives.cbc.ca/politics/provincial_ territorial_politics/clips/13358/ and Canadian Broadcasting Corporation. 1935: The gospel of Social Credit. The CBC Digital Archives Website. Last updated. 05 January 2010. [Page consulted 12 January 2010.] http://archives.cbc.ca/politics/ provincial_territorial_politics/topics/1472/

95.   Canadian Broadcasting Corporation. William 'Bible Bill' Aberhart, Social Credit pioneer. The CBC Digital Archives Website. Last updated: 05 January 2009. [Page consulted 12 January 2010.] http://archives.cbc.ca/politics/provincial_ territorial_politics/clips/13358/ and Canadian Broadcasting Corporation. 1935: The gospel of Social Credit. The CBC Digital Archives Website. Last updated. 05 January 2010. [Page consulted 12 January 2010.] http://archives.cbc.ca/politics/ provincial_territorial_politics/topics/1472/

96.   Florence Todd, who'd been a young teacher when Aberhart began his crusade, was featured in this taped interview. Canadian Broadcasting Corporation. William 'Bible Bill' Aberhart, Social Credit pioneer. The CBC Digital Archives Website. Last updated: 05 January 2009. [Page consulted 12 January 2010.] http://archives.cbc.ca/politics/provincial_territorial_politics/clips/13358/ and Canadian Broadcasting Corporation. 1935: The gospel of Social Credit. The CBC Digital Archives Website. Last updated. 05 January 2010. [Page consulted 12 January 2010.] http://archives.cbc.ca/politics/provincial_territorial_politics/ topics/1472/

97.   Canadian Broadcasting Corporation. William 'Bible Bill' Aberhart, Social Credit pioneer. The CBC Digital Archives Website. Last updated: 05 January 2009. [Page consulted 12 January 2010.] http://archives.cbc.ca/politics/provincial_ territorial_politics/clips/13358/ and Canadian Broadcasting Corporation. 1935: The gospel of Social Credit. The CBC Digital Archives Website. Last updated. 05 January 2010. [Page consulted 12 January 2010.] http://archives.cbc.ca/politics/ provincial_territorial_politics/topics/1472/

98.   Canadian Broadcasting Corporation. William 'Bible Bill' Aberhart, Social Credit pioneer. The CBC Digital Archives Website. Last updated: 05 January 2009. [Page consulted 12 January 2010.] http://archives.cbc.ca/politics/provincial_ territorial_politics/clips/13358/ and Canadian Broadcasting Corporation. 1935: The gospel of Social Credit. The CBC Digital Archives Website. Last updated. 05 January 2010. [Page consulted 12 January 2010.] http://archives.cbc.ca/politics/ provincial_territorial_politics/topics/1472/

99.   Canadian Broadcasting Corporation. William 'Bible Bill' Aberhart, Social Credit pioneer. The CBC Digital Archives Website. Last updated: 05 January 2009. [Page consulted 12 January 2010.] http://archives.cbc.ca/politics/provincial_ territorial_politics/clips/13358/ and Canadian Broadcasting Corporation. 1935: The gospel of Social Credit. The CBC Digital Archives Website. Last updated.

05 January 2010. [Page consulted 12 January 2010.] http://archives.cbc.ca/politics/provincial_territorial_politics/topics/1472/

100. The Honourable William Aberhart, 1935-43. Legislative Assembly of Alberta library. http://www.assembly.ab.ca/lao/library/premiers/aberhart.htm and Finkel , Alvin. The Rise and Fall of the Labour Party in Canada,

101. "Aberhart Declares Social Credit Would Be Real Boon To Coal Mines Addresses Large Audience," *Lethbridge Herald.*

102. Alberta Labour News reprinted in the *Lethbridge Herald,* 10 May 1934. Page 4.

103. "May be Invited to Visit Alberta." *Lethbridge Daily Herald,* 11 July 1933. Page. 5.

104. "May be Invited to Visit Alberta." *Lethbridge Daily Herald,* 11 July 1933. Page. 5.

105. "Aberhart's Startling Proposal $25 Per Month to All Over 21 Years to be Paid by the Province Under Douglas Credit Scheme." *Lethbridge Daily Herald,* Page 2. 20 March 1934.

106. The civil case, which vindicated Brownlee, involved a young country girl he had befriended. He was accused of seducing her after getting her a job as legislative clerk but no damages were awarded in the lawsuit brought by the girl's family. The scandal horrified the province.

107. More Albertans lived on farms than in cities over 2000. Cities pop was 217, 388, towns, 50, 998, MD's (farms) 371, 401, and villages 36, 994.) Municipal Affairs, Government of Alberta: http://www.municipalaffairs.gov.ab.ca/documents/ms/population1935.pdf

108. The Lieutenant Governor, William L. Walsh, appointed William Aberhart Premier and Minister of Education, effective September 3, 1935. Aberhart took his seat in the Legislature after winning the November 4 by-election for the Okotoks-High River Riding. September 5, 1937, the LG appointed him Attorney General. In the 1940 general election, he was elected an MLA for the multi-member electoral District of Calgary.

109. Canadian Broadcasting Corporation. William 'Bible Bill' Aberhart, Social Credit pioneer. The CBC Digital Archives Website. Last updated: 05 January 2009. [Page consulted 12 January 2010.] http://archives.cbc.ca/politics/provincial_territorial_politics/clips/13358/ and Canadian Broadcasting Corporation. 1935: The gospel of Social Credit. The CBC Digital Archives Website. Last updated. 05 January 2010. [Page consulted 12 January 2010.] http://archives.cbc.ca/politics/provincial_territorial_politics/topics/1472/

110. Canadian Broadcasting Corporation. William 'Bible Bill' Aberhart, Social Credit pioneer. The CBC Digital Archives Website. Last updated: 05 January 2009. [Page consulted 12 January 2010.] http://archives.cbc.ca/politics/provincial_territorial_politics/clips/13358/ and Canadian Broadcasting Corporation. 1935: The gospel of Social Credit. The CBC Digital Archives Website. Last updated. 05 January 2010. [Page consulted 12 January 2010.] http://archives.cbc.ca/politics/provincial_territorial_politics/topics/1472/

111. Scrip is a substitute for currency. Scrip certificates declare that the holder is entitled to future payment in goods or money.

112. After Lieutenant Governor Walsh's successor, Philip C.H. Primrose, died unexpectedly on March 17, 1937, Governor General Lord Tweedsmuir appointed Bowen Lieutanant Governor of Alberta. Bowen had only a few days to prepare for the new job, which became effective March 23, 1937.

113. Bill One of the 2nd and 3rd Sessions of the Alberta Legislature contained the *Bank Taxation Act. Statutes of the Province of Alberta 1937.* The Acts were referred to the Governor General October 5, 1937 after Lieutenant Governor John Bowen refused to sign it.

114. The *Credit of Alberta Regulations Act* was referred to the Governor General October 5, 1937 after LG Bowen refused to sign it. The formal name of the proposed legislation was Bill No. 8., an Act to amend and consolidate The Credit of Alberta Regulation Act. Reference: Statutes of the Province of Alberta 1937 (2nd, 3rd Session), 1938.

115. *An Act to Ensure the Publication of Accurate News and Information.* Statutes of the Province of Alberta 1937. Bill 9.1937.(Third session). Source: Bills 2nd, 3rd Sessions of the Alberta Legislature. 1938.

116. Article from October 6, 1937 Edmonton Bulletin. Source: "Great Alberta Law Cases." *Alberta Online Encyclopedia*, Alberta Heritiage foundation,

117. Irvine, William, ex-MP. "Mr. Aberhart's Figuring," *People's Weekly* reprinted in "Picked Up in Passing, for the Busy Reader." *The Lethbridge Herald.* 10 August 1937. The writer said: "Premier Aberhart must have been spending his spare time reading Alice in Wonderland."

118. On the advice of Prime Minister William Lyon Mackenzie King, John C. Bowen was appointed Lieutenant-Governor of Alberta effective March 23, 1937. This appointment was made by Lord Tweedsmuir, Governor General of Canada. The Honourable John C. Bowen 1937-1950, Lieutenant Governor, *Alberta Online Encyclopedia:* Heritage Community Foundation. Original Source: Lieutenant Governors of the North-West Territories and Alberta, 1876-1993. Legislative Assembly Office. http://www.abheritage.ca/abpolitics/people/lt_bowen.html

119. The rarely used "Royal Prerogative of thee Crown" prevents politicians from becoming too powerful or abusing their authority. Reference: *Historic Roots, Role of the Monarchy.* Monarchists Online; Governor General of Canada Website: www.gg.ca

120. "The Gospel of William Aberhart." CBC Archives.

121. Aberhart's Obituary in *Winnipeg Free Press* reprinted in *Lethbridge Herald*, 03 June 1943. Page 4.

122. Canadian Press, "Aberhart Charges Social Security Schemes Merely National Socialism" *Lethbridge Daily Herald*, 16 March 1942.

123. Canadian Press. "Board had assembly-line sterilizations." *Lethbridge Herald*, 25 June 1995, Page 7.

124. The Canada Health Act impacted the Provincial – Federal division of power by setting up federal funding for a public health care system in Canadian Provinces. http://www.canadian-healthcare.org/page2.html

125. *An Act to Amend the Sexual Sterilization Act.* Statutes of the Province of Alberta 1936-2nd Session, 1937. *Our Future Our Past.* Alberta Heritage Digitization Project. http://www.ourfutureourpast.ca/law/page.aspx?id=2914363

126. *An Act to Amend the Sexual Sterilization Act* received Royal Assent 14 April 1937. Section 7 of the Act now read: " No person shall be liable in any civil action or proceeding for anything done to him in good faith in purported pursuance of this Act, if that person is—(a). A surgeon directed to perform any operation for sexual sterilization pursuant to this act, and any person who, in connection with any such operation, acts as an anaesthetist or takes part therein or assists such surgeon in the performance thereof; (b). a person who consents to the performance of any such operation (c.) The Medical Superintendent or officer in charge of any mental hospital who causes any patient to be examined by this act. (d.) the medical practitioner having charge or direction of the Mental Hygiene Clinic who causes any person to be examined pursuant to this act. (e.) a member of the board.

127. Consent was no longer required for the sterilization of 'mental defectives. Provision was made for psychotics to give consent in the unlikely event, if they were able to consent, or if spouses, parents or guardians living in Alberta consented to the surgery.

128. "Report of the Lethbridge Nursing Mission." *Lethbridge Daily Herald.* 09 April Page 4. 1943.

129. Canadian Press. "Board had assembly-line sterilizations." *Lethbridge Daily Herald.* 25 June 1995. Page 7.

130. Chapter 47. Statutes of the Province of Alberta 1942. (Royal Assent Granted March 19, 1942.)

131. "Aberhart and the Opposition." *The Daily Lethbridge Herald.* Page Four. 05 November 1941.

132. "Bowen's Tribute." *Lethbridge Daily Herald.* 25 May 1943.

133. "Manning's Statement." *Lethbridge Daily Herald.* 25 May 1943.

134. In Commonwealth countries the First Minister is the Senior Minister in the cabinet. First Ministers usually leader of the party with the most members in the parliamentary assembly. First Ministers may also be called Premiers or Prime Ministers.

135. Test Case. BNA Act. *Great Alberta Law Cases.*

136. "Waggon" is an alternate spelling of 'wagon'.

137. Social Credit League Documents. Australia. Senator Buchanan Room. Lethbridge Public Library.

138. Irvine, William, ex-MP. Premier Aberhart must have been speeding his spare time reading "Alice in Wonderland." Irvine, Wm, Ex-Mp. *The People's Weekly Lethbridge Herald.* Tuesday, 10 August 1937.

139. Marshall, David. Premier *E.C. Manning, Back to the Bible Hour, and Fundamentalism in Canada, Religion and Life in Canada: Historical and Comparative Perspectives.* Editor: Marguerite Van Die. University of Toronto Press. Toronto, 2001.

140. Canadian Broadcasting Corporation. 1944: Ernest Manning magic.
05 September 1971.The CBC Digital Archives Website. Last updated:
21 July 2009. [Page consulted 12 January 2010.] http://archives.cbc.ca/politics/
provincial_territorial_politics/clips/9842/

141. Canadian Broadcasting Corporation. 1944: *Ernest Manning Magic.*
05 September 1971.The CBC Digital Archives Website. Last updated:
21 July 2009. [Page consulted 12 January 2010.] http://archives.cbc.ca/politics/
provincial_territorial_politics/clips/9842/

142. LaJeunesse, Ron. *Political Asylums* Muttart Foundation. 2002. Page. 72.

143. *Act to Amend the Mental Defectives Act*. 1959. Statutes of Alberta. *Our Future, Our Past*, Digital Archives. Alberta Heritage Digitization Project.

144. Canadian Press. "Doctors removed boys' testicles, trial hears procedure routine for those with Down's syndrome." *Lethbridge Herald.* 02 July 1995. Page, 7.

145. W.W. Cross served as Alberta's Minister of Public Health 1935-1940 and Minister of Health and Public Welfare 1940-1957.

146. This account of a homesteader going insane originally appeared in *The Hanna Herald*, Vol. 1, No 24, June 5, 1913: Source: Hannah. Ca, *The Doctors*. http://www.hanna.ca/Visitors/History/TheDoctors/tabid/255/Default.aspx

147. Cross, W.W. *Lethbridge Herald*. 11 December 1947.

148. Acute polio is the first stage of polio. The patient experience a high fever as the disease spreads through the body. In most patients the acute stage lasts 3 to 5 days, but it can last longer in severe cases. Source: Halsted, Lauro S. *Acute Polio and Post Polio Syndrome*. National Rehabilitation Hospital 102 Irving Street, NW | Washington, DC 20010 | 202.877.1000

149. Clarke was a member of the faculty when Cross graduated from the University of Toronto in 1915. Clarke became Dean of the Medical School in 1917.

150. Canadian Broadcasting Corporation. 1944: "Ernest Manning Magic."
05 September 1971.The CBC Digital Archives Website. Last updated:
21 July 2009. [Page consulted 12 January 2010.] http://archives.cbc.ca/politics/
provincial_territorial_politics/clips/9842/

151. The Government called Whitton as a witness to the Royal Commission investigating the social services system in Alberta.

152. International Order of Daughters of the Empire.

153. *Great Alberta Law Cases* Alberta Online Encyclopedia, ACCESS Network, CKUA Heritage Community Foundation Presents.

154. "Board Member Replaced in 1960s." *Lethbridge Herald*, 29 January 1996. Page 10.

155. *Lethbridge Herald.* 20 December 1963. Page 1. and "Donovan Ross Answers Criticisms 78 Mental Defectives Sterilized Each Year." *Lethbridge Herald*. 12-11 1963. Page 10.

156. "Donovan Ross Answers Criticisms 78 Mental Defectives Sterilized Each Year." *Lethbridge Herald*. 1963, 12-11, page 10.

157. "Donovan Ross Answers Criticisms 78 Mental Defectives Sterilized Each Year." *Lethbridge Herald.* 1963, 12-11, page 10.

158. "Some Facts on Sterilization." Editorial, *Lethbridge Herald.* 12-December 1963. Page 4.

159. *Lajeunesse,* pp. 155-159.

160. *Lajeunesse,* pp. 155-159.

161. "Infamous sterilization act hit those least able to defend." *Lethbridge Herald.* 28 March 1979. Page 49.

162. Ebner, David and Katherine O'Neill. "Alberta royalty grab stuns oil industry." Stelmach unveils new regime that will mean a potential windfall of $1.4-billion for the provincial treasury beginning in 2010." *Globe and Mail.* 26 October 2007; and "Royalties review: Alberta's new package of rates." *Calgary Herald.* 11 March 2010. Using Source: Alberta Energy.

163. "Sterilization Of Mentally Retarded Controversial Topic To Geneticists." *Lethbridge Herald.* 25 February 1969. Page 14 and Pole, Ken. "Sex Sterilization Act Comes Under Attack." *Lethbridge Herald.* 17 September 1969. Page 31.

164. Pole, Ken. "Sex Sterilization Act Comes Under Attack." *Lethbridge Herald.* 17 September 1969. Page 31.

165. *An Act to Amend the Human Rights Act.* Statutes of the Province of Alberta 1971. Statutes of Alberta.)

166. Social Credit remained the governing party in British Columbia until the party led by Premier Bill Vander Zalm's successor, Rita Johnson, was defeated in 1991. In the 21st century, Social Credit survives in Canada as in the form of obscure parties in Alberta and British Columbia. Quebec's Ralliement de Creditiste dissolved in 1978.

167. "Caouette (1917-1976) *Homme politique Crédit Social.*" Faculte des lettres et sciences humaines. Universite de Sherbrooke, Accessed at: http://bilan.usherbrooke.ca/bilan/pages/biographies/106.html Réal

168. Caouette gave a 90-minute speech describing the new leader of the Social Credit Party, Robert Norman Thompson of Alberta as a "marionette" for Premier of Alberta Ernest Manning. He claimed that, ten minutes before the 1960 leadership vote, Premier Manning had instructed him to "tell your people to vote for Thompson because the West will never accept a Roman Catholic French Canadian leader". Dufresne, Bernard, "Quebec's Socreds vote to Disown Thompson," *Globe and Mail,* 2 September 1963. Page 1.

169. Alberta Online Encyclopedia, Heritage Community Foundation. Olson, Geoffrey. "Robert N. Thompson and Political Realignment." Manning's world view impacted his politics. As a black and white thinker, he saw the world in terms of dichotomies: communism vs. capitalism as options. Evangelical Christianity vs. Atheism.

170. Statutes of the Province of Alberta 1972.

171. *Lethbridge Herald,* 08 May 1980 Page 2.

172. *Lethbridge Herald,* 08 May 1980 Page 2.

173. "Gov't Forces Couple to Separate." *Lethbridge Herald.* 07-03 Page 20.

174. Canadian Broadcasting Corporation. Trudeau mocks Lougheed. The Canadian Digital Archives Website. Last updated 27 November 2006. [Page consulted 15 January 2010.]

175. Canadian Broadcasting Corporation. West is the new East. The CBC Digital Archives Website. Last updated 19 November 2007, [Page consulted 12 January 2010.]

176. The Canadian Press. Tibbetts, Janice. *Sexual Sterilization Act* (background comment) 1992.

177. Getty`s successor, Ralph Klein, took the helm of Provincial Government on the fifth of December 1992. Klein won the Conservative Leadership over Nancy Betkowski. (As Nancy MacBeth, she later became leader of the Official Opposition Alberta Liberals.)

178. "Government in court over forced Sterilization." *Lethbridge Herald.* 14 June. 1995. Page 4.

179. 132 D.L.R.(4th) 695 Court File No. 8903 20759 Edmonton Alberta Court of Queen's Bench Veit J. January 25, 1996 Indexed as Muir v. Alberta Muir v. The Queen in right of Alberta.

180. "Provincial News." *Lethbridge Herald.* 13 June 1995. Page 10. and "Province acknowledges sterilization was wrong." *Lethbridge Herald.* 14 June 1995. Page 4.

181. Canadian Press. "Board had assembly-line sterilizations." *Lethbridge Herald.* 25 June 1995. Page. 7.

182. "Doctors removed boys' testicles, trial hears Procedure routine for those with Down's syndrome." *Lethbridge Herald.* 02 July 1995. Page, 7.

183. "Province willing to pay $60,000 to woman in sterilization lawsuit." *Lethbridge Herald.* 14 December 1995. Page 4.

184. In civil cases either the defendant or plaintiff can be awarded costs to cover lawyers fees and trial costs. Costs are awarded to the side that wins the case.

185. The Training School continues to operate on a reduced scale as Michener Centre. Most residents that remain in Michener Centre are over 50. http://www.pdd.org/ central/michener/default.shtml)

186. "Province must pay $750,000 in wrongful sterilization case." *Lethbridge Herald.* 26 January 1996. Page 8.

187. "Province must pay $750,000 in wrongful sterilization case." *Lethbridge Herald.* 26 January 1996. Page 8 and "Government Accused of fraud and trickery in sterilization case." *Lethbridge Herald.* 11 July 1996. Page 2.

188. "Province refuses to apologize to woman wrongly Sterilized." *The Lethbridge Herald.* 12 March 1996. Page 11

189. Veit, J. 1996.

190. "Government Accused of fraud and trickery In sterilization case." *Lethbridge Herald.* Page 2. 11 July 1996.

191. Flim, Leona, "No one will ever call Wayne Dad." *Lethbridge Herald.* 18 June 1995. Page 8; and "Alberta Barren." *Saturday Night Magazine.* 1997.

192. "Former training school resident upset that province won't settle out of court." *Lethbridge Herald.* 03 July Page 5.(Lorraine Bigelow).

193. "Sterilization victim doesn't trust government. Woman says she wants to avoid going to court but will if she has to." *Lethbridge Herald.* 15 March 1998. Page 17 (Donna Whittaker).

194. "Sterilization victim doesn't trust government. Woman says she wants to avoid going to court but will if she has to." *Lethbridge Herald.* 15 March 1998. Page 17 (Donna Whittaker).

195. "Sexual Sterilization Act." *The Lethbridge Herald.* 18 June 1995. Page 8.

196. "Sexual Sterilization Act." *The Lethbridge Herald.* 18 June 1995. Page 8.

197. "Province pays sterilization victim." *Lethbridge Herald.* 01 March 1996. Page 16. and "30 people file mass suit after being sterilized." *Lethbridge Herald.* 02 March 1996. Page 2.

198. "Province pays sterilization victim." *Lethbridge Herald.* 01 March 1996. Page 16.

199. "30 people file mass suit after being sterilized." *Lethbridge Herald.* 02 March 1996. Page 2.

200. "Province to compensate sterilization victims Proposed compensation package surprises lawyers for victims of Alberta's eugenics program." *Lethbridge Herald.* 10 March 1998. Page 4.

201. "Alberta wants courts to throw out lawsuits." *Lethbridge Herald.* 30 June 1996. Page 6.

202. "Government Accused of fraud and trickery In sterilization case." *Lethbridge Herald.* 11 July 1996. Page 2.

203. "Trial date set for eugenics lawsuit." *Lethbridge Herald.* 13 January 1998. Page 4.

204. "Trial date set for eugenics lawsuit." *Lethbridge Herald.* 13 January 1998. Page 4.

205. "Trial date set for eugenics lawsuit." *Lethbridge Herald.* 13 January 1998. Page 4.

206. Kiss, Simon. Express News Staff. "Feature: Our cherished charter turns 20." University of Alberta. 20 April 2002.

207. 'Province to compensate sterilization victims: Proposed compensation package surprises lawyers for victims of Alberta's eugenics program." *Lethbridge Herald.* 10 March 1998. Page 4.

208. "Province to compensate sterilization victims: Proposed compensation package surprises lawyers for victims of Alberta's eugenics program." *Lethbridge Herald.* 10 March 1998. Page 4.

209. Flim, Leona and Canadian Press. *Lethbridge Herald.* 11 March 1998. Page 3.

210. "Province to compensate sterilization victims. Proposed compensation package surprises lawyers for victims of Alberta's eugenics program." *Lethbridge Herald.* 10 March 1998. Page 4.

211. "Havelock offers to resign over sterilization mess." *Lethbridge Herald.* 13 March 1998. Page 4.

212. "Havelock offers to resign over sterilization mess." *Lethbridge Herald.* 13 March 1998. Page 4.

213. Bill Status Report for the 24th Legislature - 2nd Session (1998) Legislative Assembly of Alberta Updated to Wednesday, 09 December 1998.

214. McIlroy, Anne. "Drunk in charge." *The Guardian.* Friday 28 December 2001 16.03 GMT. Accessed at www.guardian.co.uk.

215. Socred is an informal term for 'Social credit'.

216. Ehlers, Gordon. "Money won't help the eugenics mess." Letter to the Editor, *Lethbridge Herald.* 03 April 1998. Page 17.

217. Bill 33 does not attack the mentally disabled or mentally ill. Quebeckers would been less accepting of their province's use of the 'notwithstanding clause' had it been used to override the rights of the mentally ill and mentally disabled.

218. Flim, Leona, "Future Uncertain for Victims of Forced Sterilization: Plan Withdrawal of Controversial Bill Leaves Way Unclear." *Lethbridge Herald.* 12 March 1998. Page 1.

219. "Sterilization victims left out, says lawyer." *Lethbridge Herald.* Page 5, 1998-09-10 13.

220. "Sterilization victims left out, says lawyer." *Lethbridge Herald.* 13 October 1998. Page 5.

221. Canadian Press. "Province Settles With sterilization victims." *Lethbridge Herald.* 03 November 1999. Page 4.

222. Canadian Press. "Province Settles With sterilization victims." *Lethbridge Herald.* 03 November 1999. Page. 4.

223. Canadian Press. "Province Settles With sterilization victims." *Lethbridge Herald.* 03 November 1999. Page. 4.

224. "Past minister knew nothing of eugenics." *Lethbridge Herald.* 29 January 1996. Page 10.

225. "Sterilization a Concern in the 1950s." *Lethbridge Herald.* 29 January 1996. Page. 10.

226. "Sterilization a Concern in the 1950s." *Lethbridge Herald.* 29 January 1996. Page. 10.

227. "Legislative session conflicts with Klein's fishing trip." Last Updated: Tuesday, July 18, 2006 | 9:32 AM MT CBC News Read more: http://www.cbc.ca/canada/calgary/story/2006/07/18/klein-fishing.html#ixzz0oM9a3eOe

228. Canadian Broadcasting Corporation. "Bums and Creeps." The CBC Digital Archives Website. Last updated 10 October 2008. Page consulted 12 January 2010.

229. Canadian Broadcasting Corporation. "Bums and Creeps." The CBC Digital Archives Website. Last updated 10 October 2008. Page consulted 12 January 2010.

230. "Severely normal' people don't want to talk about AISH: Klein." Last updated Friday 29 October 2004, 9:43 AM ET CBC News. cbc.ca

231. There are 75,000 American citizens living in the City of Calgary, according to Calgary Economic Development. Their source is the U.S. Consulate.

232. Marshall, David. *Premier E.C. Manning, Back to the Bible Hour, and Fundamentalism in Canada. Religion and Life in Canada: Historical and Comparative Perspectives.* Marguerite Van Die, editor. University of Toronto Press. Toronto. 2001.

233. Flanagan, Thomas. *Harpers's Team: Behind the Scenes of the Conservative Rise to Power 2007.* McGill – Queen's University Press. Canada 2007.

234. Flanagan views social welfare as 'hypertrophic' welfare state dominated by socio-distant progressive elite that wishes to remake society according to its own rationalistic vision. Flanagan, Tom, *Harper's Team*, p. 13.

235. Yearwood-Lee, Emily. *Mental Health Background Paper.* Legislative Library of British Columbia. 01 January 2008.

236. Yearwood-Lee, Emily. *Mental Health Background Paper.* Legislative Library of British Columbia. 01 January 2008.

237. "Act to Be Repealed." Canadian Press- Victoria. *Lethbridge Herald.* 21 March 1973. Page 2.

238. Canadian Press, "Government in court over forced Sterilization." *Lethbridge Herald.* 14 June 1995. Page 4. Source cited by CP McLaren, Angus, *Our Own Master Race Eugenics in Canada 1885-1945* and Canadian Press. "No Revision Is Planned In Sterilization Law." *Lethbridge Herald.* 20 December 1963. Page 1.

239. "Donovan Ross Answers Criticisms." *Lethbridge Herald.* 11 December 1963. Page 10. and *Act to Be Repealed.* Canadian Press- Victoria. *Lethbridge Herald.* 21 March 1973. Page 2.

240. Canadian Press, "Act to be Repealed." *Lethbridge Herald.* 21 March 1973. Page 2.

241. Sterilization, Policy Issue. British Columbia Association of Community Living.

242. *Lethbridge Herald*, 14 December 2000. Page 9; and Sterilization Policy Issue, British Columbia Association of Community Living.

243. "Women Sue." *Lethbridge Herald.* 14 December 2000. Page 9.

244. "Sterilized BC Man Subject of Lawsuit." *Lethbridge Herald.* 14 December 2000. Page 9.

245. McMillan, Kate, "Tommy Douglas: Not Fascist Enough!" *Small Dead Animals.* 3 January 2010.

246. Marshall, David. *Premier E.C. Manning, Back to the Bible Hour, and Fundamentalism in Canada. Religion and Life in Canada: Historical and Comparative Perspectives.* Marguerite Van Die, editor. University of Toronto Press. Toronto. 2001.

247. Recruiting both groups can be a tricky strategy. Most Evangelicals consider the Church of Jesus Christ of Latter Day Saints theologically unorthodox, but the two groups find common cause in LDS emphasis on family values.

248. E. (Mrs) v. Eve, [1986] 2 S.C.R. 388 Eve, by her Guardian ad litem, Milton B. Fitzpatrick, Official Trustee Appellant v. Mrs E. Respondent. Indexed as E. (Mrs) v. EVE. File No.: 16654. 1985: June 4, 5; Ruling: 1986: October 23.

249. *Parens patriae* is Latin. It means the jurisdiction of the courts to help and protect people with a disability.

250. E. (Mrs) v. Eve, [1986] 2 S.C.R. 388 Eve, by her Guardian ad litem, Milton B. Fitzpatrick, Official Trustee Appellant v. Mrs. E. Respondent. Indexed as E. (Mrs) v. EVE. File No.: 16654. 1985: June 4, 5; Ruling: 1986: October 23.

251. "A Tribute to the Old Nobility." *Lethbridge Herald.* 18 July 1925.

252. Intelligence tests were developed in France by Théodore Simon (1873-1961) and Alfred Binet (1857-1911). They wanted to help school children learn more easily. Binet and Simon never intended the Binet-Simon Scale to be a static intelligence. Through eugenicists like Robert M. Yerkes, Henry Goddard and Lewis Terman, intelligence tests scores became tools to identify the feeble-minded. Henry Goddard used crude intelligence tests to prove the inferiority of Eastern Europeans and Jews.

253. *Les Idees modernes sur les enfants* (1973 edition) by Alfred Binet (E. Flammarion, Paris) 1909, p. 101 and Gould, Stephen Jay. *The Mismeasure of Man.* W.W. Norton and Company. New York. 1981. Page. 166; and *Eugenics and the Power of Testing.* (Chapter 5) Facing History and Ourselves National Foundation, Inc. Brookline, Massachusetts,) 2002.

254. Binet, Alfred. *Les Idees modernes sur les enfants.*(1973 edition) E. Flammarion, Paris 1909, Page 141.

255. Binet, Alfred. *New methods for the diagnosis of the intellectual level of subnormals. The development of intelligence in children.* E. S. Kite (Trans.), Vineland, NJ: Publications of the Training School at Vineland. 1905. 1916. (Originally published 1905 in *L'Année Psychologique*, 1905. Pages 12, 191-244.

256. Goddard, H. H. (1912). *The Kallikak Family: A study in the heredity of feeble-mindedness.* Macmillan. New York.

257. Terman, Lewis M. (1916). 'The uses of intelligence tests," Chapter 1. *The measurement of intelligence.* Houghton Mifflin. Boston 1916 and Christopher D. Green Classics in the History of Psychology, An Internet Resource developed by Christopher D. Green, York University, Toronto, Ontario ISSN 1492-3173.

258. Municipal Affairs, Government of Alberta. Link: http://www.municipalaffairs.gov. ab.ca/documents/ms/population1969.pdf.

259. As many as 25 states still had permitting sterilization in the 1980s. More than 65,000 people were sterilized under these laws. McLaren, Angus. *Our Own Master Race: Eugenics in Canada, 1885-1945,* and "Government in Court Over Forced Sterilizations." *Lethbridge Herald.* 14 June 1995.

260. "U.S. mass sterilization rivalled Nazi eugenics,researchers indicate." *Lethbridge Herald.* 15 February 2000. Page 7.

261. Hubbard, Ruth and Stuart Newman. "Yuppie Eugenics." by Ruth Hubbard and Stuart Newman, *Z Magazine*, March 2002; and McLaren, Angus, *Our Own Master Race: Eugenics in Canada, 1885-1945.* Toronto: McClelland and Stewart, 1990. Reprinted Toronto: Oxford University Press, 1997.

262. Margaret Sanger, founder of Planned Parenthood, worked to limit numbers of blacks births. Her birth control clinic targeted blacks. Unlike most Canadian suffragettes she abhorred religion and despaired of women's acceptance of sentimental courting (marriage for love). "Eugenics will destroy that sentimentalism which leads a woman deliberately to marry a man who is absolutely unworthy of her and can only bring disease, degradation and death," she said.

263. "Increase in sterilizations raises moral, legal questions." *Lethbridge Herald.* 28 August 1978. Page 29.

264. "Increase in sterilizations raises moral, legal questions." *Lethbridge Herald.* 28 August 1978, Page 29.

265. "U.S. mass sterilization rivalled Nazi eugenics, researchers indicate." *Lethbridge Herald.* 15 February 2000, Page 7. and Eugenics.org.

266. "Thousands sterilized involuntarily in state's mental homes, records show." *Lethbridge Herald.* 03-04 1980. Page 20. and Eugenics.org,

267. "Thousands sterilized involuntarily in state's mental homes, records show." *Lethbridge Herald.* 03-04 1980. Page 20. and Eugenics.org,

268. Oughtred, Russell, "Doctor Charges natives used natives as guinea pigs." *Lethbridge Herald.* Saturday, 3 April, 1976.

269. England, Charles R. *A Look at the Indian Health Service Policy of Sterilization,* 1972-1976. Accessed at htttp://www.dickshovel.com/IHSSterPol.html

270. "Increase in sterilizations raises moral, legal questions." *Lethbridge Herald.* 28 July 1978 Page 12.

271. Rooney, Andy. "Moratorium on multiplication." *Lethbridge Herald.* 03 June 1987. Page 6.

272. "Young Children Within Range of Sterilization Plan." *Lethbridge Daily Herald,* 04 January 1934. Page 5.

273. *Law for the Protection of Hereditary Health: The Attempt to Improve the German Aryan Breed,* Deutsches Reich. 14 July 1933. (Also translated as *Law for the Prevention of Genetically Diseased Progeny.*) Accessed at http://frank.mtsu. edu/~baustin/nurmlaw1.html

274. "First Sterilization Order Goes Into Effect," Associated Press-Goerlitz, Germany. *Lethbridge Herald.* 05 January 1934.

275. Associated Press. "Three to be Sterilized Under German Degree." *Lethbridge Herald.* 06 March 1934. Page 1.

276. *Lethbridge Herald.* 03 September 1936. Page 5.

277. Laughlin, Harry, D. Sc., Assistant Director of the Eugenics Record Office, Carnegie Institution of Washington, Cold Spring Harbor, Long Island, New York, and Eugenics Associate of the Psychopathic Laboratory, *Model Eugenical Sterilization Law, Psychopathic Laboratory of the Municipal Court of Chicago. Sterilization in the United States.* Chicago, Illinois, December 1922. Pages 446-452.

278. *The Passing of the Great Race,* C. Scribner's Sons. New York. 1916. 1918, 1921, 1922.

279. Wire. "Eugenics for the Troops." *Lethbridge Herald.* 18 June 1936. Page 6.

280. "Military Eugenics." *Lethbridge Herald.* 24 October 1933. page 4.

281. "World Eugenics Congress." *Lethbridge Herald.* 31 August 1935. Page 4.

282. "Says Germany Has the Right System of Raising Babies.: *Lethbridge Herald.* 29 August, 1935. Page 11.

283. Crawford, Alison. "Dodge's retirement reality check." 27 March 2010. CBC News. www. cbc.ca.

284. Ninety-two percent of people over age 65 do not have dementia. Sixty-five percent of those over 85 have no forms of dementia. *Seniors and Dementia Disorders, including Alzheimer's Disease.* Canadian Mental Health Association, Ontario.

285. "Disabled Girl's Family Fights Order to Leave." Letter to the Editor. *Globe and Mail.* 23 February 2010.

286. "Genetics advances creating concerns over ethics." *Lethbridge Herald*, 03 July 1995. Page 6. and "Canada's health-care system is sliding toward nazi-style eugenics by encouraging parents to abort disabled foetuses University of Victoria academic says." *Lethbridge Herald.* 31 December 1995. Page 5.(Genome)

287. "Unhealthy foetuses may be at risk, warns health research director. Survey of geneticists finds a resurgence in eugenics." *Lethbridge Herald.* 31 December, Page 5.

288. "Unhealthy foetuses may be at risk, warns health research director. Survey of geneticists finds a resurgence in eugenics." *Lethbridge Herald.* 31 December, Page 5.

289. "Canada's health-care system is sliding toward nazi-style eugenics by encouraging parents to abort disabled foetuses University of Victoria academic says." *Lethbridge Herald.* 31 December 1995. Page 5.

290. "Many Canadians stigmatize mentally ill, poll finds." *CTV News.* 18 August 2008. http://www.ctv.ca/servlet/ArticleNews/story/CTVNews/20080818/cma_health_0 80818/20080818?hub=TopStories

291. "Many Canadians stigmatize mentally ill, poll finds." *CTV News.* 18 August 2008. http://www.ctv.ca/servlet/ArticleNews/story/CTVNews/20080818/cma_health_0 80818/20080818?hub=TopStories

292. *The Latimer Case, Canadian Council of Persons with Disabilities.* Website: http://www.ccdonline.ca/en/humanrights/endoflife/latimer/victim-murderer

293. "Most Canadians Generally Agree with Euthanasia." February 16, 2010. Source: Angus Reid Public Opinion. Methodology: Online interviews with 1,003 Canada adults, conducted on Feb. 2 and Feb. 3, 2010. Margin of error is 3.1 percent.

294. Flegel, Ken, MDCM MSc, Senior Associate Editor; and Paul C. Hébert, MD MHSc, Editor-in-Chief. "Time to move on from the euthanasia debate." 29 March 2010, *Canadian Medical Association Journal.*

295. Flegel, Ken, DCM MSc, Senior Associate Editor; and Paul C. Hébert, MD MHSc, Editor-in-Chief. "Time to move on from the euthanasia debate." *Canadian Medical Association Journal.* 29 March, 2010.

296. Beachell, Laurie, National Coordinator, Canada Council of Persons with Disabilities. "Letter to the Editor: Re: Locked in Patients Humanity for the Trapped" (25 November 2009) *Globe and Mail.*

297. CT. "Moral Question Facing Canada: More Liberal Abortion Laws Pose Problem at CBA Meet." *Lethbridge Herald.* 1963.

298. "Eugenics prompts fears of impending brave new world." *Lethbridge Herald*, 31 August1999. Page 52.

299. "Eugenics prompts fears of impending brave new world." *Lethbridge Herald*, 31 August 1999. Page 52.

300. Elder Advocates of Alberta. http://elderadvocates.ca/martha-matich-dependant-adults-act-abuse/

301. CCD Affidavit Motion for an order granting interested party status to the Canadian Human Rights Tribunal Between James Peter Hughes –complainant- and Elections Canada. Tribunal File No.: T1373/10308 Complaint No.: 20080351. March 4, 2010.

302. Levant, Ezra. "Censorship in the name of 'human rights." *National Post.* 17 December 2007.

303. "Limiting Legal Aid unjust, Review suggests 6,100 Albertans might never get their day in court." 30 March 2010. New Democratic Opposition, Alberta. http://www.ndpopposition.ab.ca/site/index.cfm?fuseaction=page. detailsandID=8103andt=8andi=48

304. "Canada Ratifies UN Convention on the Rights of Persons with Disabilities," Foreign Affairs and International Trade, Government of Canada. (No. 99—March 11, 2010—11:15 a.m. ET.

305. "Budget 2010-2011 Action Notes." Alberta Committee of Citizens with Disabilities. March 2010.

306. "Science, Morals a deadly Mixture Society still need to be on Guard Warn Legal Scholars." *Lethbridge Herald.*

307. Canadian Press. "Government in court over forced Sterilization." *Lethbridge Herald.* 14 June 1995. Page 4. (Muir was one of the 2,844 people sterilized in Alberta between 1928 and 1972 under the province's sterilization law.)

308. 2008 Variation in Turnout by Electoral Division Report. Elections Alberta: October 2008.

309. 2008 Variation in Turnout by Electoral Division Report. Elections Alberta. October 2008.

310. Report on the September 14, 2009 Calgary-Glenmore By-Election. Elections Alberta.

311. Chandler, Graham. "Losing our Bible Belt." *Alberta Views.* November/December 2001. Pages: 30-35.

312. Canadian Press. "Government in court over forced Sterilization." *Lethbridge Herald.*14 June 1995. Page 4.

APPENDICES

1. *1928 Sexual Sterilization Act* passed by the Legislative Assembly of the Province of Alberta.

2. Hitler's Euthanasia Law, September 1, 1939

3. The Nuremberg Laws on Citizenship and Race: September 15, 1935.

    a. *The Reich Citizenship Law* of September 15, 1935

    b. *First Supplementary Decree* of November 14, 1935

    c. *Law for the Protection of German Blood and German Honour*, September 15, 1935

4. *Law for the Protection of Hereditary Health: The Attempt to Improve the German Aryan Breed*, July 14, 1933 also translated as the *Law for the Prevention of Genetically Diseased Progeny*.

5. Muir *v.* The Queen in right of Alberta

6. E. (Mrs.) *v.* Eve [1986] 2 S.C.R. 388

Appendix 1.
1928 Sexual Sterilization Act passed by the Legislative Assembly of the Province of Alberta.

1928
Chapter 37.
The Sexual Sterilization Act
(*Assented to March 21, 1928*)

His MAJESTY, by and with the advice and consent of The Legislative Assembly of the Province of Alberta, enacts as follows:

1. This Act may be cited as *"The Sexual Sterilization Act."*   Short Title

2. In this Act, unless the context otherwise requires—   Interpretation

    (a) "Mental Hospital" shall mean a hospital within the meaning of *The Mental Diseases Act;*   Mental hospitals

    (b) "Minister" shall mean the Minister of Health.   Minister

3.— (1) For the purpose of this Act, a board is hereby created, which shall consist of the following four persons: Appointment of Board

    Dr. E. Pope, Edmonton.

    Dr. E. G. Mason, Calgary.

    Dr. J. M. McEachran, Edmonton

    Mrs. Jean H. Field, Kinuso.

    (2) The successors of said members of the Board shall from time to time, be appointed by the Lieutenant Governor in Council, but two of the said Board shall be medical practitioners nominated by the Senate of the University of Alberta and the Council of the College of Physicians respectively, and two shall be persons other than medical practitioners, appointed by the Lieutenant Governor in Council.

4. When it is proposed to discharge any inmate of a mental hospital, the Medical Superintendent or other officer in charge thereof may cause such inmate to be examined by or in the presence of the board of examiners.   Examination of inmate of mental hospital

5. If upon such examination, the board is unanimously of opinion that the patient might safely be discharged if the danger of procreation with its attendant risk of multiplication of the evil by transmission of the disability to progeny were eliminated, the board may direct in writing such surgical operation for sexual sterilization of the inmate as may be specified in the written direction and shall appoint some competent surgeon to perform the operation.   Surgical operation

Consent of inmate or relation necessary

6. Such operation shall not be performed unless the inmate, if in the opinion of the board, he is capable of giving consent, has consented thereto, or where the board is of the opinion that the inmate is not capable of giving such consent, the husband or wife of the inmate or the parent or guardian of the inmate if he is unmarried has consented thereto, or where the inmate has no husband, wife, parent or guardian resident in the Province, the Minister has consented thereto.

Exemption from action

7. No surgeon duly directed to perform any such operation shall be liable to any civil action whatsoever by reason of the performance thereof.

Scope of Act

8. This Act shall have effect only insofar as the legislative authority of the Province extends.

Appendix 2:
Hitler's Euthanasia Law, September 1, 1939

(1)   Berlin, den 1. September 1939

Reichsleiter Bouhler und Dr med. Brandt sind unter Verantwortung beauftragt, die Befugnisse namentlich zu bestimmender Ärzte so zu erweitern, dass nach menschlichen Ermessen unheilbar Kranken bei kritischster Beurteilung ihres Krankheitszustandes der Gnadentod gewährt werden kann.

(gez. Adolf Hitler)

In English it reads:

ADOLF HITLER

Berlin, 1 September 1939

Reichsleiter Bouhler and Dr med. Brandt are instructed to broaden the powers of physicians designated by name, who will decide whether those who have - as far as can be humanly determined - incurable illnesses can, after the most careful evaluation, be granted a mercy death.

signed, Adolf Hitler

Accessed at: http://www2.h-net.msu.edu/~german/gtext/nazi/euthanasia-eng.html

Appendix 3.
The Nuremberg Laws on Citizenship and Race: September 15, 1935

Appendix 3a.
The Reich Citizenship Law of September 15, 1935

THE REICHSTAG HAS ADOPTED by unanimous vote the following law which is herewith promulgated.

ARTICLE 1.

(1)   A subject of the state is one who belongs to the protective union of the German Reich, and who, therefore, has specific obligations to the Reich.

(2)   The status of subject is to be acquired in accordance with the provisions of the Reich and the state Citizenship Law.

ARTICLE 2.

(1)   A citizen of the Reich may be only one who is of German or kindred blood, and who, through his behavior, shows that he is both desirous and personally fit to serve loyally the German people and the Reich.

(2)   The right to citizenship is obtained by the grant of Reich citizenship papers.

(3)   Only the citizen of the Reich may enjoy full political rights in consonance with the provisions of the laws.

ARTICLE 3.

The Reich Minister of the Interior, in conjunction with the Deputy to the *Fuehrer*, will issue the required legal and administrative decrees for the implementation and amplification of this law.

Appendix 3b.
Promulgated: September 16, 1935. *In force*: September 30, 1935.

First Supplementary Decree of November 14, 1935

On the basis of Article III of the Reich Citizenship Law of September 15, 1935, the following is hereby decreed:

ARTICLE 1.

(1)   Until further provisions concerning citizenship papers, all subjects of German or kindred blood who possessed the right to vote in the *Reichstag* elections when the Citizenship Law came into effect, shall, for the present, possess the rights of Reich citizens. The same shall be true of those upon whom the Reich Minister of the Interior, in conjunction with the Deputy to the *Fuehrer* shall confer citizenship.

(2)   The Reich Minister of the Interior, in conjunction with the Deputy to the *Fuehrer*, may revoke citizenship.

ARTICLE 2.

(1)   The provisions of Article I shall apply also to subjects who are of mixed Jewish blood.

(2)   An individual of mixed Jewish blood is one who is descended from one or two grandparents who, racially, were full Jews, insofar that he is not a Jew according to Section 2 of

ARTICLE 3.

Full-blooded Jewish grandparents are those who belonged to the Jewish religious community.

ARTICLE 4.

Only citizens of the Reich, as bearers of full political rights, can exercise the right of voting in political matters, and have the right to hold public office. The Reich Minister of the Interior, or any agency he empowers, can make exceptions during the transition period on the matter of holding public office. The measures do not apply to matters concerning religious organizations.

ARTICLE 5.

(1)   A Jew cannot be a citizen of the Reich. He cannot exercise the right to vote; he cannot hold public office.

(2)   Jewish officials will be retired as of December 31, 1935. In the event that such officials served at the front in the World War either for Germany or her allies, they shall receive as pension, until they reach the age limit, the full salary last received, on the basis of which their pension would have been computed. They shall not, however, be promoted according to their seniority in rank. When they reach the age limit, their pension will be computed again, according to the salary last received on which their pension was to be calculated.

(3)   These provisions do not concern the affairs of religious organizations.

(4)   The conditions regarding service of teachers in public Jewish schools remains unchanged until the promulgation of new laws on the Jewish school system.

ARTICLE 5

(1)   A Jew is an individual who is descended from at least three grandparents who were, racially, full Jews…

(2)   A Jew is also an individual who is descended from two full-Jewish grandparents if:

(a) he was a member of the Jewish religious community when this law was issued, or joined the community later;

(b) when the law was issued, he was married to a person who was a Jew, or was subsequently married to a Jew;

(c) he is the issue from a marriage with a Jew, in the sense of Section I, which was contracted after the coming into effect of the Law for the Protection of German Blood and Honor of September 15, 1935;

(d) he is the issue of an extramarital relationship with a Jew, in the sense of Section I, and was born out of wedlock after July 31, 1936.

ARTICLE 6.

(1)   Insofar as there are, in the laws of the Reich or in the decrees of the National Socialist German Workers' Party and its affiliates, certain requirements for the purity of German blood which extend beyond Article 5, the same remain untouched…

ARTICLE 7.

The *Fuehrer* and Chancellor of the Reich is empowered to release anyone from the provisions of these administrative decrees.

Appendix 3c.

Law for the Protection of German Blood and German Honour
September 15, 1935

Thoroughly convinced by the knowledge that the purity of German blood is essential for the further existence of the German people and animated by the inflexible will to safe-guard the German nation for the entire future, the Reichstag has resolved upon the following law unanimously, which is promulgated herewith:

SECTION 1

1.   Marriages between Jews and nationals of German or kindred blood are forbidden. Marriages concluded in defiance of this law are void, even if, for the purpose of evading this law, they are concluded abroad.

2.   Proceedings for annulment may be initiated only by the Public Prosecutor.

SECTION 2

Relation outside marriage between Jews and nationals for German or kindred blood are forbidden.

SECTION 3

Jews will not be permitted to employ female nationals of German or kindred blood in their households.

SECTION 4

1.   Jews are forbidden to hoist the Reich and national flag and to present the colors of the Reich.

2.   On the other hand they are permitted to present the Jewish colors. The exercise of this authority is protected by the State.

SECTION 5

1.   A person who acts contrary to the prohibition of section 1 will be punished with hard labour.

2.   A person who acts contrary to the prohibition of section 2 will be punished with imprisonment or with hard labour.

3.   A person who acts contrary to the provisions of section 3 or 4 will be punished with imprisonment up to a year and with a fine or with one of these penalties.

SECTION 6

The Reich Minister of the Interior in agreement with the Deputy of the *Fuehrer* will issue the legal and administrative regulations which are required fro the implementation and supplementation of this law.

SECTION 7

The law will become effective on the day after the promulgation, section 3 however only on 1 January, 1936.

Nuremberg, the 15th day of September 1935 at the Reich Party Rally of Freedom.

The Fuehrer and Reich Chancellor
Adolph Hitler

The Reich Minister of the Interior
Frick

The Reich Minister of Justice
Dr. Goertner

The Deputy of the Fuehrer
R. Hess

Appendix 4.

Law for the Protection of Hereditary Health: The Attempt to Improve the German Aryan Breed, July 14, 1933

Article I.

(1.)   Anyone who suffers from an inheritable disease may be surgically sterilized if, in the judgement of medical science, it could be expected that his decendants will suffer from serious inherited mental or physical defects.

(2.)   Anyone who suffers from one of the following is to be regarded as inheritably diseased within the meaning of this law:

   1.   congenital feeble-mindedness

   2.   schizophrenia

   3.   manic-depression

   4.   congenital epilepsy

   5.   inheritable St. Vitus dance (Huntington's chorea)

   6.   hereditary blindness

   7.   hereditary deafness

   8.   serious inheritable malformations

(3.)   In addition, anyone suffering from chronic alcoholism may also be sterilized.

Article II.

(1.)   Anyone who requests sterilization is entitled to it. If he be incapacitated or under a guardian because of low state of mental health or not yet 18 years of age, his legal guardian is empowered to make the request. In other cases of limited capacity the request must receive the approval of the legal representative. If a person be of age and has a nurse, the latter's consent is required.

(2.)   The request must be accompanied by a certificate from a citizen who is accredited by the German Reich stating that the person to be sterilized has been informed about the nature and consequence of sterilization.

(3.)   The request for sterilization can be recalled.

Article III.

Sterilization may also be recommended by:

(1.)   the official physician

(2.)   the official in charge of a hospital, sanitarium, or prison.

Article IV.

The request for sterilization must be presented in writing to, or placed in writing by the office of the Health Inheritance Court. The statement concerning the request must be certified by a medical document or authenticated in some other way. The business office of the court must notify the official physician.

Article VII.

The proceedings of the Health Inheritance Court are secret.

Article X.

The Supreme Health Insurance Court retains final jurisdiction.

Appendix 5.

Muir V. Alberta Madame Justice Joanne Viet d (see Veit, 1996). Indexed as Muir v. Alberta

Muir v. The Queen in right of Alberta

132 D.L.R.(4th) 695 Court File No. 8903 20759 Edmonton

Alberta Court of Queen's Bench, Veit J., January 25, 1996

Action for damages in respect of wrongful sterilization and wrongful confinement.

P.J. Faulds and S.M. Anderson, for plaintiff. D.H. Lewis, W.C. Olthuis, R.F. Taylor and L. Neudorf, for defendant.

Veit J.:
Summary

[1]   In 1959, the province wrongfully surgically sterilized Ms Muir and now acknowledges its obligation to pay damages to her. However, the province leaves to the court the determination of how much the province should pay. The sterilization was irreversible; the testimony of Ms Muir is supported by independent evidence and establishes that the physical and emotional damage inflicted by the operation was catastrophic for Ms Muir. This injury has haunted Ms Muir from the time she first learned what had been done, through to the time when she fully realized the implications of the surgery. Her suffering continues even today and will continue far into the future. The court orders the province to pay her the maximum amount of damages for pain and suffering resulting from the sterilization allowed by the law: $250,280 as of September, 1995, adjusted to the date of issue of these reasons.

[2]   The damage inflicted by the sterilization was aggravated by the associated and wrongful stigmatization of Ms Muir as a moron, a high-grade mental defective. This stigma has humiliated Ms Muir every day of her life, in her relations with her family and friends and with her employers and has marked her since she was admitted to the Provincial Training School for Mental Defectives on July 12, 1955, at the age of 10. Because of this humiliating categorization and treatment, the province will pay her an additional $125,000 as aggravated damages.

[3]   The circumstances of Ms Muir's sterilization were so high-handed and so contemptuous of the statutory authority to effect sterilization, and were undertaken in an atmosphere that so little respected Ms Muir's human dignity that the community's, and the court's sense of decency is offended. Were there no other relevant factors, the court would order the province to pay punitive damages to Ms Muir, not by way of compensation to her for the harm inflicted on her, but rather as punishment to the province, of an additional $250,000. However, in this case, there are two reasons why punitive damages are not imposed. First, a large award has been made for aggravated damages; by itself, this award will be costly to the defendant. Second, the province voluntarily gave up what would have been a complete defence to Ms Muir's action: Ms Muir did not start her action soon enough. Had the province used this defence—called a limitations of action defence—that would have put an end to Ms Muir's claim. The effect of choosing not to use this defence is more than equivalent to an apology—it constitutes a real attempt to make things right. As a matter of policy, government apologies and initiatives of this sort to redress historical wrongs should be encouraged; punishing governments for their historical behaviour would have the opposite effect.

[4]   Ms Muir was admitted to the defendant's Provincial Training School for Mental Defectives on July 12, 1955, at the age of 10. She left the school, without having been discharged, and against the advice of the school's administration, when she was nearly 21 years old, in March, 1965. The court finds that Ms Muir was improperly detained during this decade. The particular type of confinement of which Ms Muir was a victim resulted in many travesties to her young person: loss of liberty, loss of reputation, humiliation and disgrace; pain and suffering, loss of enjoyment of life, loss of normal developmental experiences, loss of civil rights, loss of contact with family and friends, subjection to institutional discipline. The court awards her an additional $250,000 for the damages connected with the detention, plus prejudgment interest from 1965 to the issuance of these reasons.

[5]   Ms Muir claims additional aggravated damages of $125,000 relating to the detention because of the failure of the government's agents to adhere to the statutory requirements concerning admission, the use of school trainees, including Ms Muir, as human guinea pigs for drug research, the connection between the sterilization and the detention, and other abuse conduct. These elements of aggravation have already been taken into account in awarding aggravated damages for the sterilization. No award is made for aggravated damages in relation to the confinement because this would be a duplication of the earlier award.

[6]   Ms Muir also claims substantial damages because, during the time she was detained at the Provincial Training School, the government failed to provide her with the education and training that she might otherwise have achieved. While Ms Muir did have the ability to reach more than a grade 5 education, she has failed to prove that she has been, and will be, in a worse employment position as a result of the intervention of the province than she would have been had she remained out of the institution. As such, no award is made under this heading.

Summary of award

(Because certain interest items have not yet been calculated, this summary is only an approximation of the total award.)

Wrongful sterilization
Pain and suffering $250,280
Aggravated damages $125,000
Punitive damages $ 0
Wrongful confinement Pain and suffering $250,000
Interest thereon $115,500
Aggravated damages $0
Past and future loss of income $0
Total $740,780

Index

Appendix "A" Professor Robertson's report on the eugenics background of the Sexual Sterilization Act in Alberta 744

1. Background

(a) Facts

[7]   Ms Muir was born in Calgary on July 15, 1944. Her mother, to whom I will refer in these reasons as Ms Scorah, was in the 36th week of her pregnancy.

[8]   Ms Scorah was born in Poland and was a Roman Catholic. She was 14 when she married for the first time. She had married for a second time in 1942; her husband was one E.B.D. When Ms Muir was born, Ms Scorah was 20 years old. She already had given birth to three other children—one of whom had died. She was to have one other child, approximately two years after Ms Muir was born.

[9]   Ms Scorah's husband was away at war when Ms Muir was born. At the time, Ms Scorah was living with Mr. H.G. Scorah. In the application to have Ms Muir admitted to the Provincial Training School for Mental Defectives in 1953, Mr. Scorah is described as Ms Muir's father. He stated that he was 19 years old when Ms Muir was born. Whether or not Mr. Scorah was Ms Muir's biological father, he was certainly her psychological father—he was the only father she ever knew. In November, 1964, when her husband died, Ms Scorah married Mr. Scorah. Mr. and Ms Scorah subsequently separated. Ms Scorah was alive when these proceedings were commenced, but she died before the trial. Mr. Scorah also died before the trial.

[10]   Ms Scorah took Ms Muir to a provincial guidance clinic in October, 1951. Ms Muir was 7 years old at the time. Ms Scorah apparently gave Leilani's birth date as June 16, 1943. This is clearly wrong; it contradicts the evidence of the province's formal registration of birth: Document A001. Ms Scorah apparently gave Leilani's prematurity as seven months; this is also clearly wrong, as it contradicts the evidence of the province's formal registration of birth. Ms Scorah informed the guidance clinic that she had been a heavy drinker until 1949; by implication, this meant that she had been a heavy drinker during her pregnancy for Leilani. The staff of the guidance clinic at that time consisted of a family physician, a psychologist, a social worker, and a person referred to on the form as a psychiatrist; the evidence establishes that the person described as a psychiatrist, Dr. L.J. le Vann, although a medical doctor, never received full accreditation as a psychiatrist in England or in Canada.

[11]   The family had been referred to the guidance clinic because Leilani "steals 3 or 4 lunches per day from school children". Although the school attended by Ms Muir, and name of Ms Muir's grade 1 teacher, were known to the guidance clinic, there is no information about any intellectual delays suffered by Ms Muir. Indeed, nothing is reported about unusual conduct by Ms Muir, except her long-standing habit of stealing food.

[17]   No psychometric testing of Ms Muir was done in 1953.

[20]   On July 12, 1955, Ms Muir was admitted to the Provincial Training School for Mental Defectives at Red Deer. The only application form relating to her admission was the 1953 form; it was not updated. The form anticipates that a physician was to witness the signature of the person giving information, thereby confirming the information set out in the application; no physician signed the form. The form anticipates that psychometric examination of the person to be admitted has been undertaken; no testing of Ms Muir had been done.

[22] Ms Scorah, using Mr. Scorah's name, signed the following form on the day that Ms Muir was admitted to the school: "I am agreeable that sterilization be performed on my child Lellani Marie Scorah if this is deemed advisable by the Provincial Eugenics Board."

[23] The evidence establishes that Ms Muir would not have been admitted to the school if one of her parents had not signed this form. The ward admission record of Ms Muir's admission states:

Mental condition: Seems intelligent—moron

Deformities or abnormalities: 3rd finger on both hands deformed

Scars and their location: A number of very small scars on body, two scars on right knee, two scars on left knee, scar under chin

Condition of clothing: rather shabby

[24] On December 15, 1955, Dr. le Vann wrote to the psychologist at the Provincial Guidance Clinic in Calgary to ask if a psychometric was ever done on Ms Muir. On December 20, 1955, that psychologist replied:

The above named child was referred to the Provincial Guidance Clinic on November 5, 1953. An appointment was made for November 23, 1953 but the appointment was not kept.

On November 27, 1953 (the psychiatrist attached to Holy Cross Hospital) phoned to inquire about the child as the parents had told him they had been to the Clinic. Dr. Hanley, (the psychiatrist) had seen the child in consultation at the Holy Cross Hospital. He was not sure of the diagnosis but thought that there was an emotional involvement rather than a primary mental deficiency. The family had taken Marie to the Red Deer Guidance Clinic but they were not seen as an appointment had not been made.

On December 19, 1955 upon inquiring, Dr. Hanley's office informed us that there had been no further contact with this girl.

To our knowledge there has never been a psychometric given this child.

(Emphasis added.)

[25] Despite receiving this information from the Calgary Guidance Clinic some six months after Ms Muir had been admitted to the Provincial Training School for Mental Defectives (P.T.S.), Dr. le Vann did not arrange for any follow-up to Dr. Hanley's report; there was no psychometric testing of Ms Muir; there was no investigation into the possible causes of emotional involvement; there was no other action taken.

[27] In June, 1956, an administrator at the school wrote to Mr. and Ms Scorah as follows:

I am enclosing a letter from your daughter Lellani who is a trainee at this School. It has been such a long time since Lellani heard from you that she has become most anxious and has not been able to do her best work at the School. She is beginning to feel you have forgotten her and that you won't be coming to see her. As I am sure this is not the case would you please advise the Medical Superintendent when you will be coming to visit Lellani and when you will be having her home for holidays this summer.

[28]   Contact between Mr. and Ms Scorah and Ms Muir improved after this communication. Indeed, while she was a "trainee" at the Provincial Training School, Ms Muir left the school from time to time to be with her family. These visits varied in length—from a weekend to a stay of several months' duration. In November, 1956, Ms Scorah wrote to Dr. le Vann to explain why Lellani had not yet returned to the Provincial Training School. That letter contained the following comments:

Now [Lellani] has a black eye. I was sawing wood with Harley when I threw the wood to the side of me and it struck her square in the face. She does not seems to understand to stay out of the way. Heaven only knows when she really will. I pray soon.

[29]   On November 15, 1957, Ms Muir was finally given psychometric testing. She had begun to menstruate shortly before the test was administered. The test behaviour portion of the psychological examination report indicates: "Lellani is a pretty, but immature looking child, who sucked her thumb constantly throughout testing." The general findings were: verbal I.Q. 70 (borderline), performance I.Q. 64 (defective); full scale I.Q. 64 (defective). The individual scores on the tests are not recorded. The following comment accompanied these results:

The Full Scale I.Q. of 64 places Lellani in the Defective

Category. This level is considered accurate. Her top level of function would be only slightly higher.

The examination report concludes with this paragraph:

Analysis: Verbal abilities are slightly higher than those requiring visual motor co-ordination. There is comparatively little scatter on verbal scale. Her thinking is primarily concrete, although there is sporadic use of functional concepts. Her memory is fairly good; her judgment tends to be poor. She is quite observant: her score on this subtest being within the average range. Social anticipations are weak. Visual motor skills are average for her level of ability.

[30]   A clinical record, also called a progress diary, was kept of Ms Muir's experiences at the school. Although there are many reference to her laziness and impudence, there are also remarks of the following type.

January 1956 (first note after admittance in July 1955)
Lellani is doing very well at school

January 1957
Lellani has completed work for Level II in reading and number work and because of her reading ability to get new words, she is reading with others in Level III in "Friends and Neighbours". Her number work is also up to Level III standard.

[31]   In November, 1957, Ms Muir's case was brought to the attention of the Eugenics Board. The diagnosis made by Dr. le Vann was "Mental defective-moron". Under the heading "Personality, Social, Sex" there is the following entry:

"Lellani has shown a definite interest in the opposite sex."

Under the heading "Present condition", the report states, in part:

Lellani is young and needs considerably more training in self- control, good work habits and personal care habits before it is possible to consider discharge for her, and even then she will most likely need to be placed in an environment where she will receive strict supervision.

(Emphasis added.) Under the heading "Reason for sterilization", this is the complete entry: "Danger of the transmission to the progeny of Mental Deficiency or Disability, also incapable of Intelligent parenthood."

[32]   The Eugenics Board of Alberta, approved the sexual sterilization of Ms Muir on November 22, 1957. She was "passed clear" for a salpingectomy to be performed by one of a list of named surgeons; the term "passed clear" was used by the Eugenics Board to mean that no additional steps had to be performed—obtaining consents or further psychometric testing—before the actual sterilization could be done.

[33]   The Provincial Training School for Mental Defectives was not proposing to discharge Ms Muir in 1957 (when the psychometric testing preparatory to sterilization was done and the approval of the Eugenics Board for the sterilization was given) or in 1959 (when the sterilization was actually performed). Indeed, when Ms Muir left the school in 1965, it was against the advice of the medical staff.

[34]   The clinical record or progress diary entries for 1958 and 1959 are as follows:

January 1958
If she is in the mood, Lellani is a very good little worker, but she usually requires a good deal of supervision to get there to accomplish anything. Lellani works well and is making good progress in Level IV.

January 1959
Lellani is alert and is making good progress in Level V, but her working habits are rather untidy. She is usually well behaved in class.

[35]   On January 18, 1959, the government sexually sterilized Ms Muir; a bilateral salpingectomy was performed by one of a list of named surgeons; a "routine appendectomy" was performed at the same time; Dr. le Vann assisted in the surgery. A pathology report was done on Ms Muir's right and left Fallopian tubes. The entire length of both her Fallopian tubes were removed; the extent of the operation resulted in Ms Muir's sterilization being irreversible. Her record contains no mention why both tubes were removed in entirety, instead of only a small section as was done in other cases. At the same time, an appendectomy was performed.

[42]   As noted earlier, Dr. le Vann, who was the director of the Provincial Training School at the time in question was a medical doctor, but not a psychiatrist. He died before the action came on for trial. In 1950, he wrote an article for the American Journal of Mental Deficiency in which he made the following comments:

Indeed the picture of comparison between the normal child and the idiot might almost be a comparison between two separate species. On the one hand, the graceful, intelligently curious, active young homo sapiens, and on the other the gross, retarded, animalistic, early primate type individual. It is on this clinical basis that we find it difficult to associate schizophrenia as a regressive disease of the mind, if we may postulate a schizophrenic state in these idiot types. It is rather that the mind has acquired an archaic form of thinking, which in the adult is admixed with his cultural experiences and in the idiot shows itself uncomplicated and primitive with little distortion. We feel that this archaic type of thought is more extensive than has thus far been believed to be the case.

[43]   In 1959, Dr. le Vann wrote an article on the use of trifluoperazine as a tranquillizing agent in mentally defective children. In it, he makes the following comments:

Although substantial numbers of children have responded adequately to chlorpromzine, perphenazine, promazine, reserpine, or other ataractic drugs, there remain significant numbers who have not. Because of this, we continue to screen new compounds for possible use at the training school: a preliminary report, describing the effects of trifluoperazine in 33 mentally defective children exhibiting behavioral disorders, has already appeared. The present report describes the results obtained in 17 patients from the original study and an additional 25 children with behavioral and/ or convulsant disorders.

[44]   Mr. Curr, a trial witness, who worked at the P.T.S., describes Dr. le Vann as a complex person. Mr. Curr was surprised to hear the description Dr. le Vann had made of the lower grade mental defectives in the 1950 article. Mr. Curr gave examples of what he considered to be Dr. le Vann's caring attitude for inmates at the P.T.S., even if inmates were of the idiot classification.

Ms Muir currently works part-time in a Bay cafeteria in Victoria; she is a member of a union and her hourly wage is approximately $10.68 per hour. Because of the type of work she does in this cafeteria, she would not be expected to earn tips. Ms Muir lives independently, attends church occasionally, gardens, plays bingo, and enjoys needlework and reading.

[50]   In the first 15 years following her departure from the P.T.S., Ms Muir underwent many surgical and investigative procedures in order to determine what had been done to her and if it could be reversed:

– From 1971 to 1977, Dr. Faulkner was Ms Muir's family physician. In September, 1975, Dr. Faulkner referred Ms Muir to a psychiatrist, Dr. E.M. McTavish, who wrote the following after his meeting with Ms Muir:

The problems [Ms Muir] complains of and wishes help for are pretty unhelpable. She complains that she has difficulty in accepting the fact that due to sterilization in her early teens she is unable to have children. I pointed out to her that this was a fact and had to be accepted. Her unhappiness in regard to it is understandable and in no sense pathological ... The damage done to her self image and to her reproductive capacity cannot be undone.

(b) Law

(i)   Sexual sterilization legislation

[51]   Section 4(1) of the Sexual Sterilization Act, R.S.A. 1955, c. 311, empowered a medical superintendent of a mental hospital to "cause a patient of a mental hospital whom it is proposed to discharge therefrom, to be examined by or in the presence of the Board" with a view to sterilization (emphasis added).

[52]   Section 6 of the Sexual Sterilization Act established two grounds for sterilization, namely that procreation by the person under consideration:

6(1)

(a)   would result in the transmission of any mental disability or deficiency to his progeny, or

(b) involves the risk of mental injury either to such person or his progeny,

(Emphasis added.)

> (ii)   Legislation for the confinement of mental defectives

[54]   Section 5(1) of the Mental Defectives Act, R.S.A. 1955, c. 199, under the heading "Procedure Respecting Admission", provided that:

> 5(1) A person who desires to have a mentally defective person who is under his charge or control placed in an institution established for the purpose under this Act shall make application to the Superintendent, and if after due investigation and upon receipt of the prescribed forms properly completed the application is approved by the Superintendent, the mentally defective person may be admitted by the Superintendent to the institution.

> (iii)   Overview of the law of damages

[55]   This is a tort action; it must be distinguished, for example, from an action in contract. Before damages can be awarded, the court must find that a wrong has been done. The overriding objective in awarding damages in such a lawsuit is to compensate the injured person—not to punish the wrongdoer. The objective of the court is to give the plaintiff financial compensation for the damage, loss or injury that she has suffered. A court can compensate for financial losses suffered, such as the loss of income or expenses of medical treatment, or expenses to repair a car. A court can also compensate for other types of losses such as physical pain and injury to feelings. The calculation of the latter kind of damage is difficult. Money is awarded not as direct compensation for what has been lost—but as an attempt to provide what money can do—make the real loss somewhat easier to bear. Sometimes, the wrongful action has, nevertheless, had some beneficial effects on the victim; credit must be given to the wrongdoer for any savings, for example, that the victim has achieved despite the wrongful action of the defendant.

[56]   The court has the power to award damages under three headings: pain and suffering, aggravated damages and punitive damages.

(c)   Procedure

[62]   Because the events on which this lawsuit depends happened such a long time ago, the parties entered into an agreement about the use of documents at trial:

[63]   This agreement between the parties reflects law and common sense: the documents were prepared contemporaneously with the events, well before the possibility of any legal action was considered. The documents are usually the best record of what transpired. In a few circumstances, the documents are suspect; those situations will be described more fully in the reasons.

[64]   Although the defendant has tried to put all relevant documents before the court, it has been established that some of the Provincial Training School documents, stored in the sub-basement of the Michener Centre, were destroyed in a flood.

2. Witnesses

[65] The court makes the following assessments of the major witnesses.

(a) Ms L. Muir

[66] Ms Muir is not a reliable witness about the events of her childhood. This is demonstrated, among other evidence, by:

– the school attendance record which shows that, at least during one period of time during her early childhood, Ms Muir attended school regularly, rather than sporadically as she recalls;

– the evidence that suggests that she was at the Midnapore Convent for a much shorter period than she now recalls.

[67] More importantly, Ms Muir is not a reliable witness about events that occurred not long before she left the Provincial Training School. This is mainly demonstrated by the characterization as "bogus", by Ms Muir of letters that she obviously wrote. The evidence of the handwriting expert Peace, whose evidence I accept, concludes that certain letters were written by Ms Muir, even though Ms Muir does not now recall having written them. He also establishes that it was Ms Scorah, not Mr. Scorah, who filled out the application form for the P.T.S. and who wrote to Dr. le Vann.

[68] In addition, Ms Muir's recollection of her employment since she left the Provincial Training School and of her application for Canada Pension Plan benefits is not accurate.

[69] Therefore, Ms Muir's evidence about events in her childhood, and beyond, will usually only be relied on if there is independent evidence that substantially supports her testimony.

[70] There is independent evidence to support the following conclusions:

– Ms Muir had an abnormal number of scratches when she was admitted to the institution;

– Ms Muir had a very bad relationship with her mother;

– Ms Muir was denied food when she was with her family;

– Ms Muir was sterilized;

– Ms Muir's appendix was removed;

– while at P.T.S., Ms Muir was disciplined in a harsh and inappropriate way;

– while at P.T.S., Ms Muir was essentially confined;

– while at P.T.S., Ms Muir was dealt with as if she were a mental defective;

– Ms Muir was at no greater risk of having mentally defective children than anyone else in society;

– nothing in the evidence suggests that Ms Muir was incapable of intelligent parenthood;

[94] In addition to the documentary support for his conclusions, Professor Robertson's assessment of the operations of the board is largely corroborated by the evidence of Dr. M. Thompson, a former board member and geneticist. Her evidence establishes

that the powers of the board were used not in accordance with either scientific principles or legislative standards, but in support of social policy about who should be allowed to have children in Alberta. Her evidence also establishes that in most requests for sterilization that came before the board, the inmate would never be discharged, or it would be a very long time in the future before any discharge were contemplated.

[95] Professor Robertson's evidence establishes that, routinely from the 1930s on, the board frequently dealt with cases at the rate of 10 minutes per case or less. The members of the board had no information on the cases in advance of their meetings. This speed of dealing with irreversible decisions establishes that the board could not have taken the time to examine the cases in any meaningful way; it is obvious that the board relied almost entirely on the recommendation of the executive director of the institution, Dr. le Vann.

[96] Professor Robertson's evidence about the operations of the board is also largely confirmed and corroborated by the 1969 Blair Commission on Mental Health in Alberta. For example, Professor Robertson concluded that there were systemic biases in the operation of the board so that, for example, females more than males, and females from Eastern Europe and Catholics and later female natives were more likely to be sterilized. This conclusion is supported by the Blair Commission's conclusion:

Further, the sterilization of individuals with depressed I.Q. ratings attributable to emotional or delinquency or sub-cultural (e.g. Metis) factors which are capable of some degree of amelioration, is open to debate.

(Emphasis added.)

[97] His conclusion is also supported by other materials referred to in his opinion. It is obvious that much of the early eugenics movement in Canada was based on a concern by those of British stock about the potential weakening of the race by immigrants. Many early Canadian socialists, such as J.S. Woodsworth, author of Strangers within our Gates and, when he moved to Manitoba, founder of the C.C.F.—which subsequently became the N.D.P.—were much in favour of maintaining racial purity in Canada by eugenic interference with the reproduction of East Europeans. Tommy Douglas originally espoused eugenic philosophy; probably frightened by what he saw in Germany in 1936, he later turned away from eugenics. In 1944, to his great credit, as Saskatchewan's Minister of Health, he firmly rejected two reports recommending the sterilization of the feeble-minded. In Alberta also, there was great concern in some quarters about the potential negative effects of immigration; this is one of the grounds on which three of the "Famous Five"—Emily Murphy, Ms O.O. Edwards, and Ms L.C. McKinney—approved the sexual sterilization legislation which was, sadly, to have negative effects on so many women.

[98 The immigration concern which resulted in a systemic bias against those men and women from "sub-cultural" backgrounds is a factor in this case: Ms Scorah was born in Poland and was Roman Catholic.

[99] Mr. Curr's evidence also supports Professor Robertson's opinions. He testified that one of the things that the caregivers were told when a child was admitted was what religion the child was. Also, on the issue of the difference in the treatment of males and females, Mr. Curr testified that at Linden House—the model school on the

P.T.S. grounds where the best of the government's resources were concentrated, boys outnumbered girls 5 to 1.

[100] Professor Robertson's report also establishes that while there was considerable support in Alberta in 1928 for government-sponsored sexual sterilization, even then support was not unanimous. In March, 1928, for example, a Liberal politician asked what would happen if anyone suffered physical impairment as a result of a sterilization and if the board would be liable for damages or prosecution as a result of its decisions.

[112] [Dr. Thompson's] evidence conclusively establishes that the Eugenics Board did not meet the standards imposed on it by the legislation. She acknowledges that the board could not—in Ms Muir's or in many other cases—be certain that any defect of the trainee would be passed on to the trainee's offspring. Dr. Thompson testified that the board unilaterally modified the standard passed by the Legislature of Alberta; in her opinion, the legislature had set a standard that was unreasonably tough—too high to meet. Two illustrations fairly represent Dr. Thompson's approach to the sterilization determinations.

[113] Dr. Thompson was a member of the board that approved the sterilization of a boy who had a tested IQ of 76. Persons with an IQ of 70 or more were considered to be of normal intelligence. This particular boy's level of IQ rating was achieved despite a severe hearing defect; being deaf could be assumed to have had a negative impact on the education that he would have required to have done well on the verbal IQ testing. The P.T.S. report commented that this boy had no interest in the opposite sex, but that he masturbated. The report added that he required little supervision in social hygiene. It was said that he was a poor worker. Dr. Thompson was asked why she approved the sterilization of this boy. She replied that social success is a factor to be taken into account in a sterilization decision. When the school reported that he was a poor worker, she concluded that despite all the information that he was a nice quiet boy, he was not really functioning in society. She said that she was being protective of him when she decided to have him sterilized.

[114] Dr. Thompson was asked why she approved the sterilization of a male mongol child when it had been known for decades that male mongols were unlikely to reproduce. She replied that there was nothing lost by sterilizing the male mongol; she thought everyone would agree with her approach. She thought that sterilization would "make assurance doubly sure".

[115] Dr. Thompson's approach to the issue of who should be sterilized and why the legislation could be ignored is representative of the way in which the board operated.

[121] I do not accept Dr. Thompson's evidence that any interest of the trainee in trainees of the opposite sex was not a factor that was taken into account in determining if a sterilization was to be performed; it is disingenuous of her to advance that opinion. Information about interest in the opposite sex was a component of the limited information provided to members of the board. Dr. Thompson never arranged for the removal of that information. It seems clear from her evidence that persons who were brought before her were unlikely to be discharged; one can only conclude, therefore, that the sterilization was done primarily to control sexual activity in the institution rather than for any of the purposes set out in the legislation. As early as 1932, we find the following letter, written by the commissioner of mental institutions in this province to the medical superintendent of the Brandon Medical Hospital:

With respect to mental defective girls it is important to remember that, while one may take chances with a girl released from strict supervision, she still does require supervision if there are sex propensities. It is, I think, correct to say however that the only ones we have had trouble with in this respect have shown very marked tendencies to sexual delinquency before operation, but undoubtedly supervision of a general character after the operation and discharge is advisable.

[123] From the beginning to the end of its operations, concerns about sexual tendencies of the "inmates" of the P.T.S. were at the forefront of the administrators' attentions.

[124] I do not accept Dr. Thompson's evidence concerning the discussions that she had with Dr. le Vann regarding the taking of testicular tissue from vasectomized or castrated trainees: Both she and Dr. le Vann were conducting studies of "male mongols", males with Down's syndrome. She gave Dr. le Vann detailed instructions about how to take samples of the tissue that resulted from the sterilization. In all the circumstances, this constituted encouragement to Dr. le Vann to use the trainees as medical guinea pigs. This is all the more repugnant because, from the 1940s on, Dr. Thompson and the board knew, as did all those involved in genetics, that male "mongols" are infertile: their sterilization was unnecessary.

[125] Dr. Thompson's evidence demonstrates that the operations of the board, initiated on a purported scientific rationale, degenerated into unscientific practices. The decisions of the board were not made according to the standards imposed on them by the legislation, but because the members of the board, like Dr. Thompson, thought that it was socially appropriate to control reproduction of "these people".

[126] I do not accept Dr. Thompson's evidence that care was taken by the board in deciding the fate of each individual trainee brought before it. Irreversible decisions were obviously made on the flimsiest of evidence—without any true scientific investigation of the eugenics situation of each trainee. Dr. Thompson testified that most of the people who came before the board could not read, write or count and could not dress or feed themselves. The board's and the school's own records amply refute such assertions. Minimal investigation would have disclosed the abilities of the trainees who were presented for sterilization.

3. Damages for sterilization

[147] The evidence establishes that the government acted in a high-handed way when it ignored its own legislation and sterilized her before she was ready to be discharged. If the government had followed its own legislation, Ms Muir would never have been sterilized because she was never ready for discharge.

[148] Moreover, the evidence establishes that the conduct of the government in labelling Ms Muir a mental defective was high-handed and oppressive. The evidence proves beyond a doubt that the government did not follow its own legislation, practices and procedures when it labelled Ms Muir a moron. It ignored advice from an expert that Ms Muir's problems were emotional, not mental; it ignored the services of social workers and psychologists who might have assisted in obtaining information about Ms Muir's background; it failed to require compliance with the minimum safeguards which it had established—signature by a physician attesting to the validity of admission information—and psychometric testing. Before admitting her to an institution where she would be sterilized and stigmatized, the government

acknowledged that it had obtained only cursory information. This was not an emergency situation; there were alternatives that were available including foster homes and group homes.

– because the government's own standards for sterilization were ignored in Ms Muir's case, the conduct of the government was more than negligent, it was intentional. The sterilization became an assault and battery;

– the board not only authorized sexual sterilizations, and tolerated routine but medically unnecessary appendectomies, but also routinely authorized non-medically necessary processes such as biopsies of testicular tissue. In some cases, the board directed a vasectomy only, but partial castration by unilateral orchidectomy was carried out. In some cases, the board authorized the hysterectomy or oophorectomy (removal of the ovaries) in order to eliminate menstruation in females; according to the language of one typical case, the female trainees were "difficult to handle and to keep clean during menstrual periods". These operations were also ordered where female trainees masturbated or had lesbian tendencies.

[153] The defendant's actions were unlawful, offensive and outrageous. Punitive damages in the amount of $250,000 suggested by Ms Muir would certainly have been ordered had it not been for the fact that the government allowed Ms Muir to bring this action. It could have put an end to her claim; her claim was made too late, and the government could have used this delay as a complete answer to all of Ms Muir's claims. This deliberate abandonment of a complete defence is in the nature of an apology. Indeed, it is more than an apology: it is an amendment—a real effort to make things right. As a matter of public policy, this and other governments should be encouraged to recognize historical wrongs and to make fair amends for them. They should not be punished for doing so.

[154] I note also that the government recognized, in 1972, when it abolished the Sexual Sterilization Act that the former policy of government in this area was wrong.

[167] Ms Muir lived at the residential school for almost a decade. Her evidence on the conditions in which she lived is largely corroborated by Mr. Curr. The main incidents of this detention are:

– loss of privacy: as merely one example of the intrusive nature of the detention, Ms Muir's menstrual cycles were the subject of extensive record-keeping. Also, Ms Muir's correspondence from the school, and the correspondence to her, was monitored and regulated by the institution;

– loss of liberty: as merely one example of the regulation of conduct while she was detained, is the evidence that she had to have permission from the school authorities to go to different parts of the institution, such as helping in the laundry room or to help those inmates who were bedridden. Ms Muir testified that she was not allowed to leave the school premises (except for authorized home visits) until, at age 18 or so, she was sent out by the school as daily household labour in residences chosen by the school. Mr Curr's evidence on this point is especially telling because he is obviously very well disposed to Dr. le Vann; none the less, Mr. Curr gave evidence of what was really happening at the Provincial Training School on the issue of detention rather than what the reports were touting as an "open" atmosphere. Moreover, the school determined which visitors Ms Muir could have; when a Mrs. Hepner, for example, offered to take Ms Muir during a Christmas vacation, the school would not allow the visit to take place;

– imposition of institutional discipline: as merely one example of the extreme form of discipline imposed by the institution is the fact that, for punishment, Ms Muir was made to diaper adult "inmates" who had lost control of their bowel functions, and she was made to eat mush with a spoon. She was sent to wards with strait-jacketed inmates where she scrubbed floors, did other similar work, slept in a small cement room, with a rubber mattress and ate out of a tin bowl;

– administration of drugs to control behaviour: many anti-psychotic drugs were administered to Ms Muir despite the fact that she was not psychotic. Indeed, it appears from his publications in professional journals that Dr. le Vann used Ms Muir and others as a means of testing the success of different drug treatments.

Thus, the evidence clearly shows that the government is liable for Ms Muir's confinement.

Appendix 6

E. (Mrs.) *v.* Eve, [1986] 2 S.C.R. 388

Eve, by her Guardian *ad litem*, Milton B. Fitzpatrick, Official Trustee
Appellant

v.

Mrs. E. *Respondent*

and

Canadian Mental Health Association, Consumer Advisory Committee of the Canadian Association for the Mentally Retarded, The Public Trustee of Manitoba and Attorney General of Canada *Interveners*

INDEXED AS: E.(MRS.) *v.* EVE

File No.: 16654.

1985: June 4, 5; 1986: October 23.

Present: Dickson C.J. and Beetz, Estey, McIntyre, Chouinard, Lamer, Wilson, Le Dain and La Forest JJ. on appeal from the court of appeal for prince edward island

Courts—Jurisdiction—Parens patriae—Scope of doctrine and discretion required for its exercise—Whether or not encompassing consent for non-therapeutic sterilization of mentally incompetent person—Chancery Act, R.S.P.E.I. 1951, c. 21, s. 3—Chancery Jurisdiction Transfer Act, S.P.E.I. 1974, c. 65, s. 2. Family law—Mentally incompetent person—Application made for non-therapeutic sterilization of adult daughter by parent—Whether or not court authorized to grant consent—Whether or not authority to be found in statutes—Whether or not authority flowing from parens patriae power—Mental Health Act, R.S.P.E.I. 1974, c. M-9, am. S.P.E.I. 1976, c. 65, ss. 2(n), 30A(1), (2), 30B, 30L—Hospitals Act, "Hospital Management Regulations", R.R.P.E.I., c. H-11, s. 48. Human rights—Disabled persons—Mentally incompetent person—Application made for non-therapeutic sterilization of adult daughter by parent—Whether or not court authorized to grant consent—Whether or not authority to be found in statutes—Whether or not authority flowing from parens patriae power.

"Mrs. E." applied to the Supreme Court of Prince Edward Island for permission to give consent to the sterilization of "Eve", her adult daughter who was mentally retarded and suffered from a condition making it extremely difficult to communicate with others. Mrs. E. feared Eve might innocently become pregnant and consequently force Mrs. E., who was widowed and approaching sixty, to assume responsibility for the child. The application sought: (1) a declaration that Eve was mentally incompetent pursuant to the *Mental Health Act*; (2) the appointment of Mrs. E. as committee of Eve; and (3) an authorization for Eve's undergoing a tubal ligation. The application for authorization to sterilize was denied, and an appeal to the Supreme Court of Prince Edward Island, *in banco*, was launched. An order was then made appointing the Official Trustee as Guardian *ad litem* for Eve. The appeal was allowed. The Court ordered that Eve be made a ward of the Court pursuant to the *Medical Health Act* solely to permit the exercise of the *parens patriae* jurisdiction to authorize the sterilization, and that the method of sterilization be determined by the Court following further submissions. A hysterectomy was later authorized. Eve's Guardian *ad litem* appealed.

Held: The appeal should be allowed.

The *Mental Health Act* did not advance respondent's case. This Act provides a procedure for declaring mental incompetency, at least for property owners. Its ambit is unclear and it would take much stronger language to empower a committee to authorize the sterilization of a person for non-therapeutic purposes. The *Hospital Management Regulations* were equally inapplicable. They are not aimed at defining the rights of individuals.

The *parens patriae* jurisdiction for the care of the mentally incompetent is vested in the provincial superior courts. Its exercise is founded on necessity—the need to act for the protection of those who cannot care for themselves. The jurisdiction is broad. Its scope cannot be defined. It applies to many and varied situations, and a court can act not only if injury has occurred but also if it is apprehended. The jurisdiction is carefully guarded and the courts will not assume that it has been removed by legislation. While the scope of the *parens patriae* jurisdiction is unlimited, the jurisdiction must nonetheless be exercised in accordance with its underlying principle. The discretion given under this jurisdiction is to be exercised for the benefit of the person in need of protection and not for the benefit of others. It must at all times be exercised with great caution, a caution that must increase with the seriousness of the matter. This is particularly so in cases where a court might be tempted to act because failure to act would risk imposing an obviously heavy burden on another person. Sterilization should never be authorized for non-therapeutic purposes under the *parens patriae* jurisdiction. In the absence of the affected person's consent, it can never be safely determined that it is for the benefit of that person. The grave intrusion on a person's rights and the ensuing physical damage outweigh the highly questionable advantages that can result from it. The court, therefore, lacks jurisdiction in such a case.

The court's function to protect those unable to take care of themselves must not be transformed so as to create a duty obliging the Court, at the behest of a third party, to make a choice between two alleged constitutional rights—that to procreate and that not to procreate—simply because the individual is unable to make that choice. There was no evidence to indicate that failure to perform the operation would have any detrimental effect on Eve's physical or mental health. Further, since the *parens patria* jurisdiction is confined to doing what is for the benefit and protection of the disabled person, it cannot be used for Mrs. E.'s benefit. Cases involving applications for sterilization for therapeutic reasons may give rise to the issues of the burden of proof required to warrant an order for sterilization and of the precautions judges should take with these applications in the interests of justice. Since, barring emergency situations, a surgical procedure without consent constitutes battery, the onus of proving the need for the procedure lies on those seeking to have it performed. The burden of proof, though a civil one, must be commensurate with the seriousness of the measure proposed. A court in conducting these procedures must proceed with extreme caution and the mentally incompetent person must have independent representation.

Cases Cited

Considered: *X (a minor), Re*, [1975] 1 All E.R. 697; *D (a minor), Re*, [1976] 1 All E.R. 326; *Eberhardy, Matter of*, 307 N.W.2d 881 (Wis. 1981); *Grady, In re*, 426 A.2d 467 (N.J. 1981); *Hayes' Guardianship, Matter of*, 608 P.2d 635 (Wash. 1980); referred to: *Cary v. Bertie* (1696), 2 Vern. 333, 23 E.R. 814; *Morgan v. Dillon* (Ire.) (1724), 9 Mod. R. 135, 88 E.R. 361; *Beall v. Smith* (1873), L.R. 9 Ch. 85; *Beverley's Case* (1603), 4 Co. Rep. 123 b, 76 E.R. 1118; *Wellesley v. Duke of Beaufort* (1827), 2 Russ. 1, 38 E.R. 236; *Wellesley v. Wellesley* (1828), 2 Bli. N.S. 124, 4 E.R. 1078; *Beson v. Director of Child Welfare (Nfld.)*, [1982] 2 S.C.R. 716; *Re S. v. McC (orse. S.) and M*; *W. v. W.*, [1972] A.C. 24; *P (a Minor), In re* (1981), 80 L.G.R.

301; *B (a minor), Re* (1982), 3 F.L.R. 117; *K and Public Trustee, Re* (1985), 19 D.L.R.(4th) 255; *Buck v. Bell,* 274 U.S. 200 (1927); *Tulley, Guardianship of,* App., 146 Cal.Rptr. 266 (1978); *Hudson v. Hudson,* 373 So.2d 310 (Ala. 1979); *Eberhardy's Guardianship, Matter of,* 294 N.W.2d 540 (Wis. 1980); *Stump v. Sparkman,* 435 U.S. 349 (1978); *C.D.M., Matter of,* 627 P.2d 607 (Alaska 1981); *A. W., Matter of,* 637 P.2d 366 (Colo. 1981); *Terwilliger, Matter of,* 450 A.2d 1376 (Pa. 1982); *Wentzel v. Montgomery General Hospital, Inc.,* 447 A.2d 1244 (Md. 1982); *Moe, Matter of,* 432 N.E.2d 712 (Mass. 1982); *P.S. by Harbin v. W.S.,* 452 N.E.2d 969 (Ind. 1983); *Sallmaier, Matter of,* 378 N.Y.S.2d 989 (1976); *A. D., Application of,* 394 N.Y.S.2d 139 (1977); *Penny N., In re,* 414 A.2d 541 (N.H. 1980); *Quinlan, Matter of,* 355 A.2d 647 (N.J. 1976); *J. v. C.,* [1970] A.C. 668; *Strunk v. Strunk,* 445 S.W.2d 145 (Ky. 1969).

Statutes and Regulations Cited

Act for the Relief of the Suitors of the High Court of Chancery, 15 and 16 Vict., c. 87, s. 15 (U.K.)

Act to authorize the appointment of a Master of the Rolls to the Court of Chancery, and an Assistant Judge of the Supreme Court of Judicature in this Island, 11 Vict., c. 6 (P.E.I.)

Act to provide for the care and maintenance of idiots, lunatics and persons of unsound mind, 15 Vict., c. 36 (P.E.I.)

Canadian Charter of Rights and Freedoms, ss. 7, 15(1).

Chancery Act, R.S.P.E.I. 1951, c. 21, s. 3.

Chancery Jurisdiction Transfer Act, S.P.E.I. 1974, c. 65, s. 2

Hospitals Act, R.S.P.E.I. 1974, c. H-11, s. 16.

Hospitals Act, "Hospital Management Regulations", R.R.P.E.I., c. H-11, s. 48.

Mental Health Act, R.S.P.E.I. 1974, c. M-9, as amended by S.P.E.I. 1974, c. 65, ss. 2(n), 30A(1), (2), 30B, 30L.

Sexual Sterilization Act, R.S.A. 1970, c. 341, rep. S.A. 1972, c. 87.

Sexual Sterilization Act, R.S.B.C. 1960, c. 353, s. 5(1), rep. S.B.C. 1973, c. 79.

Authors Cited

Burgdorf, Robert L., Jr., and Marcia Pearce Burgdorf. "The Wicked Witch is Almost Dead: *Buck v. Bell* and the Sterilization of Handicapped Persons," 50 *Temp. L.Q.* 995 (1977).

Canada. Law Reform Commission. *Sterilization: Implications for Mentally Retarded and Mentally Ill Persons* (Working Paper 24). Ottawa: 1979.

Fitzherbert, Sir Anthony. *The new Natura brevium of the most reverend judge, Mr. Anthony Fitz-Herbert.* London: A Strahan and W. Woodfall, law printers to the King, for J. Butterworth, 1794.

Lachance, Denise. "In re *Grady*: The Mentally Retarded Individual's Right to Choose Sterilization," 6 *Am. J.L. and Med.* 559 (1981).

McIvor, Craig L. "Equitable Jurisdiction to Order Sterilizations," 57 *Wash. L.R.* 373 (1982).

McLaughlin, Paul. *Guardianship of the Person.* Downsview, Ont.: National Institute on Mental Retardation, 1979.

Norris, Christina Norton. "Recent Developments—Courts—Scope of Authority—Sterilization of Mental Incompetents," 44 *Tenn. L. Rev.* 879 (1977).

Ross, Deborah Hardin. "Sterilization of the Developmentally Disabled: Shedding Some Myth-Conceptions," 9 *Fla. St. U.L. Rev.* 599 (1981).

Sherlock, Richard K. and Robert D. Sherlock. "Sterilizing the Retarded: Constitutional, Statutory and Policy Alternatives," 60 *N.C.L.Rev.* 943 (1982).

Theobald, Sir Henry Studdy. *The Law Relating to Lunacy*. London: Stevens and Sons Ltd., 1924.

APPEAL from a judgment of the Prince Edward Island Court of Appeal (1980), 27 Nfld. and P.E.I.R. 97, 74 A.P.R. 97, with addendum (1981), 28 Nfld. and P.E.I.R. 359, 97 A.P.R. 359, 115 D.L.R.(3d) 283, allowing an appeal from a judgment of McQuaid J. dismissing an application for consent to the sterilization of a mentally incompetent person. Appeal allowed.

Eugene P. Rossiter, for the appellant.

Walter McEwen, for the respondent.

B. A. Crane, Q.C., for the intervener the Canadian Mental Health Association.

David H. Vickers, Harvey Savage and *S. D. McCallum*, for the intervener the Consumer Advisory Committee of the Canadian Association for the Mentally Retarded.

M. Anne Bolton, for the intervener The Public Trustee of Manitoba.

E. A. Bowie, Q.C., and *B. Starkman*, for the intervener the Attorney General of Canada.

The judgment of the Court was delivered by

1.   LA FOREST J.—These proceedings began with an application by a mother for permission to consent to the sterilization of her mentally retarded daughter who also suffered from a condition that makes it extremely difficult for her to communicate with others. The application was heard by McQuaid J. of the Supreme Court of Prince Edward Island--Family Division. In the interests of privacy, he called the daughter "Eve", and her mother "Mrs. E".

Background

2.   When Eve was a child, she lived with her mother and attended various local schools. When she became twenty-one, her mother sent her to a school for retarded adults in another community. There she stayed with relatives during the week, returning to her mother's home on weekends. At this school, Eve struck up a close friendship with a male student: in fact, they talked of marriage. He too is retarded, though somewhat less so than Eve. However, the situation was identified by the school authorities who talked to the male student and brought the matter to an end.

3.   The situation naturally troubled Mrs. E. Eve was usually under her supervision or that of someone else, but this was not always the case. She was attracted and attractive to men and Mrs. E. feared she might quite possibly and innocently become pregnant. Mrs. E. was concerned about the emotional effect that a pregnancy and subsequent birth might have on her daughter. Eve, she felt, could not adequately cope with the duties of a mother and the responsibility would fall on Mrs. E. This would understandably cause her great difficulty; she is a widow and was then approaching sixty. That is why she decided Eve should be sterilized.

4.   Eve's condition is more fully described by McQuaid J. as follows:

The evidence established that Eve is 24 years of age, and suffers what is described as extreme expressive aphasia. She is unquestionably at least mildly to moderately retarded. She has some learning skills, but only to a limited level. She is described as being a pleasant and affectionate person who, physically, is an adult person, quite capable of being attracted to, as well as attractive to, the opposite sex. While she might be able to carry out the mechanical duties of a mother, under supervision, she is incapable of being a mother in any other sense. Apart from being able to recognize the fact of a family unit, as consisting of a father, a mother, and children residing in the same home, she would have no concept of the idea of marriage, or indeed, the consequential relationship between, intercourse, pregnancy and birth.

Expressive aphasia was described as a condition in which the patient is unable to communicate outwardly thoughts or concepts which she might have perceived. Particularly in the case of a person suffering from any degree of retardation, the result is that even an expert such as a psychiatrist is unable to determine with any degree of certainty if, in fact, those thoughts or concepts have actually been perceived, or whether understanding of them does exist. Little appears to be known of the cause of this condition, and even less of its remedy. In the case of Eve, this condition has been diagnosed as extreme.

From the evidence, he further concluded:

[t]hat Eve is not capable of informed consent, that her moderate retardation is generally stable, that her condition is probably non-inheritable, that she is incapable of effective alternative means of contraception, that the psychological or emotional effect of the proposed operation would probably be minimal, and that the probable incidence of pregnancy is impossible to predict.

The Courts Below

5.   Mrs. E. wanted to be sure she had a right to consent to the sterilization of Eve, so she applied to McQuaid J. for the following remedies:

(a) that Eve be declared a mentally incompetent pursuant to the provisions of the *Mental Health Act*;

(b) that Mrs. E. be appointed the committee of the person of Eve;

(c) that Mrs. E. be authorized to consent to a tubal ligation operation being performed on Eve.

6.   McQuaid J. saw no problem regarding the first two remedies. These in his view were simply a prelude to the third, on which he concentrated, i.e., the authorization to consent to a tubal ligation operation on Eve. He noted that every surgical procedure requires the prior consent of the patient or someone lawfully authorized on her behalf; otherwise it constitutes battery. Though he thought a parent or a committee could give a valid consent for any strictly therapeutic procedure on behalf of a retarded person, in his view deeper issues arose where the procedure was only marginally therapeutic or, as in the present case, strictly contraceptive and specifically one of sterilization. It would deprive Eve of the possible fulfilment of the great privilege of giving birth, a result that should cause a court to act with scrupulous caution even though Eve might not be able to understand or fully appreciate this.

7. Having reviewed the Canadian and English case law and found no governing authorities, McQuaid J. considered whether the court should, in the exercise of its *parens patriae* jurisdiction, intervene on behalf of Eve. He had no doubt that the court could authorize a surgical procedure necessary to health even though a side-effect might be sterilization, and he postulated that it could also do so where the public interest clearly required it, though he found it difficult to come up with an example. However, McQuaid J. was of the view that Eve, like other individuals, was entitled to the inviolability of her person, a right that superseded her right to be protected from pregnancy. That this might result in inconvenience and even hardship to others was irrelevant. The law must protect those who are unable to protect themselves, it must ensure the protection of the higher right. He, therefore, concluded that the court had no authority or jurisdiction to authorize a surgical procedure on a mentally retarded person, the intent and purpose of which was solely contraceptive. It followed that, except for clinically therapeutic reasons, parents or other similarly situated could not give a valid consent to such a surgical procedure either, at least in the absence of clear and unequivocal statutory authority. He, therefore, denied the application.

8. An appeal to the Supreme Court of Prince Edward Island, *in banco*, was launched, and an order was then made appointing the Official Trustee as Guardian *ad litem* for Eve. The appeal was allowed. The general view of the court is set forth in an *addendum* to its notes of judgment as follows:

    In rendering judgment in this matter, we are unanimously of the opinion that the Court has, in proper circumstances, the authority and jurisdiction to authorize the sterilization of a mentally incompetent person for non-therapeutic reasons. The jurisdiction of the Court originates from its parens patriae powers towards individuals who are unable to look after themselves and gives the Court authority to make the individual a ward of the Court.

9. The court, however, differed on the evidence. A majority (Large and Campbell JJ.) was of the view, MacDonald J. dissenting, that there was sufficient evidence to warrant the sterilization of Eve. The court, therefore, ordered that:

    (a) "Eve" be appointed a ward of the Court pursuant to the parens patriae jurisdiction for the sole purpose of facilitating and authorizing her sterilization;

    (b) the Court authorizes the sterilization of "Eve" by a competent medical practitioner;

    (c) the Court reserves its approval of the method of sterilization to be followed pending further submissions of counsel as to the medically preferred surgical procedure.

10. Though the members of the court shared the general view already set forth, there were nonetheless significant differences in their approaches, particularly between that of MacDonald J. and those of the other two judges. To begin with, MacDonald J. took the position that since McQuaid J. had not dealt with the first two grounds in the application, the appeal was only as to the third ground. MacDonald J. expressed considerable doubt about the application of the *Mental Health Act*, and he added that if it did not apply, this raised questions about the burden and standard of proof the court should place on those seeking substituted consent. He, therefore, felt it would be improper for the court to address any other issue than the one strictly before it, especially when that issue was as fundamental as informed consent.

11.   In particular, MacDonald J. was concerned with the fact that no one had appeared on behalf of Eve at the hearing of the application although the judge had requested that a department of the government do so. Counsel for the provincial Department of Justice had been present, it is true, but his role was unclear, and MacDonald J. felt that McQuaid J. would not have readily reached some of his conclusions had Eve been represented. He thus felt the sole question the court could deal with was whether the court appealed from had authority or jurisdiction to authorize a contraceptive sterilization on a mentally retarded person.

12.   To that question, we saw, he replied in the affirmative, but only on a very narrow basis. In his view, the court's jurisdiction was limited to protecting those who are unable to protect themselves. In the case of therapeutic treatment, a parent or guardian could give the required consent and in default the court could intervene under its power as *parens patriae*. But when a non-therapeutic operation was involved, the court must determine whether allowing or disallowing it would best protect the individual.

13.   In MacDonald J.'s view, a court has authority to authorize the contraceptive sterilization of a mentally retarded person but only in exceptional cases. While he found it extremely difficult to conceive of sterilization as protective rather than violative, he felt it would be inappropriate to state as a binding rule that the court would never authorize sterilization for non-therapeutic purposes. If a court did so, however, it must act with extreme caution lest it open the way to abuse. Accordingly he set forth a number of criteria that must be followed in dealing with an application for the purpose. Some of these, he concluded, (in particular, the requirement that the individual proposed to be sterilized must be represented by counsel competent to deal with the medical, social, legal and ethical issues involved) had not been followed in the present case.

14.   Campbell J. took a broader view of the court's powers. The court, he thought, could exercise its parental jurisdiction by making the individual in question its ward. It was possible that the court had implied authority to bring a person within the ambit of the *parens patriae* jurisdiction by its own order, but the *Mental Health Act* provided an adequate statutory base.

15.   The *parens patriae* jurisdiction must, he stated, be exercised solely for the benefit of the mentally retarded person. Each case demanded an objective but compassionate assessment of all relevant facts and circumstances. It could not, in his view, be stated as a rule of law that the inviolability of the person supersedes the right to be protected from pregnancy. That conclusion, he felt, could only be reached by a consideration of the particular circumstances.

16.   In Eve's case, Campbell J. held, the real and genuine object of the proposed sterilization was her protection. There was no overriding public interest against it. And there was a likelihood of substantial injury to her if the operation was not performed. In his view, that injury must be assessed in its social, mental, physical and economic contexts. In the absence of permanent sterilization, the protected environment Eve enjoyed would become a guarded environment. This would deprive her of social options and relative freedom.

17.   Large J. agreed with Campbell J. that the court could exercise its parental jurisdiction through a committee appointed under the *Mental Health Act*. He also agreed with him on the substituted consent issue, but appears to have gone further. After reviewing the record, he commented:

In this unfortunate case I am unable to see how a choice between a chance pregnancy and the tubal ligation which is recommended by "Eve's" medical advisers poses any problem. I believe that the decision is first to be made by the doctor and then by the committee. I do not consider that the Courts should be concerned in each case of medical treatment or surgery which may arise in the future and would direct that "Eve's" doctor and her committee, when appointed, should be free to make a choice of whatever medical or surgical intervention is considered best for "Eve's" welfare.

18. The court, it will be remembered, had in its original order reserved its approval of the method of sterilization to be followed. After further representations, it later ordered that the method of sterilization be by way of a hysterectomy.

19. Leave to appeal to this Court was then granted to Eve's Guardian *ad litem* by the Prince Edward Island Supreme Court, Appeal Division. Subsequently this Court granted intervener status to the Consumer Advisory Committee of the Canadian Association for the Mentally Retarded, The Public Trustee of Manitoba, the Canadian Mental Health Association, and the Attorney General of Canada.

The Issues on this Appeal

20. The major issues raised in this appeal are substantially as follows:

   1. Is there relevant provincial legislation that gives a court jurisdiction to appoint a committee vested with the power to consent to or authorize surgical procedures for contraceptive purposes on an adult who is mentally incompetent?

   2. In the absence of statutory authority, does the court's *parens patriae* jurisdiction allow the court to consent to the sterilization of an adult who is mentally incompetent?

   3. What is the appropriate standard of proof to be applied in a case where an application is made to the court for its substituted consent to a non-therapeutic procedure on behalf of a mentally incompetent adult?

      Upon whom is the onus of proof?

   4. If the court has jurisdiction to provide substituted consent for a non-therapeutic procedure on behalf of a mentally incompetent adult, did the Supreme Court of Prince Edward Island, *in banco*, properly exercise its jurisdiction in granting an order authorizing the sterilization of Eve?

   5. Does the *Canadian Charter of Rights and Freedoms* protect an individual against sterilization without that individual's consent?

   6. If the *Charter* provides such protection, when will it permit the non-therapeutic sterilization of a mentally incompetent who is incapable of giving consent?

   7. Does the *Charter* give an individual the right to choose not to procreate, and if so does the court have jurisdiction to make that choice on behalf of an individual who is unable to do so?

General Considerations

21. Before entering into a consideration of the specific issues before this Court, it may be useful to restate the general issue briefly. The Court is asked to consent, on behalf of Eve, to sterilization since she, though an adult, is unable to do so herself. Sterilization by means of a tubal ligation is usually irreversible. And hysterectomy, the operation

authorized by the Appeal Division, is not only irreversible; it is major surgery. Eve's sterilization is not being sought to treat any medical condition. Its purposes are admittedly non-therapeutic. One such purpose is to deprive Eve of the capacity to become pregnant so as to save her from the possible trauma of giving birth and from the resultant obligations of a parent, a task the evidence indicates she is not capable of fulfilling. As to this, it should be noted that there is no evidence that giving birth would be more difficult for Eve than for any other woman. A second purpose of the sterilization is to relieve Mrs. E. of anxiety about the possibility of Eve's becoming pregnant and of having to care for any child Eve might bear.

Does the Court have Statutory Jurisdiction?

22.   On the application and in the Appeal Division, reliance was placed on certain provisions of the *Mental Health Act*, R.S.P.E.I. 1974, c. M-9, as amended by [the *Chancery Jurisdiction Transfer Act*] S.P.E.I. 1974, c. 65. These provisions read as follows:

2.(n)"person in need of guardianship" means a person

    (i)   in whom there is a condition of arrested or incomplete development of mind, whether arising from inherent causes or induced by disease or injury, or

    (ii) who is suffering from such a disorder of the mind, that he requires care, supervision and control for his protection and the protection of his property.

30 A (1) When a person in need of guardianship is possessed of goods and chattels, lands and tenements or rights or credits, the Supreme Court may on petition, stating the name, age and residence of the person therein alleged to be a person in need of guardianship, setting forth generally the real and personal estate, rights and credits of and belonging to that person, so far as they are known to the petitioner and the value thereof, and verified by the affidavit of the petitioner or some other credible person or

persons, order that person so alleged to be a person in need of guardianship to be examined by two competent medical men, to ascertain his state of mind and capability of managing his affairs, and the medical men shall certify their opinion thereon.

(2) If by the certificate of two medical men issued pursuant to subsection (1) it appears to the satisfaction of the Supreme Court that the person is a person in need of guardianship and incapable of managing his affairs, and that under the circumstances it would be for his benefit that the custody of his person and the management of his estate should be committed to some other person, the Supreme Court may make an order appointing some fit and proper person to be a committee of the person and estate of the person in need of guardianship and if necessary direct such allowance to be made out of the estate for the maintenance and medical treatment of the person in need of guardianship as it deems proper, and the committee shall give security by way of bond or recognizance with such sureties and in such form as the Supreme Court shall direct conditioned for the faithful performance of his duties as the committee.

30 B Every order made under subsection (2) of section 30A for the appointment of a committee has the effect of vesting the person and estate of the person in need of guardianship in the committee in the same manner as a grant to the committee of the person and estate of a lunatic made by and under the order and direction of

the Lord Chancellor of England would have done at the time of the passing of the Act 15 Victoria, Chapter 36; but when the fact the person being a person in need of guardianship is doubtful, the Supreme Court, before making the order, hold an inquiry in order that the state of the person's mind may be ascertained and until the completion of the inquiry may make such provisional order respecting the person and estate of the alleged person in need of guardianship as may seem necessary.

30 L Every act done by the committee of the estate of a person in need of guardianship under and by virtue of this Act, and every order of the Supreme Court are as valid and binding against the person in need of guardianship and all persons claiming by, from or under him, as if the person so being a person in need of guardianship had been in his sound mind and had personally done such act.

23.   The Act, as can be seen, provides a procedure for determining whether persons are in need of guardianship as defined in s. 2(n). It also gives certain powers over such persons, or at least their property, to a committee. However, it is by no means clear that the Act applies to Eve. The opening words of s. 30A(1), which provides for the psychiatric assessment of a person alleged to be in need of guardianship, at first sight at least, appear to be directed solely to persons in need of guardianship who are also possessed of property. Taken by itself, then, s. 30A(1) gives the impression that it is aimed at the management of an incompetent person's estate. Nothing in the evidence indicates that Eve has any property.

24   Section 30A(2), however, empowers the court to appoint a committee of the person as well as of the estate of a person in need of guardianship. It does not, however, expressly empower it to authorize any medical procedure, but only to make allowances from the person's estate for maintenance and medical treatment. It may impliedly empower the court to authorize medical treatment by its grant of custody, but any such implication would have to be read in light of the fact that the court's power to make an allowance for medical purposes does not extend to all medical procedures, but only to medical treatment. Eve, we have seen, is not being treated for any medical condition. The sole purpose for her proposed sterilization is non-therapeutic.

25.   Even assuming, therefore, that these provisions apply to a person who has no property, and that they confer powers beyond property management, including an implied power in a committee to authorize medical treatment, matters that are by no means free from doubt, it would take much stronger language to persuade me that they empower a committee to authorize the sterilization of an individual for non-therapeutic purposes.

26.   Finally, s. 30B provides that a committee appointed under s. 30A(2) has the effect of vesting the person and estate of the person in need of guardianship in the committee in the same manner as a grant to the committee of a person and estate of a lunatic by the Lord Chancellor of England at the time of the passing of the Island Act, (1852), 15 Vict., c. 36. That, however, does not dispel the doubts that a committee can only be appointed for a person who owns property, especially since the reference to the grant by the Lord Chancellor is to the person and estate of the incompetent, and (though this is less cogent) the Island Act of 1852 appears also to have been limited to incompetents who owned property. In any event, any relevant power the Lord Chancellor had at the time is related to the *parens patriae* jurisdiction, which I shall be discussing at length later.

27.   In a word, I am unable to see how the *Mental Health Act* much advances the case of the applicants. It does provide a procedure for a declaration of mental incompetency, at least for those who own property, but its ambit is unclear. Certainly, power to obtain an authorization for sterilization, if it exists, must be found elsewhere. It is significant that in this Court the respondent did not rely on the *Mental Health Act* but on s. 48 of the *Hospital Management Regulations*, R.R.P.E.I., c. H-11 adopted pursuant to s. 16 of the *Hospitals Act*, R.S.P.E.I. 1974, c. H-11.

28.   Section 48 of these Regulations reads as follows:

48. No surgical operation shall be performed on a patient unless a consent in writing for the performance of the operation has been signed by

(a) the patient;

(b) the spouse, one of the next of kin or parent of the patient, if the patient is unable to sign by reason of mental or physical disability; or

(c) the parent or guardian of the patient, if the patient is unmarried and under eighteen years of age, but if the surgeon believes that delay caused by obtaining the consent would endanger the life of the patient

(d) the consent is not necessary; and

(e) the surgeon shall write and sign a statement that a delay would endanger the life of the patient.

Section 16 of the Act under which it was enacted reads as follows:

16. Upon the recommendation of the Commission, the Lieutenant Governor in Council may make such regulations with respect to hospitals as may be deemed necessary for

(a) their establishment, construction, alteration, equipment, safety, maintenance and repairs;

(b) their classification, grades, and standards;

(c) their inspection, control, government, management, conduct, operation and use;

(d) respecting the granting, refusing, suspending and revoking of approval of hospitals and of additions to or renovations in hospitals;

(e) prescribing the matters upon which bylaws are to be passed by hospitals;

(f) prescribing the powers and duties of inspectors;

(g) providing that certain persons shall be by virtue of their office members of the Board in addition to the members of the Board appointed or elected in accordance with the authority whereby the hospital is established;

(h) respecting their administrators, staffs, officers, servants, and employees and the powers and duties thereof;

(i) providing for the certification of chronically ill persons;

(j) defining residents of the province for the purposes of this Act and the regulations;

(k) respecting the admission, treatment, care, conduct, discipline and discharge of patients or any class of patients;

(l) respecting the classification of patients and the lengths of stay of and the rates and charges for patients;

(m) prescribing the manner in which hospital rates and charges shall be calculated;

(n) prescribing the facilities that hospitals shall provide for students;

(o) respecting the records, books, accounting systems, audits, reports and returns to be made and kept by hospitals;

(p) respecting the reports and returns to be submitted to the Commission by hospitals;

(q) prescribing the classes of grants by way of provincial aid and the methods of determining the amounts of grants and providing for the manner and times of payment and the suspension and withholding of grants and for the making of deductions from grants;

(r) respecting such other matters as the Lieutenant Governor in Council considers necessary or desirable for the more effective carrying out of this Act.

29. As will be evident from a reading of s. 16, the purpose of the regulations is to regulate the construction, management and operation of hospitals. They are not aimed at defining the rights of individuals as such. Section 48 of the regulations (which appears to have been enacted under s. 16(k)) does not so much authorize the performance of an operation as direct that none shall be performed in the absence of appropriate consents, except in cases of necessity. The enumerated consents and necessity are at law valid defences in certain circumstances to a suit for battery that might be brought as a result of an unauthorized operation. So, for the purposes of managing the workings of the hospital, the regulations require that these consents be signed. They do not purport to regulate the validity of the consents; this is otherwise governed by law. Indeed, I rather doubt that the Act empowers the making of regulations affecting the rights of the individual, particularly a basic right involving an individual's physical integrity. For in the absence of clear words, statutes are, of course, not to be read as depriving the individual of so basic a right. In a word, the intent of the regulations is to provide for the governance of hospitals, not human rights.

30. In summary, MacDonald J. appears to have been right in doubting that the trial judge had properly addressed the threshold question of whether Eve was incompetent. In truth, however, these questions of possible statutory power only amounted to a preliminary skirmish. Argument really centred on the question of whether a superior court, as successor to the powers of the English Court of Chancery could, in the exercise of its parental control as the repository of the Crown's jurisdiction as *parens patriae*, authorize the performance of the operation in question here. It is to that issue that I now turn.

Parens Patriae Jurisdiction—Its Genesis

31. There appears to have been some uncertainty in the courts below and in the arguments presented to us regarding the courts' wardship jurisdiction over children and the *parens patriae* jurisdiction generally. For that reason, it may be useful to give an account of the *parens patriae* jurisdiction and to examine its relationship with wardship.

32. The origin of the Crown's *parens patriae* jurisdiction over the mentally incompetent, Sir Henry Theobald tells us, is lost in the mists of antiquity; see H. Theobald, *The Law Relating to Lunacy* (1924). *De Prerogativa Regis*, an instrument regarded as a statute that dates from the thirteenth or early fourteenth century, recognized and restricted it, but did not create it. Theobald speculates that "the most probable theory [of its origin] is that either by general assent or by some statute, now lost, the care of persons of unsound mind was by Edw. I taken from the feudal lords, who would naturally take possession of the land of a tenant unable to perform his feudal duties"; see Theobald, *supra*, p. 1.

33. In the 1540's, the *parens patriae* jurisdiction was transferred from officials in the royal household to the Court of Wards and Liveries, where it remained until that court was wound up in 1660. Thereafter the Crown exercised its jurisdiction through the Lord Chancellor to whom by letters patent under the Sign Manual it granted the care and custody of the persons and the estates of persons of unsound mind so found by inquisition, i.e., an examination to determine soundness or unsoundness of mind.

34. Wardship of children had a quite separate origin as a property right arising out of the feudal system of tenures. The original purpose of the wardship jurisdiction was to protect the rights of the guardian rather than of the ward. Until 1660 this jurisdiction was also administered by the Court of Wards and Liveries which had been created for the purpose.

35. When tenures and the Court of Wards were abolished, the concept of wardship should, in theory, have disappeared. It was kept alive, however, by the Court of Chancery, which justified it as an aspect of its *parens patriae* jurisdiction; see, for example, *Cary v. Bertie* (1696), 2 Vern. 333, at p. 342, 23 E.R. 814, at p. 818; *Morgan v. Dillon* (Ire.) (1724), 9 Mod. R. 135, at p. 139, 88 E.R. 361, at p. 364. In time wardship became substantively and procedurally assimilated to the *parens patriae* jurisdiction, lost its connection with property, and became purely protective in nature. Wardship thus is merely a device by means of which Chancery exercises its *parens patriae* jurisdiction over children. Today the care of children constitutes the bulk of the courts' work involving the exercise of the *parens patriae* jurisdiction.

36. It follows from what I have said that the wardship cases constitute a solid guide to the exercise of the *parens patriae* power even in the case of adults. There is no need, then, to resort to statutes like the *Mental Health Act* to permit a court to exercise the jurisdiction in respect of adults. But proof of incompetence must, of course, be made.

37. This marks a difference between wardship and *parens patriae* jurisdiction over adults. In the case of children, Chancery has a custodial jurisdiction as well, and thus has inherent jurisdiction to make them its wards; this is not so of adult mentally incompetent persons (see *Beall v. Smith* (1873), L.R. 9 Ch. 85, at p. 92). Since, however, the Chancellor had been vested by letters patent under the Sign Manual with power to exercise the Crown's *parens patriae* jurisdiction for the protection of persons so found by inquisition, this difference between the two procedures has no importance for present purposes.

38. By the early part of the nineteenth century, the work arising out of the Lord Chancellor's jurisdiction became more than one judge could handle and the Chancery Court was reorganized and the work assigned to several justices including the Master

of the Rolls. In 1852 (by 15 and 16 Vict., c. 87, s. 15 (U.K.)) the jurisdiction of the Chancellor regarding the "Custody of the Persons and Estates of Persons found idiot, lunatic or of unsound Mind" was authorized to be exercised by anyone for the time being entrusted by virtue of the Sign Manual.

39. The current jurisdiction of the Supreme Court of Prince Edward Island regarding mental incompetents is derived from the *Chancery Act* which amalgamated a series of statutes dealing with the Court of Chancery, beginning with that of 1848 (11 Vict., c. 6 (P.E.I.)) Section 3 of *The Chancery Act*, R.S.P.E.I. 1951, c. 21, substantially reproduced the law as it had existed for many years. It vested in the Court of Chancery the following powers regarding the mentally incompetent:

...and in the case of idiots, mentally incompetent persons or persons of unsound mind, and their property and estate, the jurisdiction of the Court shall include that which in England was conferred upon the Lord Chancellor by a Commission from the Crown under the Sign Manual, except so far as the same are altered or enlarged as aforesaid.

By virtue of the *Chancery Jurisdiction Transfer Act*, S.P.E.I. 1974, c. 65, s. 2, the jurisdiction of the Chancery Court was transferred to the Supreme Court of Prince Edward Island. It will be obvious from these provisions that the Supreme Court of Prince Edward Island has the same *parens patriae* jurisdiction as was vested in the Lord Chancellor in England and exercised by the Court of Chancery there. Anglo-Canadian Development

40. Since historically the law respecting the mentally incompetent has been almost exclusively focused on their estates, the law on guardianship of their persons is "pitifully unclear with respect to some basic issues"; see P. McLaughlin, *Guardianship of the Person* (Downsview 1979), p. 35. Despite this vagueness, however, it seems clear that the *parens patriae* jurisdiction was never limited solely to the management and care of the estate of a mentally retarded or defective person.

As early as 1603, Sir Edward Coke in *Beverley's Case*, 4 Co. Rep. 123 b, at pp. 126 a, 126 b, 76 E.R. 1118, at p. 1124, stated that "in the case of an idiot or fool natural, for whom there is no expectation, but that he, during his life, will remain without discretion and use of reason, the law has given the custody of him, and all that he has, to the King" (emphasis added). Later at the bottom of the page he adds:

2. Although the stat. says, *custodiam terrarum*, yet the King shall have as well the custody of the body, and of their goods and chattels, as of the lands and other hereditaments, and as well those which he has by purchase, as those which he has as heirs by the common law.

At 4 Co. Rep. p. 126 b, 76 E.R. 1125, he cites Fitzherbert's *Natura brevium* to the same effect. Theobald (*supra*, pp. 7-8, 362) appears to be quite right when he tells us that the Crown's prerogative "has never been limited by definition". The Crown has an inherent jurisdiction to do what is for the benefit of the incompetent. Its limits (or scope) have not, and cannot, be defined.

41. The famous custody battle waged by one Wellesley in the early nineteenth century sheds some light on the exercise of the king's *parens patriae* jurisdiction by the Lord Chancellor. Wellesley (considered an extremely dissolute and objectionable father due to his philandering ways and vulgar language, in spite of his "high" birth), waged a lengthy court battle to gain custody of his children following the death of

his estranged wife who had entrusted the care of the children to members of her family. In *Wellesley v. Duke of Beaufort* (1827), 2 Russ. 1, 38 E.R. 236, Lord Eldon, then Lord Chancellor, in discussing the jurisdiction of the Court of Chancery, touched upon the King's *parens patriae* power at 2 Russ. 20, 38 E.R. 243. He there made it clear that "it belongs to the King as *parens patriae*, having the care of those who are not able to take care of themselves, and is founded on the obvious necessity that the law should place somewhere the care of individuals who cannot take care of themselves, particularly in cases where it is clear that some care should be thrown round them". He then underlined that the jurisdiction has been exercised for the maintenance of children solely when there was property, not because of any rule of law, but for the practical reason that the court obviously had no means of acting unless there was property available.

42.   The discussion on appeal to the House of Lords (*Wellesley v. Wellesley* (1828), 2 Bli. N.S. 124, 4 E.R. 1078) is also instructive. Far from limiting the jurisdiction to children, Lord Redesdale there adverted to the fact that the court's jurisdiction over children had been adopted from its jurisdiction over mental incompetents. He noted that "Lord Somers resembled the jurisdiction over infants, to the care which the Court takes with respect to lunatics, and supposed that the jurisdiction devolved on the Crown, in the same way"; 2 Bli. N.S. at p. 131, 4 E.R. at p. 1081. The jurisdiction, he said, extended "as far as is necessary for protection and education"; 2 Bli. at p. 136, 4 E.R. at p. 1083. It continues to this day, and even where there is legislation in the area, the courts will continue to use the *parens patriae* jurisdiction to deal with uncomtemplated situations where it appears necessary to do so for the protection of those who fall within its ambit; see *Beson v. Director of Child Welfare (Nfld.)*, [1982] 2 S.C.R. 716.

43.   It was argued before us, however, that there was no precedent where the Lord Chancellor had exercised the *parens patriae* jurisdiction to order medical procedures of any kind. As to this, I would say that lack of precedent in earlier times is scarcely surprising having regard to the state of medical science at the time. Nonetheless, it seems clear from *Wellesley v. Wellesley, supra*, that the situations in which the courts can act where it is necessary to do so for the protection of mental incompetents and children have never been, and indeed cannot, be defined. I have already referred to the remarks of Lord Redesdale. To these may be added those of Lord Manners who, at Bli. pp. 142-43 and 1085, respectively, expressed the view that "It is… impossible to say what are the limits of that jurisdiction; every case must depend upon its own circumstances".

44.   Reference may also be made to *Re X (a minor)*, [1975] 1 All E.R. 697, for a more contemporary description of the *parens patriae* jurisdiction. In that case, the plaintiff applied to Latey J. for an order making a fourteen year old girl who was psychologically fragile and high strung a ward of the court and for an injunction prohibiting the publication of a book revealing her father's private life which, it was felt, would be grossly damaging psychologically to her if she should read it. Latey J. issued the wardship order and the injunction requested. In speaking of his jurisdiction in the matter, he had this to say, at p. 699:

On the first of the two questions already stated, it is argued for the defendants, first, that because the wardship jurisdiction has never been involved in any case remotely resembling this, the court, though theoretically having jurisdiction, should not entertain the application, but bar it in limine. I do not accept that contention. It is true that this jurisdiction has not been invoked in any such circumstances. I do not know whether they have arisen before or, if they have, whether anyone has thought of having recourse to this jurisdiction. But I can find nothing in the authorities to which I have been referred by counsel or in my own researches to suggest that there is any limitation in the theoretical scope of this jurisdiction; or, to put it another way, that the jurisdiction can only be invoked in the categories of cases in which it has hitherto been invoked, such as custody, care and control, protection of property, health problems, religious upbringing, and protection against harmful associations. That list is not exhaustive. On the contrary, the powers of the court in this particular jurisdiction have always been described as being of the widest nature. That the courts are available to protect children from injury whenever they properly can is no modern development.

(Emphasis added.)

Latey J. then cited a passage from *Chambers of Infancy* (1842), p. 20 that indicates that protection may be accorded against prospective as well as present harm. The passage states in part:

And the Court will interfere not merely on the ground of an injury actually done, or attempted against the infant's person or property; but also if there be any likelihood of such an occurrence, or even an apprehension or suspicion of it.

45.   The Court of Appeal disagreed with Latey J.'s exercise of discretion, essentially because he had failed to consider the public interest in the publication of the book, and accordingly reversed his order. The court, however, did not quarrel with his statement of the law. Thus Lord Denning, M.R., at p. 703 had this to say:

No limit has ever been set to the jurisdiction. It has been said to extend as far as necessary for protection and education: see *Wellesley v Wellesley* by Lord Redesdale. The court has power to protect the ward from any interference with his or her welfare, direct or indirect. Roskill L.J., also reinforced the broad ambit of the jurisdiction. He said, at p. 705:

I would agree with counsel for the plaintiff that no limits to that jurisdiction have yet been drawn and it is not necessary to consider here what (if any) limits there are to that jurisdiction. The sole question is whether it should be exercised in this case. I would also agree with him that the mere fact that the courts have never stretched out their arms so far as is proposed in this case is in itself no reason for not stretching out those arms further than before when necessary in a suitable case.

Sir John Pennycuick at p. 706 agreed:

...the courts, when exercising the parental power of the Crown, have, at any rate in legal theory, an unrestricted jurisdiction to do whatever is considered necessary for the welfare of a ward. It is, however, obvious that far-reaching limitations in principle on the exercise of this jurisdiction must exist. The jurisdiction is habitually exercised within those limitations.

At page 707 he added:

Latey J's statement of the law is I think correct, but he does not lay sufficient emphasis on the limitations with which the courts should exercise this jurisdiction.

46. I will be observed from the remarks of Sir John Pennycuick, as well as the words emphasized in Latey J.'s judgment, that the theoretically unlimited nature of the jurisdiction, to which I have also previously referred, has to do with its scope. It must, of course, be used in accordance with its informing principles, a matter about which I shall have more to say.

47. In recent years, the English courts have extended the jurisdiction to cases involving medical procedures. In *Re S. v. McC(orse. S.) and M; W v. W.*, [1972] A.C. 24, the House of Lords, relying in part on its protective jurisdiction over infants, approved of a blood test being taken of a husband and his wife and a child with a view to determining the paternity of the child.

48. The court's jurisdiction to sanction the nontherapeutic sterilization of a mentally handicapped person arose before Heilbron J. of the Family Division of the English High Court of Justice in *Re D (a minor)*, [1976] 1 All E.R. 326, a case that bears a considerable resemblance to the present. D, a girl, was born with a condition known as Sotos Syndrome, the symptoms of which include accelerated growth during infancy, epilepsy, clumsiness, and unusual facial appearance, behavioural problems including aggressiveness, and some impairment of mental functions that could result in dull intelligence or more serious mental retardation. D displayed these various symptoms, although she was not as seriously retarded as some children similarly afflicted. She possessed a dull normal intelligence. She was sent to an appropriate school but did not do well partly because of behavioural problems. When she was ten, however, she was sent to a school specializing in children with learning difficulties and associated behavioural problems. She then showed marked improvement in her academic skills, social competence and behaviour.

49. D lived with her widowed mother, Mrs. B., who was fifty-one, and two sisters. The family lived in extraordinarily difficult circumstances in a grossly overcrowded house with no inside toilet. The mother was described as a very hard-working woman who kept the house spotless and impressed everyone with her sincerity and common sense.

50. It was common ground that D had sufficient intelligence to marry in due course. Her mother, however, was convinced that she would always remain substantially handicapped and unable to maintain herself or care for any children she might have. Accordingly, when D was a child, her parents had decided that she should be sterilized, and when she reached puberty at ten, Mrs. B.'s concern increased; she worried that D might be seduced and give birth to an abnormal child. She consulted a doctor, who took the view that there was a real risk that she might indeed give birth to an abnormal child. He agreed that D should be sterilized and arrangements were made for the purpose. When other doctors questioned the purposes of the operation, however, a wardship application was made to the court with a view to preventing it from being carried out.

51. Heilbron J. refused to sanction the operation. After reviewing the nature of the wardship jurisdiction arising out of the sovereign's obligation as *parens patriae*, she observed, at p. 332:

    It is apparent from the recent decision of the Court of Appeal in *Re X (a minor)* that the jurisdiction to do what is considered necessary for the protection of an infant is to be exercised carefully and within limits, but the court has, from time to time over the years, extended the sphere in the exercise of this jurisdiction.

The type of operation proposed is one which involves the deprivation of a basic human right, namely the right of a woman to reproduce, and therefore it would, if performed on a woman for non-therapeutic reasons and without her consent, be a violation of such right. Both Dr. Gordon and Miss Duncan seem to have had in mind the possibility of seeking the child's views and her consent, for they asked that this handicapped child of 11 should be consulted in the matter. One would have thought that they must have known that any answer she might have given, or any purported consent, would have been valueless.

(Emphasis added.)

At page 333, she added:

This operation could, if necessary, be delayed or prevented if the child were to remain a ward of court, and as Lord Eldon LC, so vividly expressed it in *Wellesley's* case: "It has always been the principle of this Court, not to risk the incurring of damage to children which it cannot repair, but rather to prevent the damage being done."

I think that is the very type of case where this court should `throw some care around this child', and I propose to continue her wardship which, in my judgment, is appropriate in this case.

(Emphasis added.)

Later, at pp. 334-35, she expressed agreement with the consulting doctors' opinion that sterilization for therapeutic purposes was not entirely within a doctor's clinical judgment:

Their opinion was that a decision to sterilise a child was not entirely within a doctor's clinical judgment, save only when sterilisation was the treatment of choice for some disease, as, for instance, when in order to treat a child and to ensure her direct physical well-being, it might be necessary to perform a hysterectomy to remove a malignant uterus. Whilst the side effect of such an operation would be to sterilise, the operation would be performed solely for therapeutic purposes. I entirely accept their opinions. I cannot believe, and the evidence does not warrant the view, that a decision to carry out an operation of this nature performed for nontherapeutic purposes on a minor, can be held to be within the doctor's sole clinical judgment.

(Emphasis added.)

52.   Since that time, there have been several cases where the English courts have given permission to perform medical operations under the *parens patriae* jurisdiction. In *In re P (a Minor)* (1981), 80 L.G.R. 301, local authorities invoked the court's wardship jurisdiction to permit an abortion on a fifteen year old girl who had previously given birth and was caring for the first child in facilities provided by the authority. The evidence indicated that the girl was taking good care of the first child but could not cope with a second, and that the girl consented to the operation. Butler-Sloss J. authorized the abortion, despite her father's objection, on the ground that it was in the girl's best interest.

53.   More recently still, the English Court of Appeal had to consider the poignantly sad case of *Re B (a minor)* (1982), 3 F.L.R. 117. A baby girl was born suffering from Down's Syndrome (mongolism). She also had an intestinal blockage from which she would die within a very short time unless it was operated on. If she had the operation there was a considerable risk that she would suffer from heart trouble and die within

two or three months. Even if the operation was successful she would only have a life expectancy of from twenty to thirty years, during which time she would be very handicapped, both mentally and physically. Her parents took the view that the kindest thing in the interests of the child was for her not to have the operation. Nonetheless, the court, on a wardship application by a local authority, authorized the operation. Though it expressed sympathy for the parents in the agonizing decision to which they had come, it emphasized the protective quality of its jurisdiction, as the following statement by Lord Templeman, at pp. 122-23 indicates:

"The evidence in this case only goes to show that if the operation takes place and is successful then the child may live the normal span of a mongoloid child with the handicaps and defects and life of a mongol child, and it is not for this court to say that life of that description ought to be extinguished."

54. Turning now to Canada, the *parens patriae* jurisdiction has on several occasions been exercised to authorize the giving of a blood transfusion to save a child's life over its parents' religious objection. More germane for present purposes is the recent case of *Re K and Public Trustee* (1985), 19 D.L.R.(4th) 255, where the Court of Appeal of British Columbia ordered that a hysterectomy be performed on a seriously retarded child on the ground that the operation was therapeutic. The most serious factor considered by the court was the child's alleged phobic aversion to blood, which it was feared would seriously affect her when her menstrual period began. It should be observed, and the fact was underscored by the judges in that case, that *Re K and Public Trustee* raised a quite different issue from that in the present case. As Anderson J.A. put it at p. 275: "I say now, as forcefully as I can, this case cannot and must not be regarded as a precedent to be followed in cases involving sterilization of mentally disabled persons for contraceptive purposes."

55. I now turn to the American experience to which all parties referred.

The American Experience

56. The American experience in this area cannot be understood without reference to the interest in the eugenic sterilization of the mentally incompetent manifested in that country early in this century. Eugenics theory, founded upon the rearticulation of the Mendelian theories of inheritance, developed from the premise that physical, mental and even moral deficiencies have a genetic basis. In the early part of this century, many social reformers advocated eugenic sterilization as a panacea for most of the troubles that had been created by "misfits" in society. This general attitude, coupled with the evolution of surgical sterilization techniques, provoked the widespread adoption of enabling legislation. In time, over thirty states en- acted statutes providing for the compulsory sterilization of the mentally retarded; see Sherlock and Sherlock, "Sterilizing the Retarded: Constitutional, Statutory and Policy Alternatives," 60 *N.C.L.Rev.* 943 (1982), at p. 944.

57. The constitutionality of such statutes arose before the United States Supreme Court in the landmark case of *Buck v. Bell*, 274 U.S. 200 (1927). Carrie Buck, a mildly retarded woman, was the daughter of a similarly afflicted woman and had herself given birth to an allegedly retarded child. A majority of the court sanctioned her sterilization despite claims that such a course violated substantive and procedural due process as well as the equal protection rights of the handicapped. The case constituted the high water mark of eugenic theory, as the strong judgment of Holmes J. attests. He sets the tone at p. 207:

We have seen more than once that the public welfare may call upon the best citizens for their lives. It would be strange if it could not call upon those who already sap the strength of the State for these lesser sacrifices, often not felt to be such by those concerned, in order to prevent our being swamped with incompetence. It is better for all the world, if instead of waiting to execute degenerate offspring for crime, or to let them starve for their imbecility, society can prevent those who are manifestly unfit from continuing their kind. The principle that sustains compulsory vaccination is broad enough to cover cutting the Fallopian tubes. … Three generations of imbeciles are enough.

58. During the 1930s researchers and biologists began to denounce the sweeping generalizations concerning heredity in relation to mental and physical disorders. By 1937 both the American Neurological Association and the American Medical Association had criticized the overwhelming emphasis on heredity as a cause of mental retardation, mental illness, pauperism, epilepsy and other disabilities; see Burgdorf, Jr. and Burgdorf, "The Wicked Witch is Almost Dead: *Buck v. Bell* and the Sterilization of Handicapped Persons," 50 *Temp. L.Q.* 995 (1977), at p. 1007. Today, the assumptions made in *Buck v. Bell* are widely discredited; see McIvor, "Equitable Jurisdiction to Order Sterilizations," 57 *Wash. L.R.* 373 (1982), at p. 375; Lachance, "In re *Grady:* The Mentally Retarded Individual's Right to Choose Sterilization," 6 *Am.J.L. and Med.* 559 (1981), at pp. 569-70.

59. Scientific exposure of the fallacious reasoning of the eugenicists led to a waning of the initial enthusiasm for laws requiring eugenic sterilization. Along with a growing legal recognition of the fundamental character of the right to procreate, this was sufficient to trigger a reappraisal of the courts' position. Courts became extremely reluctant to order the sterilization of mentally handicapped persons in the absence of specific statutory authority; see Ross, "Sterilization of the Developmentally Disabled: Shedding Some Myth-Conceptions," 9 *Fla. St. U.L. Rev.* 599 (1981). Their *rationale* was that "the awesome power to deprive a human being of his or her fundamental right to bear or beget offspring must be founded on the explicit authorization of the Legislature …"; *Guardianship of Tulley* App., 146 Cal.Rptr. 266 (1978), at p. 270.

60. Not surprisingly, this argument has been strongly asserted by some of the parties to the present appeal. Thus, counsel for the Canadian Mental Health Association contended that the weight of authority in the United States is to the effect that there is no inherent jurisdiction in state courts, either by way of the *parens patriae* doctrine or otherwise, to order the sterilization of persons found to be mentally incompetent. For this proposition, he cited *Hudson v. Hudson*, 373 So.2d 310 (Ala. 1979) at pp. 311-12; *Matter of Guardianship of Eberhardy*, 294 N.W.2d 540 (Wis. 1980); Norris, "Recent Developments—Courts—Scope of Authority—Sterilization of Mental Incompetents," 44 *Tenn. L. Rev.* 879 (1977).

61. The proposition thus advanced would, I think, have been unassailable until a few years ago. Since 1978, however, the tide has changed significantly. The precipitating event appears to have been the decision of the Supreme Court of the United States in *Stump v. Sparkman*, 435 U.S. 349 (1978). The question at issue there was whether an Indiana judge, who had ordered the sterilization of a "somewhat" retarded child on her mother's petition, was immune from liability in a suit subsequently brought by the incompetent. On obtaining court approval, the mother had had the procedure

performed without the knowledge of her daughter who had been led to believe she was undergoing an appendectomy. The daughter discovered her deprivation when she subsequently married and attempted to have children. The Supreme Court held that the judge was immune from liability on the basis of an Indiana statute which conferred upon the Indiana circuit court original jurisdiction "in all cases at law and in equity whatsoever".

62.   Though the precise precedential value of the case has been the subject of considerable judicial and scholarly debate, *Stump v. Sparkman* appears nonetheless to have had a catalytic effect. Since that decision, the vast majority of state courts before which the question has been raised have held that they have equitable authority, in the absence of statute, to order sterilization of the mentally retarded; see *Matter of Guardianship of Eberhardy*, 307 N.W.2d 881 (Wis. 1981), at p. 887; *In re Grady*, 426 A.2d 467 (N.J. 1981), at p. 479; *Matter of C.D.M.*, 627 P.2d 607 (Alaska 1981), at p. 612; *Matter of A.W.*, 637 P.2d 366 (Colo. 1981), at p. 374; *Matter of Terwilliger*, 450 A.2d 1376 (Pa. 1982), at pp. 1380-81; *Wentzel v. Montgomery General Hospital, Inc.*, 447 A.2d 1244 (Md. 1982), at p. 1263; *Matter of Moe*, 432 N.E.2d 712 (Mass. 1982), at p. 718; *P.S. by Harbin v. W.S.*, 452 N.E.2d 969 (Ind. 1983), at p. 976; cf. *Hudson v. Hudson, supra*. Thus as McIvor, *supra*, at p. 379 concludes, despite *Sparkman v. Stump*'s weakness as a precedent, it "provides a de facto point of departure for the emerging rule recognizing equitable jurisdiction to authorize the nonconsensual sterilization of mentally retarded persons".

63.   The rationale on which state courts have acted in recent years is conveniently summarized in a passage from a pre-*Sparkman* case. In *Matter of Sallmaier*, 378 N.Y.S.2d 989 (1976), the court, basing itself on expert testimony concerning the likelihood of a psychotic reaction to pregnancy, other evidence of psychological and hygienic difficulties, and the patient's proclivity for sexual encounters with men, authorized the sterilization of a severely retarded adult woman. The court had this to say, at p. 991:

The jurisdiction of the court in this proceeding arises not by statute, but from the common law jurisdiction of the Supreme Court to act as *parens patriae* with respect to incompetents.(*Moore v. Flagg*, 137 App.Div. 338, 122 N.Y.S. 174; *Matter of Weberlist*, 79 Misc.2d 753, 360 N.Y.S.2d 783.) The rationale of *parens patriae*, as was stated by the court in *Matter of Weberlist, supra*, p. 756, 360 N.Y.S.2d p. 786, is "that the State must intervene in order to protect an individual who is not able to make decisions in his own best interest. The decision to exercise the power of *parens patriae* must reflect the welfare of society, as a whole, but mainly it must balance the individual's right to be free from interference against the individual's need to be treated, if treatment would in fact be in his best interest."

I should perhaps add that subsequent to *Sallmaier*, another New York court expressly refused to authorize sterilization in the absence of legislative guidelines; *Application of A.D.*, 394 N.Y.S.2d 139 (1977).

64.   While many state courts have, in recent cases, been prepared to recognize an inherent power in courts of general jurisdiction to authorize sterilization of mentally incompetent persons, they differ on the standard of review. Two distinct approaches have emerged: the "best interests" approach and the "substituted judgment" approach. 65. In five of the nine states in which equitable jurisdiction to authorize the non-

consensual sterilization of a mentally incompetent person is recognized, that jurisdiction is based on the inherent equitable power of the courts to act in the best interests of the mentally incompetent person; *P.S. by Harbin v. W.S.*, *supra*, (Ind.); *Matter of Terwilliger*, *supra*, (Pa.); *In re Penny N.*, 414 A.2d 541 (N.H. 1980); *Matter of C.D.M.*, *supra*, (Alaska); *In re Eberhardy*, *supra*, (Wis.) The test necessarily leads to uncertainties; see *Matter of Guardianship of Hayes*, 608 P.2d 635 (Wash. 1980), at p. 637, and in an effort to minimize abuses, American courts have developed guidelines to assist in determining whether the best interests of the affected person would be furthered through sterilization. MacDonald J. proposed a series of similar guidelines in the present case; see (1981), 115 D.L.R.(3d) 283, at pp. 307-09.

66.   How far American courts would go in allowing sterilization for purely contraceptive purposes is difficult to say with certainty, since the above decisions were at the appeal level where the question was whether courts could exercise jurisdiction. Yet the guidelines put forward in those cases suggest that the courts would have considerable latitude. The facts in *Hayes*, *supra*, where the appeal court remanded the case to the applications judge, are revealing. They are thus stated at p. 637:

Edith Hayes is severely mentally retarded as a result of a birth defect. Now 16 years old, she functions at the level of a four to five year old. Her physical development, though, has been commensurate with her age. She is thus capable of conceiving and bearing children, while being unable at present to understand her own reproductive functions or exercise independent judgment in her relationship with males. Her mother and doctors believe she is sexually active and quite likely to become pregnant. Her parents are understandably concerned that Edith is engaging in these sexual activities. Furthermore, her parents and doctors feel the long term effects of conventional birth control methods are potentially harmful, and that sterilization is the most desirable method to ensure that Edith does not conceive an unwanted child. Edith's parents are sensitive to her special needs and concerned about her physical and emotional health, both now and in the future. They have sought appropriate medical care and education for her, and provided her with responsible and adequate supervision. During the year or so that Edith has been capable of becoming pregnant, though, they have become frustrated, depressed and emotionally drained by the stress of seeking an effective and safe method of contraception. They believe it is impossible to supervise her activities closely enough to prevent her from becoming involved in sexual relations. Thus, with the consent of Edith's father, Sharon Hayes petitioned for an order appointing her guardian and authorizing a sterilization procedure for Edith.

67.   As noted, these facts indicate that the courts of the United States, in acting under the best interests test have a very wide discretion.

68.   The second approach, the substituted judgment test, raises *Charter* implications about which I shall have more to say later. This test was first applied in the context of the sterilization of a mentally incompetent by the New Jersey Supreme Court in *In re Grady*, *supra*. In affirming a lower court's grant of the petition of the parents to sterilize their adult daughter, a victim of Down's Syndrome, the court based its decision on an analysis of the daughter's rights. It began by recognizing that any court-authorized sterilization potentially violates the right to procreate, which it described as "fundamental to the very existence and survival of the race". However, the court went on to distinguish the situation before it from both voluntary and

compulsory sterilization on the ground that the individual there had not expressed a desire to be sterilized or not to be sterilized, but was simply incapable of indicating her will either way. It then reviewed the U.S. Supreme Court decisions dealing with privacy and contraception and concluded that they supported a broad personal right to control contraception which included an affirmative constitutional right to voluntary sterilization. Given that there was also a right to be free from non-consensual bodily invasions, the individual was free to choose which of those two rights to exercise.

69. The *Grady* court held that in order for this choice to be meaningful, mental incompetence should not be permitted to prevent an individual from exercising it. The court, relying on the famous case of *Matter of Quinlan*, 355 A.2d 647 (N.J. 1976), recognized judicial power to make that choice in instances where limited mental capacity has rendered a person's own right to choose meaningless. The Supreme Courts of Massachusetts and Colorado later adopted this approach in *Moe*, *supra* and *A.W.*, *supra*, respectively.

70. The primary purpose of the substituted judgment test is to attempt to determine what decision the mental incompetent would make, if she were reviewing her situation as a competent person, but taking account of her mental incapacity as one factor in her decision. It allows the court to consider a number of factors bearing directly upon the condition of the mental incompetent. Thus the court may consider such issues as the values of the incompetent, any religious beliefs held by her, and her societal views as expressed by her family. In essence, an attempt is made to determine the actual interests and preferences of the mental incompetent. This, it is thought, recognizes her moral dignity and right to free choice. Since the incompetent cannot exercise that choice herself, the court does so on her behalf. The fact that a mental incompetent is, either because of age or mental disability, unable to provide any aid to the court in its decision does not preclude the use of the substituted judgment test.

71 The respondent submitted that this test should be adopted in this country. As in the case of the best interests test, various guidelines have been developed by the courts in the United States to ensure the proper use of this test.

Summary and Disposition

72. In the foregoing discussion, I have attempted to set forth the legal background relevant to the question whether a court may, or in this case, ought to authorize consent to non-therapeutic sterilization. Before going on, it may be useful to summarize my views on the *parens patriae* jurisdiction. From the earliest time, the sovereign, as *parens patriae*, was vested with the care of the mentally incompetent. This right and duty, as Lord Eldon noted in *Wellesley v. Duke of Beaufort*, *supra* at 2 Russ., at p. 20, 38 E.R., at p. 243 is founded on the obvious necessity that the law should place somewhere the care of persons who are not able to take care of themselves. In early England, the *parens patriae* jurisdiction was confined to mental incompetents, but its *rationale* is obviously applicable to children and, following the transfer of that jurisdiction to the Lord Chancellor in the seventeenth century, he extended it to children under wardship, and it is in this context that the bulk of the modern cases on the subject arise. The *parens patriae* jurisdiction was later vested in the provincial superior courts of this country, and in particular, those of Prince Edward Island.

73. The *parens patriae* jurisdiction is, as I have said, founded on necessity, namely the need to act for the protection of those who cannot care for themselves. The courts have frequently stated that it is to be exercised in the "best interest" of the protected person, or again, for his or her "benefit" or "welfare".

74. The situations under which it can be exercised are legion; the jurisdiction cannot be defined in that sense. As Lord MacDermott put it in *J. v. C.*, [1970] A.C. 668, at p. 703, the authorities are not consistent and there are many twists and turns, but they have inexorably "moved towards a broader discretion, under the impact of changing social conditions and the weight of opinion …." In other words, the categories under which the jurisdiction can be exercised are never closed. Thus I agree with Latey J. in *Re X, supra*, at p. 699, that the jurisdiction is of a very broad nature, and that it can be invoked in such matters as custody, protection of property, health problems, religious upbringing and protection against harmful associations. This list, as he notes, is not exhaustive.

75. What is more, as the passage from *Chambers* cited by Latey J. underlines, a court may act not only on the ground that injury to person or property has occurred, but also on the ground that such injury is apprehended. I might add that the jurisdiction is a carefully guarded one. The courts will not readily assume that it has been removed by legislation where a necessity arises to protect a person who cannot protect himself.

76. I have no doubt that the jurisdiction may be used to authorize the performance of a surgical operation that is necessary to the health of a person, as indeed it already has been in Great Britain and this country. And by health, I mean mental as well as physical health. In the United States, the courts have used the *parens patriae* jurisdiction on behalf of a mentally incompetent to authorize chemotherapy and amputation, and I have little doubt that in a proper case our courts should do the same. Many of these instances are related in *Strunk v. Strunk*, 445 S.W.2d 145 (Ky. 1969), where the court went to the length of permitting a kidney transplant between brothers. Whether the courts in this country should go that far, or as in *Quinlan*, permit the removal of life-sustaining equipment, I leave to later disposition.

77. Though the scope or sphere of operation of the *parens patriae* jurisdiction may be unlimited, it by no means follows that the discretion to exercise it is unlimited. It must be exercised in accordance with its underlying principle. Simply put, the discretion is to do what is necessary for the protection of the person for whose benefit it is exercised; see the passages from the reasons of Sir John Pennycuick in *Re X*, at pp. 706-07, and Heilbron J. in *Re D*, at p. 332, cited earlier. The discretion is to be exercised for the benefit of that person, not for that of others. It is a discretion, too, that must at all times be exercised with great caution, a caution that must be redoubled as the seriousness of the matter increases. This is particularly so in cases where a court might be tempted to act because failure to do so would risk imposing an obviously heavy burden on some other individual.

78. There are other reasons for approaching an application for sterilization of a mentally incompetent person with the utmost caution. To begin with, the decision involves values in an area where our social history clouds our vision and encourages many to perceive the mentally handicapped as somewhat less than human. This attitude has been aided and abetted by now discredited eugenic theories whose influence was felt in this country as well as the United States. Two provinces, Alberta and British Columbia, once had statutes providing for the sterilization of mental defectives; *The*

Sexual Sterilization Act, R.S.A. 1970, c. 341, repealed by S.A. 1972, c. 87; *Sexual Sterilization Act*, R.S.B.C. 1960, c. 353, s. 5(1), repealed by S.B.C. 1973, c. 79.

79.   Moreover, the implications of sterilization are always serious. As we have been reminded, it removes from a person the great privilege of giving birth, and is for practical purpose irreversible. If achieved by means of a hysterectomy, the procedure approved by the Appeal Division, it is not only irreversible; it is major surgery. Here, it is well to recall Lord Eldon's admonition in *Wellesley's* case, *supra*, at 2 Russ. p. 18, 38 E.R. p. 242, that "it has always been the principle of this Court, not to risk the incurring of damage to children which it cannot repair, but rather to prevent the damage being done". Though this comment was addressed to children, who were the subject matter of the application, it aptly describes the attitude that should always be present in exercising a right on behalf of a person who is unable to do so.

80.   Another factor merits attention. Unlike most surgical procedures, sterilization is not one that is ordinarily performed for the purpose of medical treatment. The Law Reform Commission of Canada tells us this in *Sterilization*, Working Paper 24 (1979), a publication to which I shall frequently refer as providing a convenient summary of much of the work in the field. It says at p. 3:

Sterilization as a medical procedure is distinct, because except in rare cases, if the operation is not performed, the *physical* health of the person involved is not in danger, necessity or emergency not normally being factors in the decision to undertake the procedure. In addition to its being elective it is for all intents and purposes irreversible.

As well, there is considerable evidence that non-consensual sterilization has a significant negative psychological impact on the mentally handicapped; see *Sterilization*, *supra*, at pp. 49-52. The Commission has this to say at p. 50:

It has been found that, like anyone else, the mentally handicapped have individually varying reactions to sterilization. Sex and parenthood hold the same significance for them as for other people and their misconceptions and misunderstandings are also similar. Rosen maintains that the removal of an individual's procreative powers is a matter of major importance and that no amount of *reforming zeal* can remove the significance of sterilization and its effect on the individual psyche.

In a study by Sabagh and Edgerton, it was found that sterilized mentally retarded persons tend to perceive sterilization as a symbol of *reduced* or *degraded* status. Their attempts to *pass for normal* were hindered by negative self perceptions and resulted in withdrawal and isolation rather than striving to conform ….

The psychological impact of sterilization is likely to be particularly damaging in cases where it is a result of coercion and when the mentally handicapped have had no children.

81.   In the present case, there is no evidence to indicate that failure to perform the operation would have any detrimental effect on Eve's physical or mental health. The purposes of the operation, as far as Eve's welfare is concerned, are to protect her from possible trauma in giving birth and from the assumed difficulties she would have in fulfilling her duties as a parent. As well, one must assume from the fact that hysterectomy was ordered, that the operation was intended to relieve her of the hygienic tasks associated with menstruation. Another purpose is to relieve Mrs. E. of the anxiety that Eve might become pregnant, and give birth to a child, the responsibility for whom would probably fall on Mrs. E.

82. I shall dispose of the latter purpose first. One may sympathize with Mrs. E. To use Heilbron J.'s phrase, it is easy to understand the natural feelings of a parent's heart. But the *parens patriae* jurisdiction cannot be used for her benefit. Its exercise is confined to doing what is necessary for the benefit and protection of persons under disability like Eve. And a court, as I previously mentioned, must exercise great caution to avoid being misled by this all too human mixture of emotions and motives. So we are left to consider whether the purposes underlying the operation are necessarily for Eve's benefit and protection.

83. The justifications advanced are the ones commonly proposed in support of non-therapeutic sterilization (see *Sterilization, passim*). Many are demonstrably weak. The Commission dismisses the argument about the trauma of birth by observing at p. 60:

   For this argument to be held valid would require that it could be demonstrated that the stress of delivery was greater in the case of mentally handicapped persons than it is for others. Considering the generally known wide range of post-partum response would likely render this a difficult case to prove.

84. The argument relating to fitness as a parent involves many value-loaded questions. Studies conclude that mentally incompetent parents show as much fondness and concern for their children as other people; see *Sterilization, supra*, p. 33 et seq., 63-64. Many, it is true, may have difficulty in coping, particularly with the financial burdens involved. But this issue does not relate to the benefit of the incompetent; it is a social problem, and one, moreover, that is not limited to incompetents. Above all it is not an issue that comes within the limited powers of the courts, under the *parens patriae* jurisdiction, to do what is necessary for the benefit of persons who are unable to care for themselves. Indeed, there are human rights considerations that should make a court extremely hesitant about attempting to solve a social problem like this by this means. It is worth noting that in dealing with such issues, provincial sterilization boards have revealed serious differences in their attitudes as between men and women, the poor and the rich, and people of different ethnic backgrounds; see *Sterilization, supra*, at p. 44.

85. As far as the hygienic problems are concerned, the following view of the Law Reform Commission (at p. 34) is obviously sound:

   ... if a person requires a great deal of assistance in managing their own menstruation, they are also likely to require assistance with urinary and fecal control, problems which are much more troublesome in terms of personal hygiene.

   Apart from this, the drastic measure of subjecting a person to a hysterectomy for this purpose is clearly excessive.

86. The grave intrusion on a person's rights and the certain physical damage that ensues from non-therapeutic sterilization without consent, when compared to the highly questionable advantages that can result from it, have persuaded me that it can never safely be determined that such a procedure is for the benefit of that person. Accordingly, the procedure should never be authorized for non-therapeutic purposes under the *parens patriae* jurisdiction.

87. To begin with, it is difficult to imagine a case in which non-therapeutic sterilization could possibly be of benefit to the person on behalf of whom a court purports to act, let alone one in which that procedure is necessary in his or her best interest. And how

are we to weigh the best interests of a person in this troublesome area, keeping in mind that an error is irreversible? Unlike other cases involving the use of the *parens patriae* jurisdiction, an error cannot be corrected by the subsequent exercise of judicial discretion. That being so, one need only recall Lord Eldon's remark, *supra*, that "it has always been the principle of this Court, not to risk damage to children which it cannot repair" to conclude that non-therapeutic sterilization may not be authorized in the exercise of the *parens patriae* jurisdiction. McQuaid J. was, therefore, right in concluding that he had no authority or jurisdiction to grant the application.

88.   Nature or the advances of science may, at least in a measure, free Eve of the incapacity from which she suffers. Such a possibility should give the courts pause in extending their power to care for individuals to such irreversible action as we are called upon to take here. The irreversible and serious intrusion on the basic rights of the individual is simply too great to allow a court to act on the basis of possible advantages which, from the standpoint of the individual, are highly debatable. Judges are generally ill-informed about many of the factors relevant to a wise decision in this difficult area. They generally know little of mental illness, of techniques of contraception or their efficacy. And, however well presented a case may be, it can only partially inform. If sterilization of the mentally incompetent is to be adopted as desirable for general social purposes, the legislature is the appropriate body to do so. It is in a position to inform itself and it is attuned to the feelings of the public in making policy in this sensitive area. The actions of the legislature will then, of course, be subject to the scrutiny of the courts under the *Canadian Charter of Rights and Freedoms* and otherwise.

89.   Many of the factors I have referred to as showing that the best interests test is simply not a sufficiently precise or workable tool to permit the *parens patriae* power to be used in situations like the present are referred to in *Matter of Guardianship of Eberhardy, supra*. Speaking for the court in that case, Heffernan J. had this to say, at p. 894:

Under the present state of the law, the only guideline available to circuit courts faced with this problem appears to be the "best interests" of the person to be sterilized. This is a test that has been used for a number of years in this jurisdiction and elsewhere in the determination of the custody of children and their placement--in some circumstances placement in a controlled environment ... No one who has dealt with this standard has expressed complete satisfaction with it. It is not an objective test, and it is not intended to be. The substantial workability of the test rests upon the informed fact-finding and the wise exercise of discretion by trial courts engendered by long experience with the standard. Importantly, however, most determinations made in the best interests of a child or of an incompetent person are not irreversible; and although a wrong decision may be damaging indeed, there is an opportunity for a certain amount of empiricism in the correction of errors of discretion. Errors of judgment or revisions of decisions by courts and social workers can, in part at least, be rectified when new facts or second thoughts prevail. And, of course, alleged errors of discretion in exercising the "best interest" standard are subject to appellate review. Sterilization as it is now understood by medical science is, however, substantially irreversible.

90. Heffernan J. also alluded to the limited capacity of judges to deal adequately with a problem that has such general social overtones in the following passage, at p. 895:

> What these facts demonstrate is that courts, even by taking judicial notice of medical treatises, know very little of the techniques or efficacy of contraceptive methods or of thwarting the ability to procreate by methods short of sterilization. While courts are always dependent upon the opinions of expert witnesses, it would appear that the exercise of judicial discretion unguided by well thought-out policy determinations reflecting the interest of society, as well as of the person to be sterilized, are hazardous indeed. Moreover, all seriously mentally retarded persons may not *ipso facto* be incapable of giving birth without serious trauma, and some may be good parents. Also, there has been a discernible and laudable tendency to "mainstream" the developmentally disabled and retarded. A properly thought out public policy on sterilization or alternative contraceptive methods could well facilitate the entry of these persons into a more nearly normal relationship with society. But again this is a problem that ought to be addressed by the legislature on the basis of fact-finding and the opinions of experts.

91. The foregoing, of course, leaves out of consideration therapeutic sterilization and where the line is to be drawn between therapeutic and non-therapeutic sterilization. On this issue, I simply repeat that the utmost caution must be exercised commensurate with the seriousness of the procedure. Marginal justifications must be weighed against what is in every case a grave intrusion on the physical and mental integrity of the person.

92. It will be apparent that my views closely conform to those expressed by Heilbron J. in *Re D, supra*. She was speaking of an infant, but her remarks are equally applicable to an adult. The importance of maintaining the physical integrity of a human being ranks high in our scale of values, particularly as it affects the privilege of giving life. I cannot agree that a court can deprive a woman of that privilege for purely social or other non-therapeutic purposes without her consent. The fact that others may suffer inconvenience or hardship from failure to do so cannot be taken into account. The Crown's *parens patriae* jurisdiction exists for the benefit of those who cannot help themselves, not to relieve those who may have the burden of caring for them.

93. I should perhaps add, as Heilbron J. does, that sterilization may, on occasion, be necessary as an adjunct to treatment of a serious malady, but I would underline that this, of course, does not allow for subterfuge or for treatment of some marginal medical problem. Heilbron J. was referring, as I am, to cases where such treatment is necessary in dealing with a serious condition. The recent British Columbia case of *Re K, supra*, is at best dangerously close to the limits of the permissible.

94. The foregoing remarks dispose of the arguments based on the traditional view of the *parens patriae* jurisdiction as exercised in this country. Counsel for the respondent strongly contended, however, that the Court should adopt the substituted judgment test recently developed by a number of state courts in the United States. That test, he submitted, is to be preferred to the best interests test because it places a higher value on the individuality of the mentally incompetent person. It affords that person the same right, he contended, as a competent person to choose whether to procreate or not.

95.   There is an obvious logical lapse in this argument. I do not doubt that a person has a right to decide to be sterilized. That is his or her free choice. But choice presupposes that a person has the mental competence to make it. It may be a matter of debate whether a court should have the power to make the decision if that person lacks the mental capacity to do so. But it is obviously fiction to suggest that a decision so made is that of the mental incompetent, however much the court may try to put itself in her place. What the incompetent would do if she or he could make the choice is simply a matter of speculation. The sophistry embodied in the argument favouring substituted judgment has been fully revealed in *Eberhardy, supra*, at p. 893 where in discussing *Grady, supra*, the court stated:

> The fault we find in the New Jersey case is the *ratio decidendi* of first concluding, correctly we believe, that the right to sterilization is a personal choice, but then equating a decision made by others with the choice of the person to be sterilized. It clearly is not a personal choice, and no amount of legal legerdemain can make it so.
>
> ...
>
> We conclude that the question is not choice because it is sophistry to refer to it as such, but rather the question is whether there is a method by which others, acting in behalf of the person's best interests and in the interests, such as they may be, of the state, can exercise the decision. Any governmentally sanctioned (or ordered) procedure to sterilize a person who is incapable of giving consent must be denominated for what it is, that is, the state's intrusion into the determination of whether or not a person who makes no choice shall be allowed to procreate.

96.   Counsel for the respondent's argument in favour of a substituted judgment test was made essentially on a common law basis. However, he also argued that there is what he called a fundamental right to free procreative choice. Not only, he asserted, is there a fundamental right to bear children; there is as well a fundamental right to choose not to have children and to implement that choice by means of contraception. Starting from the American courts' approach to the due process clause in the United States Constitution, he appears to base this argument on s. 7 of the *Charter*. But assuming for the moment that liberty as used in s. 7 protects rights of this kind (a matter I refrain from entering into), counsel's contention seems to me to go beyond the kind of protection s. 7 was intended to afford. All s. 7 does is to give a remedy to protect individuals against laws or other state action that deprive them of liberty. It has no application here.

97.   Another *Charter* related argument must be considered. In response to the appellant's argument that a court-ordered sterilization of a mentally incompetent person, by depriving that person of the right to procreate, would constitute an infringement of that person's rights to liberty and security of the person under s. 7 of the *Canadian Charter of Rights and Freedoms*, counsel for the respondent countered by relying on that person's right to equality under s. 15(1) of the *Charter*, saying "that the most appropriate method of ensuring the mentally incompetent their right to equal protection under s. 15(1) is to provide the mentally incompetent with a means to obtain non-therapeutic sterilizations, which adequately protects their interests through appropriate judicial safeguards". A somewhat more explicit argument along the same lines was made by counsel for the Public Trustee of Manitoba. His position was stated as follows:

It is submitted that in the case of a mentally incompetent adult, denial of the right to have his or her case presented by a guardian *ad litem* to a Court possessing jurisdiction to give or refuse substituted consent to a non-therapeutic procedure such as sterilization, would be tantamount to a denial to that person of equal protection and equal benefit of the law. Such a denial would constitute discrimination on the basis of mental disability, which discrimination is prohibited by Section 15 of *The Canadian Charter of Rights and Freedoms.*

98. Section 15 of the *Charter* was not in force when these proceedings commenced but, this aside, these arguments appear flawed. They raise in different form an issue already dealt with, i.e., that the decision made by a court on an application to consent to the sterilization of an incompetent is somehow that of the incompetent. More troubling is that the issue is, of course, not raised by the incompetent, but by a third party.

99. The court undoubtedly has the right and duty to protect those who are unable to take care of themselves, and in doing so it has a wide discretion to do what it considers to be in their best interests. But this function must not, in my view, be transformed so as to create a duty obliging the court, at the behest of a third party, to make a choice between the two alleged constitutional rights--the right to procreate or not to procreate--simply because the individual is unable to make that choice. All the more so since, in the case of non-therapeutic sterilization as we saw, the choice is one the courts cannot safely exercise.

Other Issues

100. In light of the conclusions I have reached, it is unnecessary for me to deal with the *Charter* issues raised by the appellant and some of the interveners. It is equally unnecessary to comment at length on some of the subsidiary issues such as the burden of proof required to warrant an order of sterilization and the precautions that judges should, in the interests of justice, take in dealing with applications for such orders. These do not arise because of the view I have taken of the approach the courts should adopt in dealing with applications for non-therapeutic sterilization. Since these issues may arise in cases involving applications for sterilization for therapeutic purposes, however, I will venture a few words about them. Since, barring emergency situations, a surgical procedure without consent ordinarily constitutes battery, it will be obvious that the onus of proving the need for the procedure is on those who seek to have it performed. And that burden, though a civil one, must be commensurate with the seriousness of the measure proposed. In conducting these procedures, it is obvious that a court must proceed with extreme caution; otherwise as MacDonald J. noted, it would open the way for abuse of the mentally incompetent. In particular, in any such proceedings, it is essential that the mentally incompetent have independent representation.

Conclusion

101. I would allow the appeal and restore the decision of the judge who heard the application.

Appeal allowed.

Solicitors for the appellant: Scales, Jenkins and McQuaid, Charlottetown.

Solicitors for the respondent: Campbell, McEwen and McLellan, Summerside.

Solicitors for the intervener Canadian Mental Health Association:
Gowling and Henderson, Ottawa.

Solicitors for the intervener the Consumer Advisory Committee of the Canadian Association for the Mentally Retarded: Vickers and Palmer, Victoria.

Solicitor for the intervener The Public Trustee of Manitoba: The Public Trustee of Manitoba, Winnipeg.

Solicitor for the intervener Attorney General of Canada: Roger Tass, Ottawa.
Accessed at: http://csc.lexum.umontreal.ca/en/1986/1986scr2-388/1986scr2-388.pdf
March 28, 2010

BIBLIOGRAPHY

Books and Articles:

"John E. Brownlee a Biography." 1996. *Alberta History*. Dec 1.

Bidault, C. 1997. "Canada: stérilisée de force à 14 ans!" [Report on speech by Leilani Muir in Orleans, France] *La République du Centre*. October.

Brennen, Brian. 1997. *The Good Steward, the Ernest C. Manning story*. Fifth House.

"B. T. Richardson Tributes Paid to Late Premier Wm. Aberhart. Death Of a Prophet." 1943. *Winnipeg Free Press*, reprinted in the "Left Hand Corner" in *Lethbridge Herald*. May 24.

Cairney, Richard. 1996. "Democracy was Never Intended for Degenerates: Alberta's Flirtation With Eugenics Comes Back To Haunt It." *Canadian Medical Association Journal*. September 15.

Chandler, Graham. 2001. "Losing Our Bible Belt." *Alberta Views*. November/December.

Coren, Michael 2008. "Don't blame right-wing thugs for eugenics — Socialists made it fashionable," *National Post*. June 16.

Cornell, George N., "Theologians, Doctors, Scholars Queried on Troubling Issues" *Lethbridge Herald*. 1961.

Crawford, Alison. 2010. "Dodge's retirement reality check." CBC News (cbc.ca). March 27.

Darwin, Charles. 1958. *The Autobiography of Charles Darwin, 1809-1882*, with original omissions restored. Ed. Nora Barlow. London: Collins.

Elliott, David Raymond. 1987. *Bible Bill: a biography of William Aberhart*. Reidmore Books.

Flanagan, Thomas. 2007. *Harper's team: behind the scenes of the conservative rise to power*. McGill-Queen's University Press.

Flegel, Ken. MDCM MSc and Paul C. Hébert MD MHSc. 2010. "Time to move on from the euthanasia debate." *Canadian Medical Association Journal*. March 29.

Finkel, Alvin. 1972. "The Rise and Fall of the Labour Party in Alberta, 1917-42." University of Alberta.

Galton, Francis. F.R.S. 1892. *Hereditary genius: An Inquiry into Its Laws and consequences*. London and New York, MacMillan and Co.

Green, Christopher. *Classics in the History of Psychology, An Internet Resource developed by Christopher D. Green*. Toronto: York University.

Gould, Stephen Jay. 1981. *The Mismeasure of Man*. New York: W.W. Norton and Company. 166.

Grant, Madison. 1922. *The Passing of the Great Race*, New York: C. Scribner's sons.

Foster, Franklin. 1996. *John E. Brownlee: a Biography*. Lloydminster, AB: Foster Learning Inc.

Hall, David J. 2010. "Sir Clifford Sifton." *Canadian Encyclopedia*. Historica-Dominion.

Hubbard, Ruth and Stuart Newman. 2002. "Yuppie Eugenics," *Z Magazine*. March.

Kilgour, David. 1988. "Uneasy Patriots," Chapter Two, *Frederick Haultain, Forgotten Statesman*.

LaJeunesse, Ron. 2002. *Political Asylums*. Muttart Foundation.

Laughlin, Harry Hamilton, D. 1922. *Model Eugenical Sterilization Law. Eugenical Sterilization in the United States*. Chicago. Psychopathic Laboratory of the Municipal Court of Chicago, 446-452.

Levant, Ezra. 2007. "Censorship in the name of 'human rights.'" *The National Post*. December 17.

Magrath, Charles Alexander. 1910. *Canada's growth and some problems affecting it*. The Mortimer Press.

"Many Canadians stigmatize mentally ill, poll finds". 2008. CTV news. August 18. http://www.ctv.ca/servlet/ArticleNews/story/CTVNews/20080818/cma_health_080818/20080818?hub=TopStories>

Marsh, James H. "Eugenics: Keeping Canada Sane." 2010. *Canadian Encyclopedia*. Historica-Dominion. http://www.thecanadianencyclopedia.com/index.cfm?PgNm=ArchivedFeatures&Params=A2126

Marshall, David. 2001. "Premier E.C. Manning, Back to the Bible Hour, and Fundamentalism in Canada.*" Religion and Life in Canada: Historical and Comparative Perspectives*. Editor: Marguerite Van Die. Toronto: University of Toronto Press. Toronto.

McCallum, Gordon. 1944. "This Fellow Manning." *Maclean's Magazine re*printed in the *Ottawa Citizen*. October 24.

McLaren, Angus. 1997. *Our Own Master Race: Eugenics in Canada, 1885-1945*. Toronto: McClelland and Stewart. Second edition: Oxford University Press.

McMillan, Kate. "Tommy Douglas: Not Fascist Enough!" 2010. *Small Dead Animals*. January 3. http://www.smalldeadanimals.com/archives/013035.html.

McMillan, Kate. "Let's Do it for Tommy." 2007. *Small Dead Animals*. November 2. Accessed January 3. http://www.smalldeadanimals.com/archives/007340.html.

Otter, Andy A. den, 1982. *Civilizing the West: The Galts and the Development of Western Canada*. University of Alberta Press.

Pringle, H. 1997. "Alberta Barren: The Mannings and Forced Sterilization in Canada." *Saturday Night*. June, 30-74.

Robson, John. 2006. "Tommy's War on the Weak." *Western Standard*. July 3.

Robertson, Gerald. "Eugenics." *The Canadian Encyclopedia*. Historica-Dominion.

Taylor, Jeremy and Reginald Heber. "A Prayer on Behalf of Fools and Changelings." *The whole works of the Right Rev. Jeremy Taylor, Lord Bishop of Down, Connor and Dromore*. Volume 15. London: Duncan and Co., Richard Priestley. Oxford: J. Parker. Cambridge: Deighton and Son, Cambridge, 355-356.

Taylor, Jeremy and Reginald Heber. "A Prayer for Madmen." *The whole works of the Right Rev. Jeremy Taylor, Lord Bishop of Down, Connor and Dromore.* Volume 15. London: Duncan and Co., Richard Priestley. Oxford: J. Parker. Cambridge: Deighton and Son, Cambridge, 355-356.

"The Honourable E. Peter Lougheed 1971-85." 2010. Legislative Assembly of Alberta. http://www.assembly.ab.ca/lao/library/PREMIERS/lougheed.htm

"The Honourable Harry E. Strom, 1968-71." 2010. Legislative Assembly of Alberta. http://www.assembly.ab.ca/lao/library/premiers/strom.htm

Terman, Lewis M. 1916. "The uses of intelligence tests." *The measurement of intelligence.* Boston: Houghton Mifflin.

"Douglas Social Credit." The Companion to Tasmanian History. 2010. http://www.utas.edu.au/library/companion_to_tasmanian_history/D/Douglas%20Credit.htm

"The Latimer Case". Canadian Council of Persons with Disabilities. 2010. http://www.ccdonline.ca/en/humanrights/

Thomas, Lewis Herbert. 1977. *William Aberhart and Social Credit in Alberta.* Copp Clark.

Wahlsten, Douglas. 1997. "Leilani Muir versus the Philosopher King: Eugenics on trial in Alberta." *Genetica* 99, 185–198.

"Chapter 5." *Eugenics and the Power of Testing. 2005.* Brookline, Massachusetts: Facing History & Ourselves, National Foundation, Inc. Accessed January 2010.

Laws and Reports:

"Act respecting Mentally Defective Persons (Mental Defectives Act)." 1919. *Statutes of the Province of Alberta 1919.*

"Act to amend the Mental Diseases Act." 1925. *Statutes of the Province of Alberta 1925.*

"Act to amend The Mental Diseases Act." 1929. *Statutes of the Province of Alberta 1929.*

"Act to amend The Mental Diseases Act." 1931. *Statutes of the Province of Alberta 1931.*

"Act to amend The Mental Diseases Act." 1933. *Statutes of the Province of Alberta 1933.*

"Act to amend The Mental Diseases Act." 1937. *Statutes of the Province of Alberta 1936— 2nd Session.*

"Act respecting Mentally Defective Persons (Mental Defectives Act)." 1937. *Statutes of the Province of Alberta 1936—2nd Session.*

"Act to amend The Mental Diseases Act." 1956. *Statutes of the Province of Alberta 1955 —2nd Session.*

"Act to amend The Mental Diseases Act." 1959. *Statutes of the Province of Alberta 1959.*

"An Ordinance Respecting Insane persons." 1888. *Northwest Territories Ordinances.*

Alberta Liberal Caucus. 2009. "Summary of Alternative Spending Cuts." December.

Beachell, Laurie. 2009. "Letter to the Editor: Re: Locked in Patients Humanity for the Trapped." Council of Canadians with Disabilities. November 25.

Brett, Robert G., Lieutenant Governor of Alberta. 1921. "Speech from the Throne." February 15.

"Budget 2010-2011 Action Notes." 2010. Alberta Committee of Citizens with Disabilities. March.

"Canada Ratifies UN Convention on the Rights of Persons with Disabilities." 2010. Government of Canada Department of Foreign Affairs and International Trade. No. 99. March 11.

"CCD Affidavit in the Hughes Case Related Documents In the Matter of the Complaint to and in the matter of motion for an order granting interested party status to the Canadian Human Rights Commission Tribunal between James Peter Hughes, Complainant, and Elections Canada, respondent." 2010. Tribunal File No.: T1373/10308 Complaint No.: 20080351. March 4.

"Consolidated Ordinance 1898, intituled "An ordinance respecting Insane Persons," 1899. *Northwest Territories Ordinances. 4th Leg. 2nd Session. 1899. 4th Leg.*

Elections Alberta. 2008. *2008 Variation in Turnout by Electoral Division Report. Elections Alberta.* October. http://www.electionsalberta.ab.ca/Public%20Website/1012.htm).

Elections Alberta. 2009. *Report on the September 14, 2009 Calgary-Glenmore By-Election.* http://www.elections.ab.ca/Public%20Website/files/Documents/

E. (Mrs.) *v.* Eve, [1986] 2 S.C.R. 388 Eve, by her Guardian *ad litem*, Milton B. Fitzpatrick, Official Trustee *Appellant v.* Mrs. E. *Respondent* INDEXED AS: E. (MRS.) *v.* EVE File No.: 16654. 1985: June 4, 5. 1986: October 23.

"Insanity Act." 1907. *Statutes of Alberta 1907.*

Hitler, Adolf. 1939. "Euthanasia Law." Deutsches Reich. September 1.

King, David. 2007. "Notes for Remarks by David King. Eugenics and Sterilization in Alberta: 35 Years Later." Presented at the University of Alberta. April 27.

"Limiting Legal Aid unjust, Review suggests 6,100 Albertans might never get their day in court." 2010. NDP Opposition. March 30. http://www.ndpopposition.ab.ca/site/index.cfm?fuseaction=page.detailsandID=8103andt=8andi=48

"Law for the Protection of German Blood and German Honour." 1935. *Deutsches Reich.* September 15.

"Law for the Protection of Hereditary Health: The Attempt to Improve the German Aryan Breed." (Also translated as "Law for the Prevention of Genetically Diseased Progeny.") 1933. Deutsches Reich. July 14.

"Most Canadians Generally Agree with Euthanasia." 2010. *Angus Reid Public Opinion.* February 16.

"Nuremberg Laws on Citizenship and Race." 1935. Deutsches Reich. September.

"Report of the MacEachran Sub-Committee." 1998. Department of Psychology. University of Alberta. April. http://www.uofaweb.ualberta.ca/philosophy/pdfs/MacEachran%20Report4.pdf

Veit, J. (1996) Muir v. The Queen in Right of Alberta. *Dominion Law Reports*, 132 (4th series): 695-762.

Newspaper Clippings

"Aberhart Declares Social Credit Would Be Real Boon to Coal Mines." 1943. *Lethbridge Daily Herald.* May 24, Back Page.

"Board had assembly-line sterilizations — professor." 1995. *Lethbridge Herald.* June 25,7.

Canadian Press. 1970. "Banishment Ends For Mentally Ill." *Lethbridge Herald.* February 2,11.

Canadian Press. 1995. "Government in Court Over Forced Sterilization." *Lethbridge Herald.* June 14, 4.

"Credit Eugenics Protection Law: Japanese Winning Their Fight for Lining Space." 1959. *Lethbridge Daily Herald,* October 13, 27.

CT. "Moral Question Facing Canada. More Liberal Abortion Laws Pose Problem at CBA Meet." 1963. *Lethbridge Herald.*

"Eugenics for the Troops, Berlin-W. German army recruits, under a new decree, must attend four lectures on eugenics and racial topics in their first year of service." 1936. *Lethbridge Daily Herald.* June 18, 6.

"Eugenics prompts fears of impending brave new world." 1969. *Lethbridge Herald.* August 31, 52.

Galloway, John, "Sterilization" (undated clipping.) *Lethbridge Herald, Letter to the Editor.* September 3, 5.

"Government Accused of Fraud and Trickery in Sterilization case." 1996. *Lethbridge Herald.* July11, 2.

"It is proposed to examine the general basis of the plan." *Lethbridge Herald.* 1934 December 19, 3.

Lethbridge Herald. 1904. September 3, 3.

Lethbridge Herald. 1915. March 6, 4.

Lethbridge Herald. 1913. December 19, 9.

Lethbridge Herald. 1919. January 13, 3.

Lethbridge Herald. 1921. December 22, 10.

Lethbridge Herald. 1931. January 9, 10.

Lethbridge Herald. 1934. August 12, 3.

Lethbridge Herald. 1935. August 31, 4.

Lethbridge Herald. 1936. May 11, 4.

Lethbridge Herald. 1936. July 7, 4.

Lethbridge Herald. 1940. January 5, 4.

Lethbridge Herald. 1941. August 09, 3.

Lethbridge Herald. 1994. February 12, 30

Lethbridge Herald. 1995. June 14, 4.

Lethbridge Herald. 1995. July 3, 6.

Lethbridge Herald. 1995. December 31, 5.

"Reid Defends Minister." Undated. *Lethbridge Herald.*

"Military Eugenics." 1933. *Lethbridge Herald.* October 24, 4.

"Money won't help the eugenics mess." 1998. *Lethbridge Herald.* April 3, 17.

"Not entering federal politics: Not Contemplating New Political Party In Dominion, Aberhart Says." 1941. *Lethbridge Herald.* November 5.

"Program Inappropriate Banned From C. B. C." 1938. *Lethbridge Herald.* March31.

"Pussy Foot to Speak in Massey Hall Toronto" 1921. *Lethbridge Herald.* March 23, 11.

"Says Germany Has the Right System of Raising Babies" 1935. *Lethbridge Herald.* Aug. 29, 11.

"Science, Morals a deadly Mixture Society still need to be on Guard Warn Legal Scholars." (undated clipping.) *Lethbridge Herald.*

Special Legislative Correspondent. 1934. "Adjustment Changes Urged Some May Be Introduced at Present Session of Legislature." *Lethbridge Herald.* March 16, 2.

"Sterilized BC Man Subject of Lawsuit." 2002. *Lethbridge Herald. May 20,* 5.

"The Mid-thirties." 1936. *Lethbridge Herald.* July 7, 4.

Parson, Lee. 2001. "Alberta Premier berates homeless in visit to shelter." World Socialist Website. December 22. http://www.wsws.org/articles/2001/dec2001/can-d22.

Pole, Ken. 1969. "Sterilization of Mentally Retarded Controversial Topic to Geneticists." *Lethbridge Herald.* February 25, 14.

"Unhealthy foetuses may be at risk, warns health research director. Survey of geneticists finds resurgence in eugenics." 1995. *Lethbridge Herald.* December 31.

"United Church Committee in Favour of Birth Control and Sterilization." 1936. *Lethbridge Herald. September 25, 2.*

"Victim Has Mixed Feelings About Compensation." 1998. *Lethbridge Herald.* March 15, 17.

"Vulcan becoming known a centre for Douglasism." 1933. *Lethbridge Herald.* July 11, 5.

"Who'll Be Alberta Premier?" 1943. *Lethbridge Herald.* May 28, 6.

"Women Sue." 2000. *Lethbridge Herald.* December 14, 9.

Video Clips and Websites

"Alfred Binet. Eugenics In America: IQ Testing and Social Policy." 2010. Facing History and Ourselves." http://www2.facinghistory.org/Campus/rm.nsf/PrintView/9DEDE045369DD5F18525707B0075F9D7?OpenDocument

Alberta Association for Community Living. 2010. http://aacl.org/

Alberta Committee of Citizens with Disabilities. 2010. http://www.accd.net/

Alberta Disabilities Forum. 2010. http://www.adforum.ca/disability_links.html

Alberta Courts. 2010. http://www.albertacourts.ab.ca/

Alberta Law Society Libraries. 2010. http://www.lawlibrary.ab.ca

Alberta Law Society Libraries e-Resources. 2010. http://www.lawlibrary.ab.ca/eresources/selected_websites.php

Alberta Law Foundation. 2010. http://www.albertalawfoundation.org/Apply/general.html

Canadian Broadcasting Corporation. 2010. "Bums and Creeps." CBC Digital Archives Website. 2010. Last updated October 10, 2008. Accessed January 12, 2010. http://archives.cbc.ca/politics/provincial_territorial_politics/clips/2406/

Canadian Broadcasting Corporation. 1963. "Confederation in danger." CBC Digital Archives Website. Last updated August 9, 2004. Accessed January 12, 2010. http://archives.cbc.ca/politics/constitution/clips/2222/

Canadian Broadcasting Corporation. 1957. "Diversify oil market: Ernest Manning." CBC Digital Archives Website. Last Updated 16 August, 2004. Accessed April 12, 2010. http://archives.cbc.ca/science_technology/energy_production/clips/2145/

Canadian Broadcasting Corporation. 1971. "Ernest Manning magic." September 5. The CBC Digital Archives Website. Last updated: July 21, 2009. Accessed January 12, 2010. http://archives.cbc.ca/politics/provincial_territorial_politics/clips/9842/

Canadian Broadcasting Corporation. (undated). "Leduc 'blows in 300 times." CBC Digital Archives Website. Last updated: 03 February 2009. Accessed February 15, 2010. http://archives.cbc.ca/science_technology/energy_production/clips/2135/

Canadian Broadcasting Corporation. 1969. "Leduc Signals western expansion." CBC Digital Archives Website. Last updated August 16, 2004. Accessed consulted January 12, 2010. http://archives.cbc.ca/science_technology/energy_production/clips/2136/

Canadian Broadcasting Corporation. 1968. "Manning retires." CBC Digital Archives Website. Last updated 21 July 2009. Accessed January 12, 2010. http://archives.cbc.ca/politics/provincial_territorial_politics/topics/1472-9849/

Canadian Broadcasting Corporation. 1962. "1935: The gospel of Social Credit.". CBC Digital Archives Website. Last updated. January 5, 2010. Accessed January 12, 2010 http://archives.cbc.ca/politics/provincial_territorial_politics/topics/1472/

Canadian Broadcasting Corporation. 1957. 'Oil Came in with a roar.' The CBC Digital Archives Website. Last updated 03 September 2004. Accessed February 12, 2010. http://archives.cbc.ca/science_technology/energy_production/clips/2144/

Canadian Broadcasting Corporation. 1971. "1971: Peter Lougheed grabs the torch." The CBC Digital Archives Website. Last updated: July 21, 2009. [Accessed January 12, 2010.] http://archives.cbc.ca/politics/provincial_territorial_politics/clips/9843/

Canadian Broadcasting Corporation. 1979. "West is the new East." CBC Digital Archives Website. Last updated November 19, 2007, [Accessed January 12, 2010.] http://archives.cbc.ca/science_technology/energy_production/clips/2139/

Canadian Broadcasting Corporation. 1943. "William 'Bible Bill' Aberhart, Social Credit pioneer." CBC Digital Archives Website. Last updated: 05 January 2009. Accessed January 12, 2010. http://archives.cbc.ca/politics/provincial_territorial_politics/clips/13358/

"Electing Dynasties" 1935. Canadian Broadcasting Corporation. Accessed January 12, 2010. http://archives.cbc.ca/politics/provincial_territorial_politics/topics/1472/

Canadian Encyclopedia, The. 2010. Historica-Dominion. http://www.thecanadianencyclopedia.com/index.efm?PgNm=TCEandparams-A1ARTA0004558

Classics in the History of Psychology. Developer: Green, Christopher D. 2010. York University, Ontario. http://psychclassics.yorku.ca/Watson/Battle/watson.htm

Council of Canadians With Disabilities On-Line. 2010. http://www.ccdonline.ca/en/humanrights/promoting/periodic-review-2009

Complete Work of Charles Darwin Online. 2010. http://darwin-online.org.uk/

Dictionary of Canadian Biography On-line. 2010. http://www.biographi.ca/009004-119.01-e.php?andid_nbr=7514

Elder Advocates of Alberta. 2010. http://elderadvocates.ca/martha-matich-dependant-adults-act-abuse/>

Euthanasia Prevention Coalition. 2010. http://www.euthanasiaprevention.on.ca/

EugenicsArchives.Org 2010. http://eugenicsarchive.org/html/eugenics/static/themes/39.html

Galton. Org. 2010. 2010. www.galton.org

"Historical Statutes of Alberta." Our future,Our Past. The Alberta Heritage Digitization Project. http://www.ourpastourfuture.ca/lwa/browse.aspx (Historical statutes of Alberta).

"Hitler Signs an Order Authorizing Involuntary Euthanasia in Germany, October 1939." 2010. Michigan State University. http://www2.h-net.msu.edu/~german/gtext/nazi/euthanasia-eng.html

"Laughlin Model Law" History of Science. Harvard University. Ed. Alex Wellerstein http://www.people.fas.harvard.edu/~wellerst/laughlin/Laughlin_Model_Law.pdf

Library and Archives Canada. http://www.collectionscanada.gc.ca/women/

Premiers Council on the Status of Persons With Disabilities. 2010. Government of Alberta. http://www.seniors.alberta.ca/premierscouncil/

"Prime Minister Ministers Gallery." 2010. Parliament of Canada. http://www2.parl.gc.ca/Parlinfo/Compilations/FederalGovernment/PrimeMinisters/Gallery.aspx

"Trudeau mocks Lougheed." 2006. Canadian Digital Archives Website. Canadian Broadcasting Corporation. Last updated 27 November 2006. [Accessed January 15, 2010.] http://archives.cbc.ca/science_technology/energy_production/clips/2137/

"Seniors and Disability Supports." 2010. Government of Alberta. http://www.seniors.gov. ab.ca/DisabilitiesSupports/

Statism Watch.Ca. 2010. http://statismwatch.ca/1997/06/

University of Alberta Libraries. 2010. http://guides.library.ualberta.ca/law

University of Alberta. Faculty of Law. 2010. http://www.law.ualberta.ca/centres/

What Sorts. 2010. http://whatsorts.net/

Wellerstein, Alex. *History of Science. 2010* Harvard University Science Centre 371, Department of the History of Science. Cambridge, MA.02138. http://www.people.fas. harvard.edu/~wellerst/laughlin/

INDEX